COMMUNISM

STUDIES IN POLITICAL SCIENCE

THIRD EDITION

COMMUNISM

Alfred G. Meyer
UNIVERSITY OF MICHIGAN

• RANDOM HOUSE / New York

Preface to the Third Edition

• Developments in the communist world have wrought changes far more profound and rapid than any Western social scientist would have dared predict a few years ago. To account for these changes, I have undertaken a comparatively thorough revision of this book. In adding an account of most recent transformations of the communist world, I have also made minor corrections in chapters that remained relatively unchanged. Moreover, parts of the previous book were rearranged—a chapter was eliminated, others were merged—for the sake of achieving a more logical or cohesive presentation.

With regard to one sentiment expressed in the preface to the first two editions I have had second thoughts: In professing my intention to show some moral or political detachment, I had hoped to view communism outside of a narrow cold war perspective and thus to avoid some of the stereotypes fostered in our minds by the cold war. It would be foolish, however, to pretend that I am without values or biases. Indeed, the present book, like its previous versions, will show that my general attitude toward communism is as critical as is my attitude toward other political and social systems, including my own. To zealots on both sides, I know, my attitude is objectionable, and they are not likely to approve of this book.

I am grateful to Adam Ulam for suggesting some of the changes to be made. My special thanks go to Anne Dyer Murphy, an exceedingly competent editor, and a friend.

ALFRED G. MEYER

Preface to the First and Second Editions

• This introduction to communism in its various guises and functions is intended for a broad public of advanced and beginning students, policy-makers, and the proverbial intelligent layman—for anyone, in short, who wants to study the subject with a minimum of political passion. I stress my effort to achieve political detachment because I feel that much of what the general public reads about communism so caters to an attitude of disapproval that it can enlighten no one.

Some may feel that the essay style I have chosen does not suit the purposes of the book; but I believe that an author must reveal himself even when endeavoring to outline his subject and the principal controversies about it. I have tried to counteract personal interpretation by guiding the reader, at every major step, to the ample literature in this field.

I have profited from comments by Samuel Krislov, Archibald Singham, and Donald Urquidi, who read brief sections of the manuscript. Some of my statements would have been different or would not have been made prior to my 1958 trip to the USSR and Poland. For this enlightening travel I am grateful to the Inter-University Travel Grant Committee. To the administration of Michigan State University I owe thanks for releasing me from teaching for a quarter so that I could complete the manuscript. My special gratitude goes to Charles D. Lieber, of Random House, who encouraged me to write this Study, and to Mrs. Leonore C. Hauck, of the same firm.

ALFRED G. MEYER

Contents

COMMUNISM

1

Introduction

• The word "communism" means different things to different people; and its meaning may change from time to time. To some political leaders in colonial or dependent nations it may imply revolt against the white man's rule, liberation from colonialism, and rapid industrialization, aided by Soviet, Chinese, Czech, or German money, goods, or advice. To workers in some Western European countries, from Italy to Finland, it may imply defense of lower-class interests and sharp criticism of American foreign policy, if not sympathy with the Russians, the Chinese, or at least the Vietnam Liberation Front. Many a Western intellectual will regard it as a utopian ideal tarnished by inhuman practices. To the policeman it is an international conspiracy of power-mad criminals. To the citizen of any socialist country, the word connotes, in one sense, a meaningful goal his society is striving to attain within the foreseeable future and, in a broader sense, his country's entire way of life, with its rewards and its hardships. Communism means an ideal, a political movement, a method of analysis, and a way of life. It may even mean a set of attitudes which psychologists might be able to reduce to a syndrome of personality traits. Some people regard it as the product and property of Western civilization, while others see it primarily as an anti-Western revolt, or as a denial of all Western values and traditions.

Obviously, communism is protean; its meaning depends on time and place, circumstance, and on the point of view of the observer. Even its articulate ethos, Marxist theory, clothes itself in garbs of many hues. The theory itself distinguishes different levels of understanding and tries, accordingly, to speak to different publics.[1] It also views reality on different levels of concreteness or abstraction, so that it takes long-, short-, and intermediate-range views of the setting, the goals, and the strategies of the communist movement. Outsiders, meanwhile, note the tendency toward the development of an esoteric communist language which, some maintain, serves as a complicated code only the initiates know how to decipher.[2]

Because the present study is to serve as a general introduction to the subject, I am obliged to approach it eclectically, as perhaps any political phenomenon ought to be approached, if adequate understanding is to be gained. In viewing communism in its various aspects, we shall pay particular attention to a number of problems that run through these various facets of our subject: The element of change—what transformations have communist ideas and practices undergone from the time of Marx to the time of Mao? The element of diversity—what different schools of communism have arisen and which have survived? How important are the differences between communism in France and communism in Malaya, between communist revolutionaries and communist government officials? Is it meaningful to call these various political forces by the same name? Finally, we shall try to assess the nature of the much-discussed "challenge" of communism. Should communism be regarded as a threat to Western civilization, and, if so, in what way is it a threat? Is communism likely to gain adherents and make converts in the years and decades to come? If so, what makes it attractive; what elements in it appeal to people not yet committed to it?

I shall start by presenting the theory of communism; and perhaps this requires justification, because many scholars would dismiss communist theory as irrelevant. They would describe communist doctrine as a grab bag of ideas cynically used by Machiavellian manipulators at the head of communist governments and parties to justify whatever policies they choose to adopt while seeking to gain or maintain power for its own sake. I do not agree with those writers who would derive all actions of communist parties or governments from Marxist ideology. But neither is it entirely true, as many other scholars claim, that the "means have eaten up the ends." Although communism gives a great deal of emphasis to the final goal in its theories, its short-range planning and actions seem to be guided by the revisionist principle that the end is nothing, the means everything. Yet these means were derived from the ends. As Richard Lowenthal correctly says in a recent symposium on this problem, there can be no *Realpolitik* without ideological preconceptions.[3] The theory, moreover, is more than a set of goals. It is also a method of analysis, and it has remained a methodological gridwork through which its initiates view and explain reality. Finally, communism still is a definable state of mind; and the attitudes composing it are also derived in part from Marxism.

In short, communist theory is more than rationalization. Undoubtedly, the thoughts and actions of communist leaders are determined in significant measure by the intellectual heritage of Marx, Lenin, Stalin, and others. But even if this were not so, the fact remains that their ideology remains one of the strongest forces active in the world today. And therefore it must be studied by anyone trying to understand contemporary history.

However, we cannot hope to understand the strength—and the weaknesses—of communist ideas without examining communism as a system of government, a way of life, and an active political movement. Nor can we hope to grasp the meaning of communist ideas without studying the historical and political context within which they were shaped and changed. We shall therefore have to discuss the several communist societies now existing in the world. We must be aware that these societies and the governments managing them have been subject to change. Hence it will be necessary to discuss, at least cursorily, typical phases of communist rule, which may at times be as different from each other as present-day Soviet Russia is from present-day America or even from present-day China, and also the various phases of the policies of the international communist movement.

The resulting image will be complex and, for those who like easy generalizations, unsatisfactory. In order to provide a framework for all the loose pieces we shall have in our hands—and at the risk of oversimplification—let me suggest one such generalization: it seems to me that twentieth-century communism, in all its variations, can be understood to some extent if we regard it as our age's equivalent to seventeenth-century puritanism (which includes as many varying phenomena as communism).* To support this suggestion, let me draw attention to some of the innumerable parallels that can be drawn between the two phenomena.

Puritanism and communism share a number of important broad ideas and political goals. Both claimed to strive for liberty and against tyranny, even though in the name of liberty both set up starkly autocratic regimes. Both claimed to fight for equality and human brotherhood and against the privileges or abuses of ruling classes and hierarchies; yet both set up societies marked by gross inequalities of reward, and in their ideologies they found justification for such inequalities. Both claimed overriding justification—be it God's will or historical inevitability—for destroying institutions they regarded as artificial, unnatural, or imposed. Both, finally, claimed that their aim was to carry out the ideals of revolutions that had preceded them by a century or more. The puritans gave themselves their name because their avowed aim was to fulfill, or purify, the Reformation; whereas communism promises to fulfill the broken promises of the French Revolution.

Puritanism as well as communism are theories of salvation and damnation, incorporating the notion of inevitability (predestination). Both movements fought (or fight) for an invin-

---

* Similarities can also be seen between communism and later forms of puritanism, for instance, Victorianism.

cible cause, guided and strengthened by a Holy Writ that played a central role in shaping the minds of entire generations. Both the puritans and the communists are fully convinced that "objective reality" or "God's will" can be known through careful study of the scriptures. Both movements developed their thought into complicated and involved systems of ideas that include theories of history, human nature, society, and the entire universe, and provide standards for behavior, including a theory of leadership and obedience. In both cases, moreover, the revolutionary zeal of the educated spokesmen appealed to broad strata of the lower, underprivileged classes, who were exhorted to despise and destroy the prevailing authorities; yet, once the leaders had installed themselves in power, that same zeal caused them to impose intolerable conditions and superhuman standards of performance on the citizens.

In both puritanism and communism we have, I think, cases of liberational movements gone sour and pessimistic, movements that therefore are marked by strange ambivalences in judgment and contradictions in both goals and methods. For both, an intellectual point of departure is the belief in the sovereignty of the autonomous human personality; in one case it is the individual in his direct relationship to his God, in the other case it is the proletariat in its crucial role in history. But in both cases serious doubt has arisen. For the puritans, this implied a renewed emphasis on original sin; for the communists beginning with Lenin, the belief that the working class by itself could never attain consciousness. In both movements, the practical consequence was that the earlier democratic conception that men would freely and spontaneously choose the road to (heavenly or earthly) salvation gave way to the idea that the elect, the vanguard, the chosen few would have to force the masses into salvation. Yet, while the individual (or the class) is regarded as weak and untrustworthy, while the movement has little faith in the autonomous personality, it still burdens the individual with grave responsibility for his actions and thoughts. Distrust in human nature or an emphasis on original sin is accompanied by the attempt to make every man into a fully rational being or into a saint, while the gloomy realization that this task might be impossible drives the movement to manipulation, coercion, and terror, carried out in both cases by an organization of the elect which coöpts its members, while going through the motions of elections or other democratic procedures. In organization, in procedure, in the purges they carried out, and in their actual and pretended relationship to government authorities (once a puritan or communist government has been created), the organization of the elect and the Communist Party bear striking resemblances to each other.

The underlying pessimism is expressed in the conviction that Satan (or capitalism) will surely defeat the cause of righteousness if the movement relents for but a little moment in its zealous devotion to the dogma, in its intolerance of deviation and laxness. Indeed, the devil lurks behind the most angelic masks, and both the puritan and the communist are therefore witch hunters, who tend to explain untoward developments by the weakest of all social theories—the conspiratorial theory. At the basis of the deep pessimism that characterizes both puritanism and communism is, perhaps, the fact that both these revolutionary movements were only partly successful, that they were forced to *coexist* with their enemy. Theoretically, neither movement was prepared for prolonged coexistence during which it might be obliged to have friendly or at least normal relations with the enemy. Both were profoundly disturbed by the experience.

Coexistence fortified the tendency of both puritans and communists to see everything in black and white and to divide mankind into friends and enemies, recognizing no shadings or positions in between truth and falsehood. Both are totalitarian in that they seek to infuse every realm of human endeavor with the spirit of their movement. Everything a man may do has religious (or political) significance. No pursuits are undertaken for their own sake, but must be given the spirit of *partiinost'*.* Precisely because the movements are forced to accommodate "temporarily" to coexistence with

---

* For an explanation of this term, see pp. 104–105.

the foe, they must banish all thoughts of lasting or meaningful accommodation. Because of this pessimism and the resulting ambivalence, the urge to cleanse out what is rotten and wrong is given a note of frantic urgency. Every action counts. Everything that is done is decisive.

Despite the otherworldly orientation of the puritans and the lofty humanism of communist doctrine, both movements must be characterized as intensely materialistic and secular. The principal orientation of both can be said to be *accumulation,* that is, economic growth. And just as the American puritans went forth into the wilderness to carry civilization to the aborigines, so communism is the pioneer movement which in our century seeks to civilize (in the material sense) the underdeveloped nations, which aims to bring social mobility and the spirit of work to indolent cultures. There is about both movements the same missionary spirit, the same desire to liberate all mankind from evil and sloth.

In both cases, finally, this mission is carried out with an almost inhuman earnestness, with a complete lack of a sense of humor, and a stern intolerance of frivolousness and hedonism. The drabness of Soviet towns, the stark utilitarianism of Chinese communist garments, the primness of Soviet sex morality are as puritan as they could be and remind us vividly of the pictures we have seen of America in the days of her Western pioneers. In both cases, the individual is to be serious, thrifty, and single-minded in his devotion to the goal of accumulating wealth.

Future historians may find also that neither the puritan dictatorship nor its twentieth-century analog can sustain itself indefinitely. The strains and the human cost of terror and thought control become excessive. To ease the strain and maintain the societies they have created, both systems may be bound to transform themselves, however gradually, into more pluralistic and more open societies.

The similarities I have pointed out have been noticed by previous observers.[4] But they deserve mention nevertheless because I think that the comparison gives us a rather unusual view of communism, an angle of vision that might help to explain features and relationships which might otherwise

remain puzzles. In addition, I must confess that I find the
déjà-vu feeling this perspective gives me a bit reassuring;
for the comparison suggests that communism might not be
as novel, as strange, or as alien to Western traditions as it
appears to most of us, and as many of its adherents would
like to make it seem. At the same time, as a decidedly anti-
puritan person, I find that this view adds support to the
antipathy I feel toward various features in the development
of communism, even though it does help to explain them.

Let us then analyze the growth, the ideas, and the way of
life of this twentieth-century puritanism, beginning with its
own Good Book, the writings of Karl Marx and Friedrich
Engels.

Although I am beginning with an exposition of Marxist
doctrine, I do not wish to imply the existence of a causal
chain from doctrine to institutions. There is a much more
complicated reciprocal relationship between ideas and politics; and at all its stages of development, the doctrine itself
can be understood only as a response to real social problems.
Hence an introduction to Marxist theories should properly
begin with the Industrial Revolution, the French Revolution, and the social and political problems resulting from
both.

2

Marxist Theory

• The emergence of nineteenth-century industrial society brought massive social dislocation and misery. Technological progress made entire classes of small producers and distributors obsolete, impoverished them, degraded them in the social scale, and forced them into the burgeoning cities, where unspeakable working and living conditions awaited them. Socialism as a mass movement began as the rebellion of the working class against their misery. Sporadic, almost aimless uprisings, such as those of the weavers in Silesia, the machine-wrecking Luddites in England, or the numerous working-class rebellions of 1848, mark the beginnings of the socialist movement. As a political theory, it developed when the workers' lot was contrasted with the liberal rhetoric prevailing at the time. Its point of departure was the assertion that the ideals of the American and French revolutions— liberty, equality, brotherhood, and the right to a human existence—had been betrayed; and that the promise of these revolutions could be fulfilled only if political rights were matched by social and economic equality, by wiping out the difference between rich and poor. Beyond this, we cannot generalize about advocates or theorists of socialism. They have differed sharply not only over the definition of the kind of society that would rectify these ills but even more over the methods that would bring it into existence. They have included atheists and believers, pacifists and terrorists, criminals and saints, authoritarians and anarchists, and all shadings in between. The variety of socialist schools that has developed in the last 170 years is made clear to us when we realize that, in the vague sense I have given to the word, almost everyone today is a socialist or has accepted socialist ideals.[1]

Communism regards itself as the legitimate heir of all that is valid and good in the socialist tradition It looks upon the working-class revolts of the early nineteenth century as the beginnings of its own movement and regards the first socialists, beginning with Gracchus Babeuf, as precursors of its most honored prophets, Marx and Engels (who, incidentally, preferred to call themselves communists rather than socialists, in order to emphasize their disagreements with other socialists).

The precursors of Marx and Engels are often referred to as "utopian socialists." This term was used by the Marxists themselves in criticism of both the detailed descriptions of the coming socialist society which earlier theorists had given and their failure to indicate how these societies might be brought into existence.[2] In contrast, Marx and Engels regarded their communism as scientific socialism. They claimed to have proven that the coming of socialism was inevitable; and their entire doctrine is an attempt to support this assertion. Marxism can therefore be defined as that school of socialism which seeks to prove that socialism is inevitable.

As we shall see a little later, Marxists support this assertion partly by moral argument: capitalism so degrades the individual, so frustrates his potentialities for creative development, that life under it is hell on earth, a mockery of all the ethical commands associated with the Christian-Liberal tradition. But man still retains his innate ability to shape a good life for himself, through socialism.

Marx and Engels, however, denied that they were moral philosophers or prophets preaching reform to an evil society. When they asserted the inevitability of socialism, they used the word "inevitable" in a descriptive (or, as they would have put it, scientific) sense. The existing system, they thought, simply could not last, and all the conditions necessary for the birth of socialism had come into being. The core of this doctrine was and remains the Marxist description of capitalism and the "laws" governing it—that is, the manner in which the system functioned. According to these laws, capitalism was well suited to ensure economic growth in the early industrial age; and Marx therefore assigns the most important place to capitalism among the stages in the march of human progress. No social philosopher, perhaps, has rivaled the songs of praise that Marx and Engels sang to capitalism in their *Communist Manifesto*. At the same time, however, Marxism asserts that the same laws that made capitalism advance the progress of mankind would bring misery, chaos, crisis, and final breakdown to the mature capitalist society. Institutions, habits, and intellectual traditions that had once strengthened the system would burden and fetter it intolerably and would hasten its collapse.

The fundamental law governing the Marxist model of capitalism is that of the market. In basing his analysis on this law, Marx follows in the footsteps of Adam Smith and other "classical" economists. He differs from them on several counts. For one thing, he places market economies into historical perspective by pointing out that they were preceded by different systems. There are societies in which men produce only to satisfy their immediate needs or those of their masters. Under capitalism, however, they produce marketable commodities; and all their economic activity is guided, even dictated, by the market. Another assertion distinguishing Marxism from classical economic theories is that under capitalism the labor power of the "immediate producers"—the workers—is bought and sold as if it were a commodity. Therefore, the very lives of people who are compelled to work for a living are subject to the laws of the market. Life has become a market place, with human work, human emotions, human spirit bought and sold as a commodity.

To Marx, this transformation of human labor power into a commodity is the specific feature which distinguishes capitalism from all other market economies and therefore from all other modes of production as well. Since, according to Marx, human labor is the only creative force, its subjection to the laws of the market introduced into that market a curious element both constructive and disruptive: a commodity which, through the creation of values, could not only reproduce itself but could create far more than its own market value.

Before we pursue this, we must note one other line of argument connected with the definition of capitalism as that mode of production in which human labor power has become a commodity. I have in mind the attempt Marx and Engels made to show beyond any doubt that capitalism was an exploitative system. To do so, they again followed in the footsteps of classical economics by incorporating in their market theory a theory of value. Most Western economists today do not take the Marxist theory of value seriously and tend to regard the very notion of value as meaningless. They have usually failed to see, however, the crucial role which the Marxist theory of value plays, not as a concept in economic analysis, but as a description of *social* relationships in a market economy; and of particular significance here is the relationship between capitalist and worker, because, on the basis of his particular definition of value and the classical laws of the market, Marx could argue that the workers, selling their labor power at its true value, were nevertheless cheated out of a portion of what their labor produced.

From the concept of human labor as a commodity producing surplus value and from the relationship of this human commodity to the "dead" commodities (materials, machines, and so forth) used in production, Marx derived additional laws governing both the growth and collapse of capitalism. These laws describe capitalism as a system compelled by its inner dynamic to accumulate capital at an ever-increasing rate and to invest it in new enterprises even though a constantly falling rate of profit made investment more and more difficult. The force of these laws was further seen to drive increasing numbers of capitalists to their ruin, swelling the ranks of the propertyless proletariat. Fiercely competing with each other, the workers would drive down the market value of human labor power, creating additional misery for the proletariat. Capitalism was therefore a system that had, through technological and social progress, led mankind to the threshold of an era in which the material needs of all humanity could be filled, if only the technological achievements could be used rationally. But the laws governing capitalist production had caused the system to become entangled in hopeless difficulties: a free-enterprise system in which all individuals operated blindly and helplessly; a productive capacity that could not be used; surplus human beings who could not be employed; surplus commodities that could not be sold nor given away, even while poverty was increasing. These and similar problems, Marx and Engels believed, capitalism could not possibly solve without destroying itself. Inevitably, therefore, the system would collapse, and socialism would rise from the ruins. This death and rebirth of society would take the form of a revolution in which the proletariat would expropriate the capitalists and reorganize the economy on completely different, and rational, principles. Society would then be able to satisfy all men's material needs. Inequality and exploitation would be abolished. Oppressive institutions and inhuman behavior would become superfluous and dysfunctional and would wither away. As a matter of fact, all institutions, habits, traditions, beliefs, behavior patterns, and the like, now confining and constraining human beings and preventing them from freely being themselves, would become superfluous. For, having become fully rational, all men would also become convinced that their own private interests could be satisfied only if they were identified with the interests of all. Men would become like brothers. Their relations with each other would be free and easy and spontaneous. This belief in the coming brotherhood of men led many communists in the years immediately following the Russian Revolution to believe that law courts and the police, money and wages, sexual morals and the institution of the monogamous family, and many other elements of social life would disappear in the very near future.

Crucial to this vision of inevitability was the belief that the proletariat would be equipped to destroy the old and

erect the new. And, in Marxist theory, the working class is
indeed endowed with education, rationality, discipline, organization, and other qualities which, taken together, transform them into a Chosen People who will lead mankind into
an earthly Promised Land.

This image of the proletariat and the society within which
it exists is based upon several important assumptions. There
is, first, Marx's insistence that social studies are a science. To
use his and Hegel's terminology: History proceeds in accordance with laws, *gesetzmässig*, and because of this it can be
understood by men. This belief in man's ability to understand history is based, in turn, on the axiom that man is rational and therefore potentially free, freedom being defined
as the ability to shape one's destiny and to develop one's inherent potentialities to the fullest extent.

The question that arises at once is one which Rousseau
asked in the first page of his *Social Contract*: If man is free,
why is he everywhere in chains? In the same spirit, Marx
might have asked why man's fate is not freely made by him
but is determined by his environment, even though man is
rational. Rousseau's answer is that civilization corrupted and
enslaved man. Marx's reply is rather similar. In his theory,
man is the animal that *produces*—which means that man
strives intelligently and purposively to master the forces and
resources of nature. Except on the most primitive level, however, production is an organized activity, not of individuals,
but of societies, which in conformity with their technological
and scientific achievements develop social structures and institutions as a framework or machinery for carrying out the
activity of production. For Marx, the history of mankind is
the development of different modes of production, that is,
of different types of social structures, from primitive and inefficient to highly complex and efficient ones, all of which
must be seen primarily as machineries designed to master
the forces of nature and to ensure man's survival and comfort.

The most important principle of social structuring, in
Marx's theory, is the class structure. Marxism maintains that
the division of labor in all societies has led to the develop-

ment of classes, the different classes being defined by their relations to the essential means of production. And, since control over these means of production confers decisive power over the entire community, the class that wields such control is not only playing a different role in the economy, it also plays a different political role by becoming the ruling class.[3]

Marxism contains a theory of lag: although a correspondence can be traced between class structure and technology and general mode of production, these "forces of production" are seen as developing on and on while the "production relations" show tendencies toward becoming rigid and self-perpetuating. Human progress is conceived as proceeding at varying speeds. New forces of production win over older, and "lower," forces. A new ruling class controlling these new forces establishes itself and builds social institutions corresponding to the new mode of production. Once in power, however, the new ruling class seeks to perpetuate its rule even if it is made obsolete and superfluous by further economic progress. The class structure becomes a drag on further progress. The superstructure of institutions, ideologies, and habits, which once was part of the forces of progress, now paralyzes further development. The forces and relations of production are in conflict with each other. Man's past actions dominate the present generation. They do so all the more easily because men, according to Marx, are not, as a rule, aware of their state of subjection to the forces of the past. They believe they are masters of their fate even while they have only a false consciousness of the relationships that constitute the mainspring of their respective societies. This false consciousness, which Marx called ideology, enables men to live in unjust and moribund societies. But it also prevents them from seeing the impending doom of these societies.

Thus man's freedom is only potential. But Marx believed that it could be realized. All his doctrine is based on a yearning for freedom and on the assumption that history is continual progress in the realization of freedom, a movement toward a society worthy of man. This vision of progress is related to a humanist ethic based on the principle that "man, for man, is the highest being," and that therefore everything which pains or degrades him must be abolished. Like all socialists, Marx denounced the free-enterprise system for having betrayed liberal values. Unlike some of them, however, he went further and criticized *all* societies, past and present, for having betrayed basic human values. His doctrine calls for the most radical criticism of social institutions. Just as Rousseau and the romantics had contended that civilization is evil and spoils human nature, so Marx held that human relationships in civilized society—torn as it is by class conflict—are false, evil, unworthy; and that, in such a society, man is *alienated* from nature, his fellow man, and even himself. Class societies dehumanize man. Marx's moral indignation at such alienation pervades all his writings, especially those that preceded his economic analysis of capitalism. He was a radical humanist before he became a Marxist.

In contrast, however, to present-day critics of mass culture and the bureaucratic society, Marx was an optimist. As a matter of fact, his doctrine is the last example of the great optimistic ideologies that have succeeded each other in the Western tradition; it is, in that sense, the direct heir of liberalism.[4]

This optimism is based on the idea that mankind can solve all its problems without divine assistance, because of man's essentially rational nature. Marx's view of human nature is Promethean; Marx sees man as capable, like Prometheus, of defying the gods and stealing their fire to provide himself with the warmth of material comfort and the light of knowledge. Marxism is an arrogant ideology, and religious thinkers in our day often condemn it as a "secular religion." In their view man is afflicted with original sin and therefore forever unable to solve all his problems. They regard the intention to create the good life on this earth as presumptuous and blasphemous, and they point out that the attempt to carry out this intention, condemned in advance to failure, must lead to totalitarian tyranny.*

---

* Assuming that in fact secular religion tends to impose dictatorship on the people in its attempt to create an earthly paradise, we must be aware at the same time that heavenly religion, by

Marx and Engels, however, had no such fears. To be sure, they foresaw and even welcomed a period of violence and dictatorship that would link capitalism with communism. Meaningful change, in their eyes, could not but take the form of revolution. No ruling class, they thought, had ever given up or would ever give up their power without a desperate struggle. Nor could the change from one mode of production to another proceed without the old superstructure of institutions and beliefs being smashed. History, they held, progresses in leaps; where certain features lag behind the development of the means of production, there must be sharp breaks with the past and a thorough overhauling of the social system, through terror and violence. They condoned this violence because it would be coercion of the few by the many, of the exploiters by the exploited, of the ruling class by the people. They also implied that the period during which this dictatorship of the working class would prevail would be brief. Finally, whatever dictatorial or totalitarian features the dictatorship of the proletariat would entail, Marx and Engels regarded it as but the transition to the Good Society, an inevitable albeit regrettable means to a moral end.

We must ask ourselves on what facts or presuppositions Marx and Engels based this glowing optimism. Was it not in conflict with their ambivalent appraisal of civilization, that is, with their belief that the material progress of mankind had led to the increasing dehumanization of man? To be sure, if man's alienation is a consequence of the division of labor, the class struggle, and the unequal distribution of the means of production, then it follows that alienation might be cured once private property and the class struggle have been abolished. If it is correct to trace the growth of oppressive institutions and deceptive ideologies to the special needs of class-torn societies, then surely it follows that tyranny, exploitation, and superstition are likely to wither away once the class struggle is a feature of the past. Even within the terms of Marxist ideas, however, it is by no means obvious

---

postponing paradise to the hereafter, falls into the danger of being indifferent to human misery which could be alleviated by rational action.

why the revolution leading to such a classless society should ever occur; or why, if indeed the working class seizes power, it will know what to do with it to ensure that leap into the realm of freedom which Marx and Engels foresaw. On the contrary, if they were right in saying that man is dehumanized under capitalism and that the worker has been transformed into a commodity, a marketable piece of equipment, how could they impute to these same workingmen that rationality which would make the coming of socialism inevitable?

The answer is that, according to Marxist theory, the proletariat is so absolutely alienated that the mechanism by which the ruling classes have usually managed to divert the attention and stultify the minds of the exploited no longer functions. The worker under capitalism has been estranged so relentlessly from what sociologists today call primary organizations and loyalties that his consciousness can free itself from deceptive ideologies. Having been dehumanized, the worker becomes aware of his dehumanization and understands the social system that has produced him. When men become conscious of themselves as commodities, they will feel the urge to abolish that mode of production which makes them commodities. They will also have the power to do so. Marx and Engels attributed to the working class not only full rationality (born out of unprecedented misery) but also a number of qualities that would enable them to be successful in their striving to abolish capitalism. For one thing, the proletariat in the period of mature capitalism would constitute the overwhelming majority of the population. Moreover, they would be well organized, having learned the virtues of cooperation in the capitalist machine shop, where work proceeded in cooperative fashion. By drafting them into their armies, the ruling classes had also trained the proletariat for warfare, and by educating them in at least an elementary way had further equipped them for the coming role as revolutionaries and rulers. Finally, Marx and Engels assumed that as the class which by its physical labor with modern machines was the only really productive class in capitalist society, the proletariat was also well prepared to expropriate the means of production and assume command over them.

This image of the working class as combining rationality with power and therefore inevitably bound to lead mankind into the Promised Land is a bold attempt to reconcile the gloomy theory of alienation with the Promethean image of man. It must be regarded as the cornerstone of Marxist theory.[5]

We recognize in this image a variation of a dream that is at least as old as Socrates. He believed that true goodness cannot be theoretical but must be expressed in works: one cannot know virtue without practicing it. Something akin to this belief is inherent in the Marxist belief that the self-consciousness of the proletariat will impel it to act. But Marx also shared the idea of Socrates' pupil Plato that ideas remain ineffectual if they are not backed by power. This insight into the problem of power caused Plato to wish for a philosopher who was either himself a king or whose advice was accepted by a king. In Marx the awareness of the problem of power led to the statement that ideas become effective only when they get hold of the masses. Neither philosophy nor action is effective by itself; they must work together. It is not enough, wrote Marx, that the idea strive toward realization; reality should also be receptive to the idea. And it is this coincidence of revolutionary thought with revolutionary action that Marx saw in the working-class movement on the eve of the Revolution of 1848.

The reader might miss a treatment of Marxist philosophy in this short sketch, especially since almost any other treatment of Marxism, be it by communists or by Western scholars, would begin with an outline of dialectical materialism. The reason I am omitting such an outline is that Marxism is a social theory, not a universal philosophy. Marx was interested in human relationships and social institutions; he dealt with nature only insofar as it was part of human society, and he had use for philosophy only to the extent that it was identical with scientific method. He held, moreover, that every realm of existence must be understood in terms of its own laws; hence he did not contend that the methods and insights he advanced in his social theories were applicable to biology, physics, or general philosophy. There is, in short, a decidedly positivistic strain in Marxism. And yet, neither Marx nor Engels could escape or deny the profound influence which Hegelian philosophy exerted on them, a philosophy which focused its sights on concepts of reason and freedom and had developed a highly esoteric combination of ontology and logic, called dialectics.[6] In negating these elements of Hegelian philosophy, Marx nonetheless retained and transformed it. In his view, moral philosophy was inadequate or meaningless if it did not coincide with, or even take the form of, revolutionary action designed to change reality. He saw philosophy and politics, thought and action, science and moral postulates, as coalescing, as Plato had hoped they would fuse in the philosopher-king. And just as the Platonic utopia demands a philosopher-king, so the entire structure of Marxist ideas is held together by the belief that the proletariat does indeed represent the merger of theory and practice. This belief, in turn, is the keystone of that "materialist" (read: sociological) dialectics into which Marx transformed Hegel's philosophy of reason. However, moral philosophy which becomes incarnate in the revolutionary proletariat, and a dialectic of reason which is "stood on its feet" and then becomes the history of human institutions have turned into a denial of abstract philosophy. Any attempt to abstract a universal philosophy from Marxism is therefore a distortion, and I should be prepared to argue this even though Engels himself, in violation of all his own positivistic statements, was the first to attempt this distortion.[7]

3

European Marxism,
1848–1914

• The evidence is not altogether conclusive, but the impression prevails that when Marx and Engels wrote the Manifesto of the Communist Party in 1847, summarizing their views with marvelous conciseness, they were momentarily expecting the end of capitalism. They thought that their ideas were but the articulation of actual feelings, of the actual consciousness shared by vast masses of proletarians who were prepared for revolutionary action and were waiting only for some historic event or for action by the enlightened leadership to set events in motion. Marx and Engels knew, as many other politically conscious people in Europe knew, that a revolution was brewing. They thought it would be the revolution of the proletariat.[1]

In fact, however, the working class played a comparatively negligible role in most of the upheavals that shook Europe in 1848. Moreover, in the subsequent years and even decades, the development of the working-class movement gave Marx and Engels little encouragement to expect the proletariat to rally to the banner of their ideas. Working-class parties were slow in getting organized; and when they did, their leaders (and followers) were not necessarily committed to Marxist doctrines.

This failure of the 1848 revolution, and the seeming un-

willingness of the masses to become fully conscious (in the
Marxist sense of the term) led to soul searching on the part
of the fathers of the doctrine and caused them to make adjustments in their thoughts concerning the nature of capitalism, the aims and morphology of the revolution, and the
strategy to be employed by the proletariat. Explanations had
to be found for the failure; contemporary political constellations had to be examined for this purpose; and, in both cases,
Marx and Engels were forced to pay closer attention to concrete phenomena at odds with the more abstract grand design of their theoretical model. Recognition of precapitalist
features still affecting current politics was not, of course, regarded as a refutation of the theory, but it did complicate
the task of analysis, self-orientation, and evaluation. Similarly, instead of preparing for the final act of revolution, as
Engels, particularly, had done with joyous alacrity in 1848,
Marx and Engels now felt compelled to study and discuss
strategies that might prepare the ground for revolution and
lead toward it; and here again short-range plans were likely
to come into conflict with long-range expectations. Or, at
least, the strategy of Marxist politics was obliged to consider
measures and attitudes that the original theory of revolution
simply had not incorporated—alliances with other radical
movements, foreign policy problems, the evaluation of constitutional democracy from the point of view of the proletariat, and so forth. Various ranges of strategy were developed,
and different aims—minimal, maximal, and in between—
were formulated. In retrospect, many of these changes appear drastic when compared to the dreams of 1848; and one
scholar has dramatized the contrast by stating that after
1848 Marx "became what is nowadays called an ex-Commu-
nist." [2]

Yet these drastic changes did not imply any fundamental
changes in the grand conception. Rather, they can be regarded as refinements, concretization, elaboration, and extension of the doctrine. The intense and ceaseless intellectual
activity of research, writing, and debating in which Marx
and Engels engaged to the end of their lives, without ever
completing their major task of systematic exposition, was

solidly founded on the ideas they had elaborated in common in the five years or so before 1848.

This unfinished job of elaboration and extension made Marxism more complex, ambiguous, and fragmentary, hence more subject to controversial discussion, misinterpretation, and vulgarization. There are, indeed, many scholars who claim that the process of misinterpretation and vulgarization was begun by Engels himself. They would point out that Engels' book against Dühring is filled with naive and shallow passages that do violence to Marx's sophistication, and that his attempt to apply Marxist ideas to the realm of natural science is based on gross misunderstanding. Against this argument, we have indications that Marx approved of the anti-Dühring manuscript. Be that as it may, however, Marxism has certainly not always been well understood, even by its own most devoted followers. Indeed, it seems to be fashionable among Marx scholars today to distinguish carefully between (a) the thoughts of Karl Marx and (b) Marxism in its various forms. The first important school that misunderstood and misrepresented Marxism were the theoreticians of the European socialist movement in the generation preceding World War I, the spokesmen of the Second International. Even though many of them battled fiercely to defend the letter of what had already become the Marxist Holy Writ against any attempts to revise or criticize it, Marxism in their hands became something quite different from the ideas of its founder. They turned his revolutionary radicalism into a comparatively tame search for gradual reform; for his fighting spirit they substituted something akin to fatalism; and instead of the contempt he had for liberal democracy, his followers had an honest veneration for constitutional government. The subtlety of Marxist dialectics became the shallow determinism which non-Marxist scholars have always had an easy time refuting.[3]

These disciples also perverted Marx's ideas by extending them—as Engels had begun to do—from social science into natural science and general philosophy. Marxist dialectics, a complex set of heuristic devices that had served to make Marx sensitive to subtle and involved relationships, is far

too esoteric in language and complicated in ideas to become
the ideology of a broad political movement. Nor did it fit
the scientific concepts and prejudices then dominant in the
educated world. For these and other reasons, the concep-
tual tools of Marx were abstracted from their context and
transformed into an utterly inadequate philosophy, called
"dialectical materialism," that was a caricature of Marx's
thinking. Finally, the notion of the unity of theory and practice, central to Marxist ideas, was almost totally forgotten.
Marxists no longer understood the importance which Marx
and Engels had attributed to proletarian consciousness in
their theory of revolution; and the notion of class consciousness itself was given a very different meaning. We shall see
that some of these misinterpretations have found their way
also into contemporary communist thought, while others
have been rejected.

In trying to explain this process of vulgarization, we have
called attention to the fragmentary state and the complexity
of Marxist thought, as well as to the intellectual preconceptions of the Victorian age. We might have added that the
jargon of Hegelianism presented a formidable obstacle to the
understanding of Marxist ideas. But the most important reason for the transformation was undoubtedly the changing
nature of the working-class movement.

Marxism found a mass basis only in the last two decades
of the nineteenth century. For only then did the growing labor movement in Continental Europe adopt Marxism as its
guiding ideology. By that time, however, the proletariat was
quite different from the one described in the *Communist
Manifesto*. Far from being impoverished, it was beginning
to obtain its share—however modest—of the material benefits being reaped by the business community in these decades. Moreover, whether because of the continued agitation
for constitutional reform, or for whatever other reasons, the
working class was given the franchise, formed political parties, and began to participate in constitutional politics.

Instead of being absolutely alienated, therefore, significant
sections of the working class, and especially their political
leaders and trade-union officials, began to feel themselves

part of a functioning social system that only needed to be improved to be altogether acceptable. From revolutionists they turned into reformists and constitutional democrats. Abandoning the plan to smash the existing system, they began to strive for improvements in working and living conditions, and equal political rights. And in the end, when an international war forced them to decide between their loyalty to their class and their loyalty to their country, most of them, at least for the time being, abandoned internationalism and chose patriotism.

There was therefore a growing gap between the revolutionary theory and the reformist practice of the Marxist movement, which sooner or later would call for serious readjustments. Most of those who were aware of the discrepancy sought to revise Marxist ideas to bring them into line with current political strategies, although a handful of radical leaders tried in vain to revise the movement's political program to bring it back into line with revolutionary theory.* Those who did not see, or did not wish to see, the divergence of doctrine and practice were forced to align them by reinterpreting and misinterpreting Marxist thought. This process of reinterpretation gradually merged with that of revision; and both have gone on apace ever since the end of the last century. The result has been that democratic socialism has almost completely divorced itself from Marxist theories.

---

* Even these radicals, of course, were forced to make adjustments in the theory. We shall come back to these adjustments when we discuss the communist theory of imperialism.

4

Principles of Leninism

• The gap between theory and practice was even wider in prerevolutionary Russia than in Russia after the revolution. The tsarist empire must be characterized as a relatively backward society, a term that is not meant to imply moral or cultural superiority of other nations, but denotes only one thing, technological inferiority and the resultant lower productivity. Nor does it imply that the country did not have its share of highly educated, cultured people who made important contributions to science, art, and philosophy. Russia before the revolution of 1917 was backward because in the nations of Western and Central Europe she faced neighbors who had more productive economies and therefore were also stronger militarily and politically. In stressing the nicely measurable economic backwardness, I do not, of course, wish to minimize related cultural and political differences, such as the almost universal illiteracy of the Russian people through the nineteenth century or the prevalence of an autocratic political system of the kind that the French and American revolutions had done away with more than a hundred years before.

Economically advanced nations are usually regarded by their less-fortunate neighbors as presenting a threat to themselves, and much of Russia's history can be explained in terms of reaction to the technological superiority of the West.

The great dilemma faced by political leaders in underdeveloped areas is this: What they regard as the threat of economically advanced nations can be mitigated only by adopting the technology which is at the basis of the presumed threat. For a nation that wishes to maintain its established culture and traditional way of life, the need to "westernize" is extremely painful. But the rulers of old Russia were well aware of this need, and some of Russia's tsars were nothing less than revolutionaries who tried to transform radically the society over which they ruled. To be sure, while they sought to introduce Western technology, science, and administrative skills, they did not wish to endanger their own rule. Consequently, their aim was to westernize selectively; but in this they did not succeed. On the contrary, with Western technology and administration came Western progressive ideas and movements of reform.

Old Russia was ruled by emperors who claimed absolute power. Their arm of government was a civil and military bureaucracy, the officers of which were recruited mainly from the landowning aristocracy, a privileged leisure class whose wealth was measured not only in land but also in serfs. They had obtained their privileges as compensation for services rendered to the tsars. But in the eighteenth century they were freed of their service obligation while retaining their privileges. Indeed, service itself became a privilege of the nobility. After the nobles were freed of their duties, the serfs remained in bondage for about another hundred years. They were released only in the second half of the nineteenth century. But the land they were given at this time was so inadequate that they remained in economic bondage to their old masters. Constantly on the brink of economic ruin and smarting under legal discrimination, the Russian peasants, constituting about nine-tenths of the population, were therefore a dissatisfied class and potential fomenters of revolution.[1]

Toward the end of the nineteenth century, industry began to develop in Russia and a working class grew which found itself laboring and living under very poor conditions, thus forming another revolutionary class, which was easy to organize and from the very beginning was conscious of its grievances. With the growth of industrialism, a middle class of merchants, capitalists, and well-educated professional people also arose. This class at once sought to participate in the political process and began to advance such aims as free enterprise and democracy. In tsarist Russia such aims, too, were revolutionary. These various revolutionary groups were joined by representatives of Russia's numerous national minorities, who demanded equality, autonomy, self-determination, and similar rights which tsarist Russia denied them. These classes were revolutionary in the sense that their grievances were deep and the system was unable or too dilatory to satisfy them. My calling them "revolutionary" does not, however, mean that Russia's peasants, workers, and growing middle class were active in fomenting revolution or even desirous of overthrowing tsarism. On the contrary, the vast majority of Russians doubtless felt that their needs and hopes could and would be satisfied by the tsar and his government. Only dramatic crises of confidence jolted sufficient numbers out of this belief to cause revolutionary upheavals.

Russia had witnessed rebellion, unrest, and revolution throughout the ages. But the revolutions of 1905 and 1917 were unique because in them for the first time the entire people, or at least the vast majority, participated actively or tolerated the upheaval passively. These revolutions were different also because, unlike most previous rebellions Russia had witnessed, they were fought in the name of ideals imported from the West: the ideals of liberalism and socialism. Finally, in 1917, these ideals were being propounded and translated into programs and strategies by organized political parties well known to the broad masses of the population.

Nineteenth-century Russia had proved to be curiously receptive to the most radical Western ideas; and, beginning in the 1880's, Marxism began to exert tremendous influence on the minds of revolutionary intellectuals. Out of local conspiratorial organizations, which often began to coalesce with the spontaneously growing labor movement, a Marxist party was born which by 1903 emerged fully organized, though troubled by serious disagreements. In fact, we can easily agree with Leopold Haimson, who says that the Russian Social-Democratic Labor Party in 1903 was stillborn: the disagreements dividing the party in the very beginning of its history became more and more acute. Factions developed into separate parties; and the contending leaders finally found themselves on opposite sides of the barricades.

These disagreements can be traced to the difficulties that inevitably arose when attempts were made to apply Marxist ideas to Russia. It should be obvious that the thoughts of Marx and Engels about the nature of the revolution or about political strategy could not serve as an adequate guide to their Russian disciples. Marxism was the product of Western conditions and Western developments; and many features of Russian society did not correspond to the Marxist model. Marx and Engels had relied on a large and mature proletariat to seize power when the number of capitalists had been reduced to a minimum. In Russia, however, the number of workers was small in comparison with the total population. Moreover, capitalism, far from being on the decline or even at its peak, was still growing. The number of people engaged in business was small; not, however, because competition had ruined most of them, but, rather, because Russian capitalism was still in its beginnings. Russia remained overwhelmingly a country of peasants. Who was to serve as the historical moving force in such a country? Who was to play the revolutionary role most Marxists wanted to be played?

And what kind of revolution was it to be? It could not very well be expected that a proletarian revolution in Russia—or any revolution whatsoever—would usher in the socialist society predicted by Marx and Engels. Russia's peasant society could not produce that abundance of industrial products which, in Marxist theory, is one of the essential preconditions of socialism. Hence even a proletarian revolution in Russia would have to have different results from those expected in the West.

Every one of these and related questions raised controversies that created and exacerbated division in the Russian Marxist movement. Obviously, it would not be possible

within the framework of this study to trace any of these controversies. Since our topic is communism. we must, in any
event, largely disregard the arguments of noncommunist
Marxists. Hence we will not be able to discuss the views of
the mensheviks at all. But even the bolsheviks' views can be
summarized only in the sketchiest manner.[2]

Bolsheviks and mensheviks agreed that in Russia the working class must fight for not one but two revolutions—the
bourgeois and the proletarian one. Their political program
thus gave unprecedentedly sharp emphasis to the Marxist
distinction between maximal and minimal goals. The bolsheviks' minimum program aimed to destroy tsarism and the
rule of landlords, and to establish a "democratic republic,"
that is, a constitutional, representative government, in which,
to be sure, social legislation providing for social security,
minimum wages, maximum hours, and the like, was to pro-
tect the working class against excessive exploitation. Only
after this stage had been reached would it be advisable to
begin preparations for the proletarian revolution that would
usher in the socialist society.

This step-by-step approach to socialism was dictated by
the developmental theory of Marxism, which sees history as
a logical unfolding of stages, where the contradictions or
inconsistencies inherent in each stage determine the nature
of the succeeding one. Few Marxists even in Russia were
prepared to admit the possibility that any major stage might
be skipped altogether, though in practice communist theory
was to come close to this position, as we shall see.

The communists' endeavor to help establish a "democratic
republic" in Russia can be explained by another argument as
well: Communism was convinced (and communists today
tend to have similar convictions) that constitutional democracy was more desirable than the tsarist police state or any
other autocratic government.

The communist attitude toward democracy is highly complex. In the sense of popular government, democracy is, of
course, part of the ideal toward which Marxism and Leninism are striving. The idea of the withering away of government in favor of some sort of anarchic communalism is but

the most radical formulation of democratic ideals, as Marx himself was eager to point out. It was to be accomplished by abolishing the rule of special interests (ruling classes), which alone, in the eyes of Marx, made the existence of repressive governmental institutions necessary. Once classes were abolished, repressive institutions would become unnecessary and would gradually disappear. In Marxist theory, the fulfillment of the liberal ideal is thus seen as a by-product of the fulfillment of socialist ideals. All these notions live on in present-day communist thought. As a matter of fact, the concept of the withering away of the state is receiving renewed attention in Soviet theoretical literature, since the Kremlin has announced that the transition from socialism to communism is now in process.[3]

But there has been controversy within the communist camp over the question whether the classless society, and the democracy that goes with it, can be attained through democratic processes of representative, constitutional government. On the one hand, Marxism is based on the belief that the working class is rational. A consequence of this belief is a general faith in democratic processes; and for this reason Marxist politicians have generally been in favor of constitutional government, widening of the franchise, civil liberties, and the like. These rights and advantages might have to be won by a revolution (which would, of course, be the bourgeois revolution). But, once won, they would assure the victory of the proletariat. Or, rather, once constitutional democracy was fully realized, the proletariat, constituting the vast majority of the people, would be in power. Engels could therefore say that the democratic republic would be the specific form of the dictatorship of the proletariat.

The Russian communists, however, could not follow Marx and Engels all the way in these thoughts. For in Russia, where the proletariat was still in the minority, the democratic republic would not spell proletarian rule. Yet, untrammeled democracy could nonetheless be very useful to the proletarian movement as a stepping stone toward the proletarian dictatorship, and for this reason it was the main plank of the minimum platform. We can best understand this if we realize that Russian revolutionary intellectuals instinctively contrasted the word "democracy" with autocracy and bureaucracy. To them, it therefore signified not so much constitutional government or any government whatsoever, but rather the absence of restraint and direct rule by the masses. Like Marx, they interpreted the concept of democracy in the spirit of Rousseau, i.e., as that direct rule of the people of which Hamilton, Madison, and most of the other American Founding Fathers were so keenly afraid. According to Marxist theory, however, the absence of governmental restraints in capitalist society could mean only open class warfare; for the absence of such restraints would cause all the contradictions of capitalism to come to the surface and clearly divide society. Democracy therefore becomes synonymous with civil war. Such a clear and open struggle, however, would be desirable because it could end only with the victory of the proletariat.

To be sure, communist strategy also took into account the fact that democratic government can be equated with constitutional, representative government, which customarily provides political liberties for all citizens; and the establishment of such a government in place of more authoritarian forms is desirable because the communist movement, like all interest groups, would like to operate as freely as possible. Moreover, the mere struggle for political liberties would benefit the communist movement whether it was successful or not. Success would give desired advantages. Failure could be used for the purpose of buttressing the communists' argument that under capitalism democracy will always be imperfect.

Hence communism fights with unrelenting vigor to establish and perfect constitutional democracy. Win or lose, the fight will pay off. And yet, we can detect a certain hesitancy about this, a certain preference for losing the fight. For communism has remained highly suspicious of the liberties granted under constitutional government. While democratic institutions might be regarded as an aid in revolutionary struggle, communists warn that a Marxist should never fall victim to "constitutional illusions," that is, to the belief that capitalism can be overthrown and socialism established without violence and revolution. Bourgeois democracy, wrote Lenin, "is always narrow, hypocritical, mendacious, and false; it always remains democracy for the rich, a bluff for the poor." [4] While he criticized those of his comrades who did not recognize the advantages of utilizing the freedoms of representative government, he was even more critical of those who thought that the fight for democratic liberties was an end in itself. Such an overemphasis of the minimum program, he thought, amounted to a betrayal of the proletarian revolution. Communism thus has a highly ambivalent attitude toward piecemeal gains: they are useful and must be used; but they also threaten to corrupt those who gain advantages from them.

The precise relationship of their minimum goal to the final and over-all aims of the movement was not the only problem troubling the Russian communists. Circumstances also caused them at various times to redefine the minimum goal itself: although in their purist moods communist theoreticians have asserted that there is no essential difference between various types of capitalist society, practical politics impelled them at other times to voice a preference for one or another such type as the minimal goal to strive for. Furthermore, it has always been a thorny problem for them to decide precisely what forces in underdeveloped societies such as Russia were to carry out this bourgeois revolution. Russian communists were agreed that in their country the *bourgeois revolution* would have to be carried out or at least initiated and led *by the proletariat*—a curious but extremely important variation on the original Marxist theme. But, obviously, a proletariat constituting a small minority could not by itself carry out this revolution. Who should be its allies? And how should such allies be attracted to the party of the proletariat? In answering these questions communism has played it by ear; but, after a good deal of controversy, the Russian pattern of 1917 has emerged as the school solution: according to this pattern, the proletariat is to carry out the bourgeois revolution aided by the land-hungry peasantry, by dissatisfied national or other minorities, and possibly even by sections of the liberal middle class wherever this class can be expected to be ready for revolutionary action. In colonial countries, virtually every class might be deemed a suitable ally. The proletariat is to attract these auxiliary forces by adopting their specific grievances and aspirations as planks in its own political platform and is to promote these aspirations in the most vigorous and radical fashion, so as to steal all other revolutionary parties' thunder. Communist programs in underdeveloped countries therefore typically include demands for radical land reform and for national self-determination.

While stressing the need for alliances and for the theoretical and political flexibility that would make such alliances possible, communist doctrine stresses even more the idea that in all such political arrangements the proletariat must retain a leading role. Proletarian hegemony in the bourgeois revolution, paradoxical as it may sound, is demanded by communist strategy for several reasons. For one thing, Lenin was convinced that, in Russia at least, the bourgeoisie was not interested enough in "its own" revolution to promote it without being pushed by the working class; or, as a variant of this, he tended to believe that precisely because of vigorous proletarian initiative the bourgeoisie was not interested. In any event, he assumed that the bourgeoisie could not be expected to promote the bourgeois revolution. And, once the revolution had begun, the bourgeoisie could be expected to work against it or to betray it by making compromises with the old ruling class. Finally, he argued that proletarian hegemony in the bourgeois revolution would ease the transition to the next stage—the proletarian revolution.

We are touching here yet another problem concerning the relationship between the two revolutions: How can the party make sure that the transition from the bourgeois to a socialist society is effected most swiftly and efficiently? For, after all, as soon as it has been reached, the minimum goal turns into an obstacle, into something hostile that must be overcome; or, at best, it is regarded as a stepping stone toward the higher goal. In no case, however, is it something desirable in its own right. On the contrary, the longer the phase between the bourgeois revolution and the proletarian revolution lasts, the more time given the bourgeois regime to entrench itself, the more difficult will it be to complete the series of revolutions. Communist theory has remained ambiguous about this problem. Estimates of the desirable or probable time span that would seperate one from the other have ranged from Vladimir Lenin's "era of world wars and revolutions" to Leon Trotsky's hope that the two revolutions might merge and occur simultaneously, an idea which was based on thoughts vaguely expressed by Marx and Engels in the *Communist Manifesto*. (Even the Trotskyist term "permanent revolution" was used by Marx and Engels in this context.) In between we have another idea of Lenin's, namely, that the democratic republic established by the proletariat in the bourgeois revolution would slowly but surely "grow over" into socialism.

The Marxist-Leninist program for Russia was further refined and complicated by linking it with the expected world revolution—partly in order better to justify revolutionary action by the Marxist movement in a backward country. Many of the daring schemes constituting the Russian communist program were so bold a departure from the original Marxist scheme that many other Marxist theoreticians looked upon Lenin's party as a group of unprincipled adventurers lusting for power regardless of the consequences. They argued that Russia was in no wise prepared (or "mature") for a proletarian regime, and that therefore a Russian revolution carried out under proletarian hegemony could not but lead to failure and would discredit the entire Marxist movement.

Communists agreed that a proletarian revolution in Russia alone made no sense. Yet when the chance came to seize power, they seized it in the name of the proletariat. But, whether or not they were in fact unprincipled adventurers, they did have a theoretical justification for their action. I have called the arguments they used the theory of the spark. Just as Lenin insisted that the working class as the most conscious element of society would set the bourgeois revolution

in motion by its own initiative, so he asserted that the proletarian revolution in Russia (doomed to failure if it were an
isolated event) would spark a world-wide chain reaction of
proletarian revolution. This world revolution, in turn, would
ensure the success of socialism even in such a backward
country as Russia. Here we see that even in Lenin's view the
bourgeois and the proletarian revolutions have merged into
one event.

The Party

Marx and Engels were concerned primarily with prognoses,
that is, trends of development they thought they recognized
in present-day reality; this preoccupation resulted from necessity, not choice. Lenin, however, stressed plans and wishes,
goals and desiderata. Marx and Engels were confident that
reality would develop toward the goal. Lenin knew what the
goal was and made the most determined efforts to reach it.
To be sure, they all asserted the inevitability of socialism.
But I think that we can detect a subtle change in this notion
of inevitability. For Marx and Engels it had been a concrete
certainty of events to come in the immediate future. For
Lenin it was far more theoretical than that. And theory in
this case was always in danger of being divorced from practice. Theoretically socialism was inevitable; any convinced
Marxist was sure of that. But practically it would take careful planning and adjustments to make it come about. Theory,
in short, was no longer an expression of what was, that is,
scientific analysis and description; instead, it had become a
guide to action, a method of analyzing and understanding
reality in such a fashion that it could be used for the attainment of the goals the theory had developed.

By emphasizing goals, communism prepared to discard
the means, procedures, and patterns of development that
Marx and Engels had foreseen or described. The validity of
their scheme of evolution was never challenged directly, but
in the hands of communist political leaders it became more
and more schematic and abstract. At the same time, communist theory gave even greater emphasis than Marx and

Engels had given to theory itself as a creative force in history.

Communism is a school of Marxism which assigns a tremendously important role to rational understanding, which they call *consciousness*. To communists it is the most essential force in history. For, without scientific knowledge, or, rather, without leadership by people possessing such knowledge, chaos and disaster instead of socialism might be the outcome of history.

Communism complements its demand for proletarian hegemony with the equally insistent striving for the hegemony of consciousness. Hegemony over what? Over insufficiently developed consciousness, that is, over instinct, habit, tradition—in short over any political action which is not based on the scientific (read: Marxist) understanding of reality. Communist theory defines nonconscious political action as *spontaneous;* and the hegemony of consciousness is therefore to be established over spontaneity.

Conceptually, this is not different from the Marxist theory, in which the proletariat was assigned its Chosen People role precisely because consciousness was attributed to it. Because Marx did attribute consciousness to the working class, however, he had no need to differentiate theoretically between consciousness and spontaneity. The *Communist Manifesto* refers to the party as an organization providing theoretical and practical leadership and mentions bourgeois intellectuals who, by virtue of their enlightenment and insight, break away from their own class and provide this leadership for the proletariat. But the implication remains nonetheless that the spontaneous emergence of class consciousness in the proletariat itself is inevitable. Consciousness and spontaneity coincide in the theory of Marx and Engels.

In Leninist theory they do not. On the contrary, by itself (that means spontaneously) the working class would never attain consciousness. Consequently, it would never be able to carry out its historic task, or at least not alone.

Nonetheless, consciousness must guide the proletariat. And if the working class by itself cannot attain it, it must be found elsewhere. Lenin asserted that it was possessed by ed-

ucated people, intellectuals such as he. It is they whom consciousness compels to prepare and lead the proletariat in the
revolutions that have to be staged in Russia. They are expected to provide this leadership by devoting their entire
lives to the task, becoming revolutionaries by profession.
They are the ones who should form the party, which Lenin
conceived as consciousness incarnate or institutionalized, the
Ecclesia Militans of history, the general staff of the proletarian revolutions. And, because Leninism relies so firmly on
consciousness for deliverance, it must rely with equal fervor
on the strength and the survival of the party in which consciousness has become flesh. Come what may, the party must
be preserved. Without it the proletariat is nothing. Without
it everything is lost.

A general staff by itself, however, cannot wage nor win
a battle. A party formed only by the enlightened few is unable to win revolutions. To do so, the vanguard of the proletariat must be sure that the rank and file of the working
class will act according to its commands. In addition, the
party must aim to go beyond the working class in attracting
the allies which, as we have seen, the proletariat in backward countries needs.

All political parties seek to gain adherents and become
decisive majorities. In order to do so, parties customarily
try to develop programs and voice slogans that respond to
the felt or anticipated needs of potential political adherents.
They try to voice the will of the people or of important
groups within the people.

The Communist Party cannot gain adherents quite so
simply. Since it believes that it is the repository of consciousness, while the people, including even the proletariat, are in-
capable of defining their own interests, the party obviously
cannot let the "spontaneous" feelings of the masses determine policy. On the contrary, its consciousness, and the goals
and policies derived from it, must somehow be instilled in,
or imposed on, the people whom the party wishes to lead.
What is required, then, is an educational job; and indeed the
party regards its most important function to be the education

of the proletariat. The consciousness which the party possesses must be given to the working class.

Communist theorists refer to this educational work as "propaganda," but they do not wish to imply by the use of this word irrational, tricky, or deceptive means of persuasion. On the contrary, propaganda denotes the painful and lengthy effort of so educating the proletariat that it understands and absorbs Marxist theory in all its ramifications and complications. For only this constitutes consciousness. There are, however, means short of this difficult process, which the party uses to gain adherents. There are, for instance, the important first steps of the educational effort, measures designed to wake up the masses and plant the first seeds of consciousness in their minds. These first steps are short and simple messages—slogans—dramatizing the workers' grievances and providing greatly simplified explanations for them. Collectively, these primitive efforts to arouse resentment against capitalism and faith in communism are called "agitation." Its messages are no more meant to be deceptive than those of propaganda; they are only simplified truths which even simple minds can grasp.

Education to consciousness, however, is not enough. Communist theorists have great difficulty deciding how much effort and time is required to raise the workers' level of consciousness. Estimates have varied according to circumstances. In times of revolution or impending revolution, the party has tended to be optimistic about this problem. At other times, its leaders were aware of the difficulties they faced in educating the masses.

Yet the party needs the masses to carry out its policies. Moreover, communism is impatient Marxism, which cannot afford to wait for the proletariat to become mature, just as in Russia it could not wait until the society had finally caught up with Western Europe in its development. At least one Western scholar maintains that this "impatience" was inherent in the Marxist movement long before Lenin and therefore Marxism, by the very mood it expresses and by the structure of its principal ideas, is suited primarily or only to countries in the very early stages of industrial and capitalist development.[5] In the communist (bolshevik) branch of the Russian Marxist movement, this impatience is the result of suppressed but strong and persistent doubts concerning the inevitability of socialism, doubts which in their turn are related not only to the unpropitious Russian environment but also to those changes in the nature of the working-class movement that led to the changes in Western Marxist doctrines (see Chapter 3). More generally yet, these doubts are a product of that era of "imperialism" which, as we will see, communist theory analyzes as the current stage of capitalist development. All these doubts have, as I phrased it above, made the idea of the inevitability of socialism more "theoretical."

Under the impact of the transformation of capitalism into imperialism and of the working class into an antirevolutionary interest group, Marxist theorists in the West abandoned revolutionary change. The Leninist solution of the same problem was different. Unwilling and, under Russian conditions, probably unable to abandon revolution as the means to attain socialism, communism found itself compelled to supplement the time-consuming method of education with more immediately effective manipulation of the masses. The party formulates goals and strategies. All that the masses have to do is to act according to the party's directives. To the communist it does not really matter whether or not the masses understand what they are doing. It may be desirable and preferable, but it is not essential.

Communism attributes consciousness to an elite of professional revolutionaries organized in the party. This party almost desperately feels the urge to act, so as to make its theory come true. Hence the masses, and in particular the proletariat, which in Marxist theory was the main agent of historic change, now turn into the main tools of such change. They become instruments in the hands of the conscious vanguard, raw material of revolutionary history, which must be molded and shaped and sent into action according to the party's plans.

The party's principal means for working with this human

raw material is not, as many might suppose, propaganda (now meaning the use of irrational or deceptive means of persuasion), even though in fact there is no firm line between honest conviction and calculated appeal in the propaganda and agitation messages of communism. Moreover, many policies (apart from propaganda or education) are adopted by the party, not for their own sake, but only because they are apt to attract followers and sympathizers; or because not adopting them would disillusion those whose sympathies already are with the party. As a matter of fact, communism is often torn by a sharp dilemma: Should the party remain true to its convictions even though its orthodox stand will alienate its followers; or should it be flexible, opportunistic, obedient in some fashion to grass-roots opinion, in order to attract the masses? Unwilling to wait until the masses become conscious, the party has usually decided that some concessions to their opinions must be made. Propaganda, in the sense of manipulation, thus plays its role. But another method of manipulating the masses is far more important and desirable, because it requires no concessions to grass-roots spontaneity. That method is organization.

Lenin, in some ways rather old-fashioned, was nonetheless up-to-date in a number of ways. One trait that made him a pioneer of twentieth-century politics was his insight into the crucial role of organization. Lenin realized that in modern industrial society (if not everywhere else) man is never an isolated individual. All human activities, economic, political, recreational, educational, and so forth, are carried out in and through organizations and associations. Each individual is a functioning member of society only as a member of the various groups to which he belongs. And much of his behavior is influenced by these groups. Lenin concluded from this that masses of people could be influenced and manipulated most effectively if the manipulators were in control of the organizations and associations to which these masses belonged. Once the party controlled them, these organizations would become transmission belts (to use Lenin's phrase) conveying the will and impetus of the party leaders to the masses. Organization would be a system of wires the party could pull to set the people dancing to its tune. In this relationship, the lack of consciousness on the part of the masses did not really matter.

The Leninist party is therefore far more than a small elite of professional revolutionaries organized as leaders because they consider themselves conscious. It is also an educational institution aiming to raise the working class to the level of consciousness; and, finally, it is the center of a vast network of auxiliary organizations, reaching, ideally, into every part of society in an attempt to control the entire associational life of broad masses of the population. The party's ideal is, of course, to dominate all of society in this indirect fashion. Needless to say, this dream comes close to being realized only after the party has come to power, Then, however, it becomes one of the guiding principles of communist government.*

Decision-making Processes

The manipulative attitude with which we have become acquainted here is at the basis of the party's ideas on organization, and it pervades and shapes the party's political strategy. The party views not only the working classes as political raw material that should be organized and controlled; it similarly views all forces, arrangements, institutions—in short, everything that exists in contemporary society. In principle, the communist is ready and eager to regard everything as a potential instrument which, if wielded correctly and kept under control, can serve his party's and the movement's interests. Here we see a tendency toward the dissolution of the Marxist scheme of action into Machiavellian opportunism and amoral ruthlessness. And yet, this flexibility of strategy, this readiness to adjust action to the given environment, is neither unprincipled nor un-Marxist. Whatever the communist may do, he feels guided by principles insofar as he wants to work for the proletarian revolution and for socialism. Meanwhile, whatever his strategies,

---

* See Chapter 8.

the communist can remain a Marxist as long as he keeps
analyzing his environment in Marxist terms. Whatever he
does, Marxism remains a guide to his action as long as it
guides his thinking.*

Communist theorists would strongly repudiate the in-
ference that their movement is immoral or even amoral; on
the contrary, they would stress the moral probity of communism and would claim that communist morality is the only
valid morality of the contemporary world. They would point
out that communism is based on, and in a broad sense
guided by, moral indignation over capitalist inhumanity and
by moral ideals concerning a society worthy of man; and
communists are ever ready to measure others by their moral
yardstick. The communist movement, moreover, is eager
and impatient to make its ideal into reality. It wants action
and success. Success in an evil world, however, is attainable
only by working within that world and using the means that

---

* Other writers disagree with this, having reduced communism
to purely Machiavellian principles of expediency or to a code of
behavior derived from irrational attitudes closely akin to paranoia (see Nathan Leites, *A Study of Bolshevism,* Chicago, 1953).
These writers see communism as pursuing only one aim—power
unlimited in scope and area. In their view, communism is absolutely unprincipled and immoral, the ideology serving only as rationalization of the urge to dominate. Most popular and journalistic books on the subject take this line, which I believe is based
on inadequate understanding of the nature and history of bolshevism. A good example of such journalistic work is the much-
ballyhooed book by H. and B. Overstreet, *What We Must Know
About Communism* (New York, 1958). Once this view is accepted, the study of the development of communist ideas becomes, of course, quite irrelevant. The difficulty of defining the
relationship between ideas and political action in the communist
world may not be apparent to journalists; but its recognition by
scholars is attested by the great number of articles devoted to it
recently, and by the strongly hypothetical tone of many of these
articles. See Daniel Bell, "Ideology and Soviet Politics," with
comments by George Lichtheim and Carl J. Friedrich, in *Slavic
Review,* vol. XXIV, No. 4 (December 1965), pp. 591–621,
and a discussion by Alfred G. Meyer, David Joravsky, Frederick
C. Barghoorn, Robert V. Daniels, and Morris Bornstein in *Soviet
Studies,* vol. XVII, No. 3 (January 1966), pp. 273–285, and
vol. XVIII, No. 1 (July 1966), pp. 2–19 and 66–80.

are at the movement's disposal. The *practical* morality of the communist movement is therefore a morality of expediency: whatever works is moral; whatever does not, is immoral. Whoever because of moral scruples fails to act resolutely to bring socialism nearer is a traitor to the morally just cause of communism. Whoever overcomes his "petty-bourgeois" moral scruples, whoever is unafraid to dirty his hands in the noble work of removing obstacles in the path of moral progress, is worthy of praise. Communism thus adopts the old maxim first attributed to the Jesuits, that the end justifies the means. A Westerner's first instinct is to point out that this contradicts prevalent Western notions of morality.[6] But I am not convinced that this is so. After all, we, too, argue that for the defense of certain ethical values we must be prepared to kill. We are ready to scrap conventional morals for causes we consider to be just. I suspect therefore that the main disagreement between the communists and their antagonists is over the ends, not over the means. Perhaps the communists are just more defiant and frank in stating the problem clearly and facing up to a morality of expediency.

At the same time, the manipulative attitude makes it more and more difficult to make decisions and to determine precisely what the proper Marxist course would be. The reason for this is that the manipulative attitude is linked with a profound ambivalence toward everything that exists. Everything—classes, groups, nations, institutions, attitudes, traditions—everything is potentially useful to the party. But everything is at the same time part of the hated present. Everything is both an obstacle and a stepping stone on the road to progress. And Marxist theory, being highly abstract, cannot really guide the party leader in deciding how positively or negatively he is to judge any phenomenon at any particular time. After all, Marx and Engels themselves did not always agree on such appraisals.

This ambivalence is intensified by the fact that the communist thinks on several levels of abstraction at one and the same time. Not only that, he must plan his course of action on several different levels—maximum and minimum programs; strategy and tactics; action based on principles as against that which is an accommodation to special circumstances; action in different locales. Obviously, various courses of action are open to the party in any one situation, all of them fully consonant with Marxist-Leninist theory.

To prevent paralysis or chaos, therefore, more than theoretical skills (consciousness) is required. According to Lenin's principles, consciousness must be linked to an efficient decision-making machinery so as to make sure that in every case the correct decision is made. And that for every situation there is one and only one correct decision Lenin was convinced, even though it seems, in the light of what we have discussed above, this conviction cannot be reconciled with the ambivalent (dialectical) and multilevel approach to reality characterizing Marxism. To be sure, Marx and Engels themselves, however prone they were on the basis of their method to regard the world in contradictory terms, were often as dogmatic as Lenin when discussing courses of action. In their cases, too, we get the impression that they recognized only one solution to a problem as correct.

Lenin, moreover, was a rare type of revolutionary: a revolutionary with a bureaucratic mind. Such a combination is rare because most revolutionaries so hate the bureaucracy of the social system they want to overthrow that they come to hate all officialdom. Certainly, in the political thought of Western liberalism, which is suspicious of all governmental authority, this is true; and Marxism, being an heir to the liberal heritage, shares its antibureaucratic bias in the main. Lenin, however, as a rule did not share it. He seems to have felt that there was something inherently rational in good bureaucratic organization; that such organization, when put to work, would produce correct decisions, especially when it consisted of conscious people. It may very well be that this faith in rational organization only covered up his desire to create a governmental apparatus completely subservient to him; perhaps he was organization-happy because it suited his purposes. I for one believe that this is part of the truth. Yet it is true also that Lenin's preoccupation with principles and problems of centralized bureaucratic organization is in tune with the beliefs and preconceptions of Marx and Engels.

After all, as prophets of the cult of rationality and the good life in this world, they praised not only the machine age, but also collectivism and large-scale, centralized administration. In their eyes, these were aspects of up-to-date civilization, and they would be preserved and fostered in the socialist society.* To this one must add that Lenin's entire schooling in Marxism and Marxist party politics came from the leading Marxist party of the late nineteenth century, the German Social-Democratic Party. It is from this party, the first modern mass party, and an important pioneer of political mass organization, that Lenin learned the organizational principles he imposed on his branch of the Russian movement. Still, Lenin's motivation is rather irrelevant. What does matter, for the history and development of communism, are the principles of organization which emerged.

Lenin wanted the party to be a striking organization which could be totally committed to any action as quickly as possible. He wanted this organization to be absolutely centralized and subject to firm control by its leaders. He wanted its organization to be hierarchical, following the command principle of armed forces, where the chief virtue of the lower ranks is discipline and obedience. Comparison of the party with a military organization is not a far-fetched idea attributable to Western critics. On the contrary, Lenin made it clear that military organization was the pattern according to which he wished the party to be organized. Communist ideologists have a predilection for military terminology. The revolutions they promote are battles to be fought and won; the societies within which they occur are fronts in a global war; the workers are the rank-and-file soldiers; other classes furnish reserve troops; and the party is the general staff.

But the conception of the party as a disciplined bureaucratic body was in sharp conflict with another principle of organization: the democratic one. That the proletarian movement should organize itself and manage its own affairs democratically follows logically from the assumption that the

---

* If I have drawn a contradictory picture of Marxist attitudes toward bureaucracy, I have done so in the awareness that one must not expect political philosophies to be altogether consistent.

proletariat is conscious. And if that assumption is replaced by one which attributes consciousness only to the party elite, then democracy should reign within that vanguard of the elect. For, surely, where everyone is conscious, everyone's voice should be heard; and everyone's counsel is of equal worth. Not even Lenin ever saw fit to repudiate this argument.

Bureaucratic-authoritarian principles of organization thus were in conflict with democratic ones. Lenin attempted to resolve this clash by a formula: the party, he argued, should be governed in accordance with the principle of "democratic centralism."

The formula symbolizes the desire to merge both principles. According to Lenin, party policies should be formulated by absolutely free discussion and deliberation, with every party member entitled to participate either directly or through freely elected representatives. The formal structure of the party corresponds to this, in that the sovereign body which, in theory, determines policy is the party Congress of delegates representing the entire membership. All executive organizations of the party, such as the Central Committee and its numerous subsidiary or servant organizations, are, formally, accountable to the Congress. In addition to providing for free discussion of all pending questions, the democratic element of democratic centralism was meant to give each individual party member freedom to criticize. Indeed, Lenin once defined democratic centralism as "freedom to criticize and unity in action." The centralistic principle of "unity in action" was to prevail only after policies had been adopted and had become party law. Then, after every member had had his opportunity to speak up, all dissent was to be suppressed and the party was to display monolithic unity. Any sign of disagreement at such a time was to be regarded as a breach of discipline and punished by expulsion. A party committed in action could not tolerate dissenters within its ranks.

Thus freedom to criticize was obviously to be sharply circumscribed. But exactly how to circumscribe it remained a problem. To be legitimate, said the party leaders, criticism should be constructive. But what is the criterion of constructiveness? Criticism, said the party rules, should focus on the execution of adopted policies rather than on the policies themselves. *What* was being done should be beyond criticism; only *how* it was being done could be a matter of dispute. But the borderline between policy formulation and policy execution does not exist except in textbooks. In practice it is meaningless. Moreover, who is to have the right to challenge policies that have been in force for a long time, or for any length of time? Somebody must be able to point out that circumstances have changed and that measures once adopted unanimously have outlived their usefulness. Someone must be authorized to prepare agendas for meetings and congresses and thereby indicate what problems deserve to be discussed. But, according to the rules of centralism and discipline, such suggestions ought not to be made by any member while the party is committed in action. Yet, is not the party always committed? Is there ever a moment when dissent is not dangerous and a breach of discipline and unanimity?

In reality, the cards were stacked overwhelmingly against democratic principles. Lenin may have paid lip service to them; he may even have been completely sincere in his praises of party democracy. But he was also highly impatient with criticism and dissent. He was contemptuous or perhaps even fearful of Russian intellectuals and their proverbial knack for interminable and aimless discussion. He wanted action rather than words, results instead of dreams. And to attain these aims he favored centralism and authoritarianism.

In addition to Lenin's tremendous prestige within the party, two devices became important in curbing democracy. One was a rule outlawing "factionalism," adopted at the Tenth Congress of the Russian Communist Party in 1921, which had the effect of atomizing all dissent. Disagreement and criticism could still be voiced; but it had to be voiced by individuals. The formation of dissenting groups, the writing of minority reports or rival platforms, even the organization of minority discussion groups were outlawed as treason against the party. These formal curbs on the freedom of discussion were supplemented by an increasing tendency on the part of the leaders to control the membership through the party's administrative organs, to make the representative gatherings more and more subservient to the party bureaucracy, to pack them with yes men, and the like. Centralism consequently won a complete victory over party democracy. This was true of the Russian Communist Party and, for a long time, also the communist parties throughout the world. But, for reasons to be discussed later in this book, it is no longer true today.

World View

The composite picture of the Leninist or communist, as Lenin himself visualized him, is that of a radical, revolutionary Marxist imbued with loathing for capitalism and yearning for socialism, and in a hurry to attain his goal; ruthless in his methods and opportunistic (Lenin would have said, flexible) in his strategies; absolutely loyal to his party and its leaders, and filled with holy intolerance of any ideas or even facts that might shake his loyalty; intolerant also of any political leader, especially one calling himself a socialist or communist, not in total agreement with the party; and ever eager to deepen his own consciousness, yet disciplined and obedient as a party servant. When Lenin talked about "hard" Marxists or "hard" bolsheviks, he had in mind that combination of determination and devotion, lack of squeamishness, adaptability, and loyalty. As we shall see when discussing the history of the party, he did not always get the kind of following he wanted; the party also, at various times, attracted people who had some, but not all, of the desired traits. (The picture is complicated further by the fact that the kinds of virtue that Lenin demanded of his disciples after the party acquired political power are significantly different from those of the model revolutionary.) The ideal bolshevik, however, is foremost "hard" and radical—a simple syndrome of traits which distinguishes him from adherents of most other parties of either the right or the left. To make the image more complete we shall have to describe his general world view. By that I mean not his philosophy but his image of society in the twentieth century. To the communist, ours is the age of *imperialism;* in order to understand what this implies, we should determine what the term "imperialism" means in communist writings. For this purpose, we shall have to begin by sketching the circumstances under which the term gained currency.

The word began to be used around the beginning of our century, when the expansion of the European powers into economically backward and politically defenseless areas of Asia and Africa had reached its peak. New colonial empires were established at that time; spheres of influence and domination were carved out; and fierce rivalries developed between the European powers in their competition for areas of domination.

For the Western world in general, this was a period of rapid economic growth through the work of ever-larger industrial and financial corporate structures, of quickly rising living standards, and increasing national consciousness. For the Marxist movement, it was a time of puzzlement and soul searching, because so many features of their contemporary world corresponded less and less with the Marxist model as they understood it. The decline of capitalism seemed remoter than ever. The revolutionary spirit of the working class was yielding to the tendency to strive for reforms within the existing system. The entire timetable of Marxism seemed hopelessly upset. Where the spirit of revolution was still alive, it was in relatively backward countries, in which proletarian revolutions did not make much sense according to a strict and dogmatic reading of Marxism. All these developemnts required explanation; and the communist theory of imperialism was an attempt to provide it.[7]

Reduced to the simplest terms, this explanation runs as follows: Instead of having developed its internal contradictions and tensions to a point where a revolutionary break must occur, capitalism has found a way out of these contradictions, even though previously they were thought to be insoluble. The way out is expansion throughout the world in search of cheap raw materials, ready markets for commodities and for excess capital, and, most important, cheap labor which can be exploited in unprecedented measure. This expansion of capitalism is called imperialism.

In his attempt to describe the social processes going on in his time, Lenin further defined imperialism. He described it as an intensification of all those features that Marx and Engels had attributed to capitalism. In his law of the concentration of capital, Marx had described how the small entrepreneur is inevitably wiped out by his larger competitors and capital is concentrated in fewer and fewer hands. According to communist theory, this concentration has proceeded apace and has led to the development of *monopoly capitalism*. Similarly, the fate Marx and Engels predicted for the majority of the middle classes, namely, transformation into proletarians, has, according to Lenin, become reality; almost everyone outside a small power elite is a helpless cog in a vast commercialized machine dominated by monopolists.

But if indeed the tendencies seen by the writers of the *Communist Manifesto* have reached their peak, what is to explain the failure of the revolutionary movement and the staying power of capitalism? The communists' reply is that this intensification of various essential features of capitalism has temporarily eased some of the strains under which the system labored. First of all, the reign of monopoly and the increasing interference of centralized government in the economy reduce the anarchy which, according to Marx and Engels, characterized free-enterprise economy. Monopoly capitalism and state capitalism, as the communists call the modern Western systems, are guided and planned. Further, they argue, monopoly has grown so strong in its grip on the system that it can afford to make political concessions to the lower classes and thus tie them more firmly to the status quo. Moreover, monopoly capitalism, by exploiting backward areas, reaps such enormous profits—communist theory calls them superprofits—that it can bribe the proletariat (or at least its leaders) also with economic concessions, that is, with a rising standard of living. One of the fundamental laws of capitalist development in Marxist theory, the law of the

increasing misery of the masses, is thus substantially modified. Finally, the workers have been corrupted also by the
fierce nationalism which, as a result of imperialist competition, has been fostered within each imperialist nation. This
nationalism, to which according to Lenin the working-class
leadership especially has fallen victim, has corroded international proletarian solidarity and made the workers' movement
a pawn in the hands of the ruling classes.

The chances for a proletarian revolution therefore seem
more remote than ever. But communist theory resurrects
the optimism of Marx and Engels by uncovering new tendencies toward the eventual breakdown of capitalism and new
revolutionary forces to speed up the process and carry it forward to construct a socialist commonwealth. This new theory
of doom and renascence forms the core of the theory of imperialism.

According to communist thought, the "contradictions" of
capitalism have been overcome within the Western nations
only to reappear on a global scale. Within any one nation,
the anarchy of capitalist production may have been reduced
to a minimum. But sharp and deadly competition lives on
between international monopolies and between the various
imperialist nations; and on a global level capitalism is therefore as anarchic as ever. Analyzing this competition in some
detail, Lenin came to the conclusion that it could be resolved
only by war; and the inevitability of imperialist wars, that is,
wars between various capitalist nations, remained an axiom
of communist theory until very recently, even though the
course of world history since 1917 had given rise to the nag-
ging fear that a counter tendency might exist: ever since the
birth of a communist regime in Russia, communist leaders
have ever been in fear of a world-wide alliance of all imperialist nations in a crusade to wipe out Soviet Russia. For several decades this fear of an all-imperialist bloc and of "capitalist encirclement" played an important role in communist
ideology.

Further contradictions of capitalism are seen in imperialism. For instance, capitalism, according to communist theory, has saved itself from collapse by exporting capital into

underdeveloped areas. But, as industrial civilization engulfs the entire globe, it becomes more and more difficult to dispose of the faster and faster accumulating surpluses. Soon there will be no new frontiers nor safety valves. Moreover, by exporting capital, the West also exports capital*ism* with all its stresses and its inherent revolutionary potential to areas hitherto untouched by Western history. Not only competition but also those other features Marx had seen in capitalism—exploitation and domination of man by man and a resulting struggle of classes—reappear on a global scale. The new class struggle which develops in the age of imperialism, according to communist theory, is more complicated than the conflict between capitalists and proletarians was in the nineteenth century. The old struggle persists, although it is mitigated temporarily in the imperialist countries. And it now goes on everywhere, even if only under the surface. In addition, however, world society is now divided into the exploiters and the exploited in yet another fashion: the new exploited populations are entire nations, namely, those backward, underdeveloped peoples on whom the capitalist world has been encroaching. Modern communist theory attributes to them the same relationship to the exploiter nations as the proletariat was to have to the bourgeoisie. The class struggle is thus partly transformed into an international conflict.

This picture, which has been drawn in very simplified strokes, has interesting implications for the over-all theory of revolution of Marx and Engels. One concept that was very important to their earlier followers was that of *maturity:* conditions had to be ripe for a proletarian revolution before working-class action made sense; capitalism had to be highly developed as a social system, and industrial technology had to be sufficiently advanced to provide a decent livelihood for all. Then conditions would be mature for the proletarian revolution. Now this concept is virtually turned upside down. Industrial capitalism and the revolutionary movement are seen not as developing in direct but in inverse proportion to each other. Highly developed industrial countries get stuck in the rut of imperialism, while the revolution develops in backward countries. *Consciousness is more important than*

the maturity of conditions. This is one of the implications of
the communist theory of imperialism.

Another implication is the theory of "combined development." The sharp line drawn above between exploiter nations and exploited nations does not imply that either type is
homogeneous. To be sure, in the imperialist world the class
struggle may be stifled; but it is taken for granted by most
(not all) communists that eventually it will erupt with renewed vigor. Meanwhile in the underdeveloped nations a
far more complicated class conflict rages. For in these societies the fight of the proletariat against the bourgeoisie goes
on simultaneously with the struggle of peasants against landlords, bourgeois against traditional rulers, caste against caste,
nationality against nationality. Thus backward societies, in
the communist view, combine features which in the West
characterized different stages of development. Noncontem-
poraneous elements here are telescoped so as to coincide in
time, because modern civilization, through Western imperialism, has been superimposed on societies hitherto untouched
by Western developments.

To the revolutionary strategist this phenomenon opens up
exciting new perspectives for action. It makes possible
unique combinations of social forces; it creates political constellations of new and ever-shifting character, which have to
be examined anew in each country. And this necessity to regard every underdeveloped country as unique in its social
problems gives theoretical justification to all the pragmatism
and seeming opportunism of communist parties. The strategies and tactics used by Marx and Engels, which used to be
copied slavishly by their earlier followers, have ceased to be
obligatory.

Not only do strategies and tactics become more flexible on
the basis of such theories, however; the whole conception
of the revolution changes profoundly. First of all, in the
communist view, the revolution is no longer to be carried
out by the proletariat alone but by an alliance of the Western proletariat with the underdeveloped nations and the colonies and dependencies. Its point of departure, its origin, is
no longer the condition of the working class but the condi-

tion of all mankind, seen as victims of imperialism. The crucial point of Marxism, that conditions have to be ripe for revolution, has been amended, as we have seen. The maturity of capitalism now is seen to lead to revolution, not in the capitalist world, but somewhere else. The aims of the revolution also have changed. In the *Communist Manifesto*, the proletariat was to seize the means of industrial production in the name of society and utilize them in collectivist fashion for the benefit of all. The aim of the new revolution must be different; for in underdeveloped areas there is little that can be seized, and current means of production will not suffice to satisfy the material needs of those societies. The revolution of the colonial world has as its immediate aim the destruction of imperialism. It is to weaken the rule of capital not only in the colonies but also in the home countries by knocking the props from underneath the tottering system. Having accomplished this negative task, the coming world revolution is to proceed toward an even more difficult undertaking, which is to *build* modern industrial civilization in the underdeveloped areas, to copy the achievements of the capitalist West, in order to emancipate all mankind from it. For this, strong communist governments are required; hence it would be foolish to expect that the revolution will lead at once to the withering away of oppressive institutions. On the contrary, the emerging communist states will have to emphasize dictatorship, sacrifice, and continued alienation, for entire nations will have to be reeducated to be made fit for the machine age. In this fashion, the revolution, which in the minds of Marx and Engels was to have been a comparatively brief interlude, albeit violent and bloody, now assumes much greater dimensions in time by becoming an entire era of what communists call "socialist construction." Communism thus has turned into an ideology of modernization; and communist societies must be defined primarily as massive attempts at rapid economic and cultural development.

I shall deal with the theory and practice of communist governments in subsequent chapters, but will first go off on what might appear to be a tangent—a brief history of the Russian Communist Party. Since the Russian party was the

first party within the revolutionary Marxist movement to
come to power and remained the only one for several
decades, its early experiences were for a long time regarded
as exemplary for the entire communist world. Moreover, this
was Lenin's party; and since Lenin is regarded as the founding father of modern communism by all of its adherents, the
history of this party constitutes an integral part of the movement's doctrinal heritage and tradition.

5

History of the Russian Communist Party up to the Death of Lenin

• A knowledge of doctrine and the environment in which it was worked out is insufficient to give us an adequate understanding of communism. Knowledge of the history of the party as a political organization, and of the major personalities that helped make this history, is essential to understanding, for major events and milestones in the history of the party have had a lasting impact on it. This is partly because communism itself is very history conscious and tends to see present-day problems in terms of historical parallels and precedents. There is perhaps no other way of life in which historical memory (true as well as distorted) has played so important a role as a means of educating the younger generation. Or are there other creeds which use a history textbook as their main political primer and catechism? One other history textbook which has played a similar role is the Old Testament.

Russian intellectuals, disaffected and critical, were ever eager to slake their thirst for ideas about history and society and to show their disapproval of Russian conditions by adopting the most radical ideas they found in the West. The curious consequence was that the first foreign language into which Marx's major work was translated was Russian. Marxism quickly became well known among radical intellectuals

and gained adherents. Young men and women met in conspiratorial groups to study and discuss Marxist literature and
tried to establish contact with the working class. From the
very beginning, some of the most important leaders of the
new movement found themselves spending most of their lives
in Western Europe, out of reach of the tsarist police and in
touch with the Marxist parties of the West. With the exception of a brief period around 1905, the center of the Russian
Marxist movement from its beginnings to the revolution of
1917 was to be found in Munich, Geneva, or other Western
cities rather than in Moscow or St. Petersburg.

Emerging at a time when the Marxist movement in the
West was entering a period of serious disputes, the Russian
group was almost at once involved in struggles for the preservation of the orthodox creed. Men like Plekhanov, Aksel-
rod, Martov, and Lenin, who belonged to the first generation
of Russian Marxists, first sharpened their ideological weapons against those who maintained that Marxism was not applicable to Russia. These were primarily the Russian *narodniks*,[1] who had vague ideas about a particular native peasant
socialism that might be developed in their country without
Russia's having to go through a phase of capitalist development. Hardly had the Marxists succeeded in emerging from
these arguments with renewed confidence in their own theory when they were forced to defend it against the Russian
equivalents of the revisionists, groups opposing all political
activity on the part of the working class as premature (the
economists) or at least condemning all underground, subversive activity (the legal Marxists). These disputes, which
in their acrimoniousness foreshadowed many subsequent arguments, were also the beginning of a never-ending process
in which generation after generation of leaders were eliminated from the Russian movement.

Among the faithful, meanwhile, important discussions set
the stage for future developments and future conflicts. At
stake were the formulation of a party program and the shape
of the party organization; and both questions were intertwined not only with each other but also with personality
conflicts and struggles for influence. Obviously questions re-

garding the relationship between intellectuals and workers within the party, between the party and the labor unions, between constitutional and subversive political activity, between the party headquarters and the party press, between the Russian party and the workers' movements of Russia's national minorities—all were questions that concerned both organization and party programs.

Having been founded, formally, at the otherwise rather unimportant Congress at Minsk, in 1898, the party came together in 1903 for its first major gathering in its Western-European exile. At this Second Congress the antagonism that had been developing burst into the open. The Congress turned out to be a stormy one. One group of delegates stalked out; friendships were broken; and, most important, the two major factions, mensheviks and bolsheviks, emerged, which were to divide the party perpetually. The Russian Social-Democratic Labor Party thus came out of its first important meeting split in two. There is a good deal of evidence, though perhaps none that is conclusive, that the split was deliberately provoked and engineered by Lenin, who was alarmed at the stand taken by his antagonists within the party leadership on a whole number of policy questions. Lenin always considered it all-important to have a party which followed correct policies; and if the party as it existed at any given moment did not, then it would be better to destroy it, or, rather, split it so as to cast out those who in his opinion were misleading it. In the eyes of his antagonists, these attempts were tantamount to wrecking the party for the sake of attaining exclusive command over it. In their eyes, Lenin was willfully destroying proletarian unity and therefore wrecking the working-class movement. Lenin's own view was, of course, that he was only cleansing the movement of dangerous, misguided leaders who in effect were betraying Marxism. We see that there was an irreconcilable clash of views here. And yet, for almost another decade after the Second Congress, the two factions nominally remained in the same party.

The war of 1904 and, much more, the revolution of 1905 seemed at first to provide an opportunity for patching up the

rift. For the masses of workers, students, and others who
during the revolution associated themselves with the Marxist
movement, the struggles and disputes among the leaders
were often meaningless; some of them had not even heard
of mensheviks and bolsheviks. Among the rank and file of
party members, there was a tendency toward unity. This
was strengthened by the fact that the revolution temporarily
eclipsed the leaders, most of whom had difficulty getting
into Russia from their places of European exile and were
able to assume command only in the last stages of the revolution. One exception was Leon Trotsky, who emerged in
the revolution as one of the most glamorous figures of the
Russian Marxist movement. Finally, the revolutionary upheavals themselves rendered some of the controversies obsolete and senseless. In some of the most important events of
the revolution, such as the armed uprising that took place in
Moscow in December of 1905, bolsheviks and mensheviks
collaborated without great difficulties.

Once the revolution was defeated, however, disputes broke
out with renewed vigor. Bolshevik post-mortems conflicted
with menshevik ones. Even greater were the conflicts over
the lessons to be drawn from the experience and over the
strategies, tactics, programs, and organizational patterns to
be adopted on the basis of these lessons. The so-called Unity
Congress of the party, held in Stockholm in 1906, where
these matters were discussed, deepened the rift. So, finally,
did the bitter disputes that broke out over party finances, including not only the unorthodox manner in which the bolsheviks obtained their funds, such as bank robberies and
holdups, but also the question of who should dispose of the
funds.[2]

Struggles over control of finances appear to have led also
to the first major rift in the leadership of the bolshevik faction, that is, between Lenin on the one hand, and Bogdanov
and Krasin on the other—the triumvirate which in the years
immediately after the 1905 revolution constituted the command of the bolsheviks. Conflicts over funds were complicated by philosophical disputes and by controversies over
attempts either to widen or to mend the split within the en-

tire Marxist camp. Lenin fiercely attacked those bolsheviks who sought a reconciliation and were prepared to make compromises with the mensheviks; and he resisted with equal vehemence the efforts of people standing between or above the two factions, such as Trotsky, to pave the way for a reconciliation.

The years 1910–1912 mark the breakdown of reconciliatory efforts and the emergence of the bolshevik faction as virtually an independent party openly rivaling the mensheviks in trying to obtain funds, gain control over the labor movement, establish a press, and set up an underground organization within the Russian empire. The milestone of autonomous organization was the party Conference of Prague, in 1912, which was a purely bolshevik undertaking, the only outsiders being police spies who at that time had succeeded in infiltrating even Lenin's Central Committee.

The years between 1905 and 1917 were, on the whole, difficult for the entire Marxist movement in Russia. We have mentioned the intrigues and nasty disputes which racked its ranks and the police spies who managed to penetrate into its innermost councils. These were, moreover, years of defeat. The revolution had failed; reaction reigned supreme. Many Russian intellectuals were disillusioned with revolutionary activity, and many veteran fighters left the movement forever. The party was reduced to very small size, and it was in financial trouble. Its leaders were in exile abroad or in Siberian banishment. The working-class movement, as a thing apart from the party, was declining. Strikes and other workers' activities began to increase only around 1912, and many communist historians regard 1912 as a turning point in the history of their movement. But the major turning point in the history of bolshevism was the outbreak of the World War I. For the gap between bolsheviks and mensheviks became unbridgeable as a result of differences over the party's attitude toward the war.[3]

The outbreak of hostilities had shown that Marxist dogmas or hopes concerning international proletarian solidarity had been little more than phrases and that national loyalties were stronger than class consciousness. Most working-class

leaders, albeit with some reluctance, supported their countries' war effort. Lenin nevertheless urged the working class
to turn their military weapons against their own ruling
classes, fraternize with their fellow workers across the
trenches, and turn the war into a world revolution. During
the war, while living in Switzerland, he tried to rally like-
minded comrades around him, helped organize conferences
for the purpose, swore undying enmity to all those Marxists
who had supported the war, and made plans for founding a
new international organization of all truly revolutionary parties. The handful of men and women who came to his support, together with those who had been with him since about
1909, formed the bulk of the bolshevik leadership when the
revolution of 1917 broke out.

Lenin was joined in 1917 by a considerable number of
Marxists who had hitherto refused to be identified with bolshevism but who now supported Lenin because they were
attracted by the uncompromising radicalism of his stand.
These people include Leon Trotsky and a large number of
brilliant leaders forming his entourage, who had previously
tried to conciliate bolsheviks and mensheviks, as well as some
outright mensheviks, as, for instance, the future commissar
for foreign affairs, G. V. Chicherin. As a result of this influx
of new blood into the highest ranks of the party in 1917,
party membership became more heterogeneous in outlook
than ever before; and, corresponding to this heterogeneity,
the democratic representative institutions of the party acquired greater weight in decision making than they had ever
had. Moreover, one of the newcomers, Trotsky, came close
to rivaling Lenin as the leader of the bolsheviks, though he
never quite equaled him in authority. He was popular with
the rank and file and was better known to outsiders than
anyone except Lenin; but the old-timers in the party tended
to regard him with suspicion and envy.[4]

During 1917, when the range of attitudes and policies expressed by bolshevik leaders widened and leadership to some
extent diffused, some of the comrades-in-arms who had stuck
by Lenin most faithfully during the difficult interrevolution-

ary years found themselves out of tune with him. During the eight months between the fall of tsarism and the bolshevik seizure of power, Lenin's attitude was marked by uncompromising radicalism. His policy was to endorse sweepingly the most radical demands voiced by Russia's lower classes. He endorsed the peasants' demand for the immediate distribution of the landlords' estates. He came out in favor of giving the workers control over the factories. He supported the cry of Russia's national minorities for national self-determination, including even separation from the Russian state. And he advocated measures to end the war immediately. Lenin's radicalism in 1917 implied uncompromising resistance to the caretaker government that had instituted itself in the spring. He demanded its replacement by a government of popular action committees (soviets) in which only the revolutionary parties were represented. Furthermore, he showed an absolute intolerance of revolutionaries who were satisfied with, or for any reason preferred, compromise.

In short, Lenin from the very beginning was unwilling to regard the overthrow of tsarism as an end in itself or even as a major achievement giving time to pause. Instead, he saw it as a mere beginning, a prologue to further revolutionary events, an opportunity for quick advances, and he was eager to get done with the further tasks as quickly as possible. In advancing such ideas, he was at first far ahead of most of his closest friends and associates. They were unprepared for, and frightened by, his sweeping program and sought to prevent or soften what they thought would be rash, adventurous actions. Some, like Stalin, rallied around Lenin after a while. Others became ever more alarmed. Their conflict with Lenin came to a head in October of 1917, when, from his Finnish hiding place, he bombarded the Central Committee with messages urging them to prepare an armed uprising at once with the aim of overthrowing the provisional government and establishing a Soviet regime. Two of his closest associates, Zinoviev and Kamenev, publicly dissociated themselves from such a course of action and were virtually read out of the party by Lenin. Yet they had done little more than express openly the doubts shared by many of their comrades.*

Once the bolsheviks had seized power in the name of the Soviet (at that time they were in the majority in this body), the heterogeneity of party leadership and the prevalence of open debate within this group were intensified by the fact that the first few years of communist rule brought acute problems that no one had anticipated. Crises can unify the group they confront; but they can also have divisive effects; the grave problems faced by the party in the first few years of its rule did both.

At the root of the problems was the fact that the Communist Party had come to power with the firm expectation that this event would produce a world-wide chain reaction of proletarian revolutions; and this world revolution in turn would ensure the immediate advent of socialism even in Russia. We shall have more to say about these expectations in the following chapter. It took only a few months of Soviet rule to convince at least Lenin that these ideals were not going to be attained immediately. With the gradual ebbing of hopes for a general European revolution, his government was not only forced to think of its own preservation; it also had to postpone the Good Society as far as domestic measures were concerned. The grim fight for survival in the civil war which broke out in the summer of 1918 required the abandonment of democratic ideals and the imposition in their stead of strict military discipline; and the economic ruin following in its wake forced Lenin to take the most stringent measures to save his regime from collapse. Moreover, it dawned on the communist leaders that the vigor with which substantial por-

---

* No account, however brief, of the Russian revolution would be complete which does not at least mention theories current to-day which depict the bolshevik victory and the entire history of the party as the work of agents in the pay of sinister outside forces, especially German intelligence, but including among others the tsarist secret police. The most comprehensive summary of these theories can be found in Stefan T. Possony, *Lenin: The Compulsive Revolutionary* (Chicago, 1963).

tions of the lower-class population of Russia had fought for the revolution did not necessarily imply that they were in general on a high level of literacy, education, or productivity. On the contrary, the human material at the disposal of the party was on an abysmally low cultural level—hardly the basis for the ideal communist society.

Some of the repressive measures taken during the civil war were defended by many communists as attempts to create immediately the communist or socialist society. Each new measure of nationalization and centralization, each new tightening of controls, was praised as the harbinger of true socialism. But other members of the party saw in these steps a betrayal of the ideas for which they had fought, and Lenin had to impose every such measure against vigorous opposition from leading party members. The ideas of 1917 thus served both to justify the civil-war measures (known in the history books as "war communism") by stirring expectations of the immediate attainment of socialism and to criticize them as a violation of communist ideals. It appeared that Lenin's left-wing followers, who had been the most sanguine in their expectations in 1917, tended to be the most critical of war communism and simultaneously to harbor the greatest illusions abouts its results. In contrast, the old-time Leninists, who had resisted their leader in 1917, were less burdened with idealistic hopes and with squeamishness. Consequently, war communism did not present them with such acute ideological problems.[5]

Once the civil war was won, the party, in a sudden about-face, made substantial concessions to free enterprise and other capitalist features; and once again the membership was jolted and perturbed, and many of them retained serious misgivings about the new policies which they regarded as a retreat from socialist principles. These heated debates, in the course of which Lenin was outvoted more than once in the Central Committee, prompted him to curb dissent and discussion within the party by the measures described above and by such devices as control over recruitment, assignments, and other personnel policies. Because of these steps

68   COMMUNISM

to silence dissenting members, the doubts arising over the
concessions made after the end of the civil war remained
unexpressed in the main while Lenin was still alive. But they
were to erupt all the more forcefully when illness and death
removed him from the scene and the curtain rose on a new
act in the history of Russian communism.

This sketch of the history of the Russian Communist Party
can, of course, offer no more than a few highlights of an involved and complex development. In summary: The party
grew up as a tightly organized and self-conscious faction
within the Russian Social-Democratic Labor Party; it strove
to gain full control over the Russian working-class movement
with the aim of making its own policies prevail; and its
leader did everything within his power to make it into an
organization whose every move was well under his own control, rejecting and casting out all persons and groups who
refused to submit to such control.

After the revolution, the effort to convert the working-class
movement into an efficient and tightly controlled political
machine (in Russian: *apparat*) was extended to the international working-class movement. On the basis of plans
Lenin had conceived during World War I, he created an
international league of communist parties, the Third, or
Communist, International, the by-laws of which were drafted
so as to resemble closely those of the Russian party and to
give control over membership and policies of all its constitu-
ent parties to Lenin and his Russian colleagues. The Communist International, with its numerous auxiliary organizations, thus quickly became a global extension of the Russian
*apparat.**

Yet when Lenin became ill, the problems of party policy,
organization, and personnel were by no means solved. A
number of fundamental differences in attitude divided the
party along policy lines. The resulting formation of factions
was complicated by personal antagonisms and friendships
between different groups of leaders. Finally, the death of

---

* See Chapter 9.

the leader, in whose hands most lines of control and command had been concentrated, brought out serious unresolved problems of party government and precipitated a deep and prolonged crisis within the party. We shall give a brief account of it in the next chapter.

6

Phases of Soviet Rule

• The history of communism comprises not only the growth of the party but also the development of the state and the society over which that party has been ruling for more than four decades. Because Soviet Russia for many years was the only country under the rule of a Communist Party, all the world regarded her as an experiment in socialist government —and so did the communists themselves. Consequently, the history of Soviet Russia has become part of the heritage of communism everywhere. It is an experience which in some fashion all adherents of the movement share and which they take into consideration, willingly or not, whenever and wherever they map out governmental policies. In this introductory essay we can do no more than provide a brief outline of the main phases of Soviet rule in Russia.

One thing that will emerge from this chapter is the changing nature of the Soviet regime. Its basic aims and activities, its institutions and the entire social structure beneath these institutions, have several times undergone radical transformations. Hence to speak about *the* Soviet government or *the* Soviet society is misleading, since there has been a succession of markedly distinct social and political systems. To be sure, there are continuities within this recurrent change. From its beginnings to our day, the Soviet Union has been ruled by one and the same political party. This ruling party

has continually expressed its allegiance to one and the same
official doctrine. Hence there has been political and ideological continuity. I would argue, however, that these continuities are formal rather than real. For one thing, the membership and organization of the party, as well as its place and
functions within Soviet society, have changed as much as the
society itself; further, although the words of Marxism-Leninism rarely change, the meaning given to them, and the
relationship between doctrine and politics, have not remained
the same, as I shall try to show.*

The bolsheviks expected their revolution to result in a
world-wide chain reaction of proletarian revolutions, which,
they assumed, would ensure the birth of a global (or at least
all-European) socialist commonwealth. The kind of socialist
commonwealth Lenin envisaged is described in some detail
in his unfinished *The State and Revolution,* which he wrote
in the fall of 1917 and which echoed sentiments widespread
in his party at that time. In it he visualized that the creation
of a soviet state would at once lead to the expropriation of
capitalists and landowners and therefore to the abolition of
commodity production (i.e., production for the market). It
would lead to classless society, in which the material wants
of all could be fully satisfied. Since by working for the common good all members of society would be working directly
for themselves, they would, Lenin foresaw, gladly give their
energies for production; no longer would there be incentive
problems. Moreover, the need for men to dominate or exploit
other men would disappear, and hence institutions of coercion and government, such as armies, police forces, courts,
and bureaucracies, would disappear. The people would manage their communal affairs spontaneously, directly, rationally. The administration of the industrial establishment, in
turn, would be reduced to simple tasks of accounting and
controlling, tasks so simple that they could be performed by
anyone. Since these would be all the "governmental" tasks

---

* For an elaboration of my argument about the changing nature of Soviet society, see my chapter "The Soviet Political System" in Samuel Hendel and Randolph L. Braham, *USSR Fifty
Years Later: The Promise and the Reality* (New York, 1967).

remaining to be done, any "female cook" could run the government; and administrative responsibilities could therefore
be rotated among all.

These sanguine expectations held by the bolsheviks in the
last months of 1917 were not merely propaganda designed
to justify their seizure of power. On the contrary, the bolsheviks were convinced that this ideal society was within
reach, and it took some of them years to shed such beliefs.
Since then, the blueprint Lenin provided for a classless and
stateless society has become a source of embarrassment to
the party, a symbol of unfulfilled dreams or broken promises,
an idealistic mirror that mocked the face of an exceedingly
drab reality.*

For developments took a different turn. The workers of
the West did not take up the cue tossed them by the Russian Revolution. The bolshevik regime of Russia remained
isolated and harassed. Within the country, a protracted and
bitter civil war broke out, and in the narrow territory remaining under Soviet rule uncooperative, hostile elements
abounded. The regime truly had its back to the wall. It won
the civil war partly because substantial sections of the peasantry and the national minorities joined the workers in supporting the regime actively or passively, or at least showed
themselves more hostile to the counterrevolutionary forces
than to the Red Army, and partly because the bolsheviks
adopted stringent emergency measures to keep themselves
in power. They imposed the strictest military discipline on
the entire population, including their own supporters and
party members. Like commandants of a besieged fortress,
they commandeered every ounce of available human and

---

* Although Lenin's book on *The State and Revolution* is often
assigned to students to acquaint them with the writings of Lenin,
I should like to stress its unrepresentative nature. I should
go so far as to say that it is the most unrepresentative, the
most untypical work of all that Lenin has produced; it is an
aberration from his customary thought pattern. See Robert V.
Daniels, "The State and Revolution: A Case Study in the Genesis
and Transformation of Communist Ideology," in *The American
Slavic and East European Review*, vol. XII (February 1953),
pp. 22–43.

material resources for the civil-war effort, disdaining neither to rob the peasant of his produce by force nor to employ tsarist officers, capitalist entrepreneurs, and other "bourgeois specialists." Ruling by stark terror, with the support at times of ignorant and dissolute mobs who often abused the power so suddenly thrust upon them, smashing existing institutions and assigning loyal revolutionaries to administrative jobs for which they were altogether unprepared, improvising and fumbling, they yet found this to be the time for brave cultural experiments in many fields, most of them based on the notion that the brotherhood of all men was about to become reality. Antagonizing countless supporters, they yet managed to inspire an entire generation of Russian youngsters with heaven-storming enthusiasm, with the readiness to sacrifice everything to the building of a world without exploitation and inequality, a socialist commonwealth that would begin as soon as the civil war would be won. This was the heroic period of the Russian Revolution, usually referred to as the period of war communism, a period in which all the worst fears of antirevolutionary men in Russia and in the West were confirmed by the excesses of the Red Terror, the insolence of drunken or ragged proletarians, and the muddle of communist bureaucracy, while the image which Soviet Russia presented to her sympathizers abroad was still one of unsullied revolutionary pioneering.

Yet the ruthlessness of the civil-war emergency measures exhausted the credit of the bolshevik regime among many of its supporters. By the time the civil war was won, the regime was therefore close to political collapse. In addition, seven years of foreign and civil war had brought unspeakable economic ruin to the country. Drastic measures were required to restore the economy and pacify at least parts of the population. The measures adopted for the purpose are known as the New Economic Policy, or NEP. They consisted in the reintroduction of private enterprise in agriculture, trade, crafts, and small manufacture, with only foreign trade, major industries, and political rule remaining firmly in the hands of the party and its government. (Concessions made to Western business firms allowing them to exploit Soviet resources or build up manufacturing enterprises made no serious dent in these monopolies.)

The NEP meant a relaxation of bolshevik terror. Members of the old ruling classes remained disfranchised and discriminated against; but they were at least permitted to make a living. Workers still enjoyed privileges over the members of other classes, but economically the NEP benefited well-to-do peasants and small businessmen. Bold experiments were still conducted by the party in various cultural fields; but other currents in art, literature, science, and mores were at least tolerated. To the average Soviet citizen looking back to this period in the 1930's or 1940's, the years of the NEP must have appeared like a veritable golden age. After the hardships of the heroic period, normalcy seemed to have returned.

Yet this normalcy did not look attractive to many members of the Communist Party. To be sure, they had adopted the NEP as a necessary retreat; they had said, with Lenin, that they were accepting it "seriously and for a long time"; but nonetheless not all had accepted it gladly. True, most party members had had enough of civil war, terror, and heroism for a while. But not all were comfortable in the humdrum tasks of gradual economic reconstruction and of teaching illiterates the ABC's or with the patient tolerance shown to peasants, small businessmen, and foreign concessionaires. The men at the head of the party had spent their lives in an agonizing struggle for a lofty goal. Most of them could not possibly be satisfied unless there was a chance to make that goal—socialism—reality.

Conflicting schools of thought developed within the Russian Communist Party concerning the manner in which socialism might be made to come about. One group, usually considered to be the right wing of the party, developed an almost Fabian theory of inevitable gradualness, based on thoughts expressed in Lenin's last articles and speeches. They held that the uneasy compromise between socialism and free enterprise would give way to pure socialism in the course of a slow, organic evolution and that in similar fashion the social basis of the regime, that is, the "alliance" between workers and peasants, would gradually "grow over" into a purely proletarian society. The economic transformation, entailing the gradual waning of free enterprise and other capitalist features, would come about as the result of free competition between capitalism and socialism, and not through coercion or governmental arbitrariness. The most outspoken among them therefore argued that the free-enterprise features of the NEP ought to be fostered and encouraged rather than curbed. Precisely the free unfolding of capitalism—perhaps with constitutional democracy added—would hasten the growth of socialism. The party's chief role in this process, they tended to think, was that of promoting the cultural revolution, that is, the transformation, by education, of Russia's ignorant, backward masses into informed, sophisticated, responsible citizens. The cultural revolution, they thought, was the most essential prerequisite and the surest guarantee of the eventual victory of socialism over capitalism.

The people who developed gradualist views were of different types. The chief theoreticians of gradualism appear to have been antitotalitarian idealists such as N. N. Bukharin who in the period of war communism (if not before) had become suspicious of violent and authoritarian methods. In their attempts to provide their political views with ideological support, they interpreted Marxism in strictly determinist fashion, leading to the conclusion that it is impossible to go against economic laws or to skip historically predetermined stages of development, and that it would be foolish or criminal to attempt it. Similarly, Marxist dialectics was transformed by Bukharin into a theory of equilibrium which supported his reluctance to engage in daring and radical political experiments. Theoreticians such as he were supported by a host of party bureaucrats who seemed loath to jeopardize the interests of their political machine for the sake of bold new adventures, people whose vested interest in the existing system made them timid if not conservative.[1]

Against the gradualists stood those party leaders who argued that the NEP was a danger which must be overcome by daring measures. It was a political danger because the dominating position taken in the national economy by the successful peasant and small businessman sooner or later would be transformed into political dominance, so that the proletarian regime was in danger of being swamped by the petty bourgeoisie. Economically the NEP was dangerous, they held, because Soviet Russia was threatened with the prospect of getting stuck in economic backwardness. Socialism, they argued, was possible only in a modern industrial society; and the first task of the communist regime would therefore have to be to erect a modern industrial structure.

The spokesmen for the left wing of the Russian Communist Party—outstanding among them were Leon Trotsky and Eugene Preobrazhenski—gave dramatic emphasis to their theory by calling for a policy of *primitive* (or *primary*) *socialist accumulation.* Primary accumulation, in Marxist theory, is that sanguinary process of robbery, piracy, conquest, extortion, and other violent means through which society accumulates the material resources and "free" labor that enable the capitalist mode of production to develop. In the words of Marx, it is "an accumulation not the result of the capitalist mode of production, but its starting point"; and he adds that it "plays in Political Economy about the same part as original sin in theology." [2] Marx describes it with loathing and moral indignation, concluding that capitalism comes into the world "dripping from head to foot, from every pore, with blood and dirt." [3] This then was the image Trotsky and Preobrazhenski evoked in demanding a policy of primitive socialist accumulation. They argued that just as capitalism could arise only after surplus wealth and a surplus population had been accumulated, so the creation of an industrial base was the essential prerequisite for building socialism. In addition, industrialization was the only policy that could prevent the revolution from being overwhelmed by peasants and NEP men (small businessmen). They warned that the policy they were advocating would require harsh measures and dictatorial discipline. The resources to be invested in industrialization would have to be provided by Russia's population through forced savings. And yet they argued that the task could be accomplished without living standards falling drastically and without a renewal of the Red Terror of civil-war days. Whatever the measures and the methods, however, the revolution would be lost if it did not industrialize.

On the very left wing of the party, there were small groups of leaders who argued that the revolution had already been lost or betrayed, that it had followed a cycle similar to that of the French Revolution, in which the radical Jacobin dreams of equality and justice had been destroyed by the Thermidorian reaction and the ensuing Bonapartist dictatorship. According to such men as Shliapnikov and Sapronov, leaders of the ultraleftist opposition, the ideals of 1917 had been betrayed by the Communist Party itself. Instead of socialism, a mixture of capitalist free enterprise and industrial dictatorship had been set up, they argued; instead of proletarian rule, rule by the party, and not even the entire party at that, but only the handful of leaders constituting the core of the Old Guard. These men, ardently committed to the anarcho-syndicalist dreams of 1917, ultimately came to the conclusion that a third revolution (third after the two revolutions of February and October of 1917) was needed, this one to be a genuine proletarian revolution to overthrow the dictatorship of the party and to establish a genuine socialist workers' democracy.

As we shall see, these divergent views concerning the most desirable or necessary development of the Russian Revolution were linked with equally conflicting policy lines concerning the policies of the international communist movement. Disputes over policy and ultimate goals, moreover, led to discussions in virtually every other field of learning, thought, and action; and the 1920's, more than any other period, therefore witnessed a thorough and highly controversial reexamination of Marxism and Leninism in all its details, a debate that was far more open than any similar disputes within the party were later allowed to be. For the student of communist political systems anywhere, it is interesting and important to study these debates because similar problems are likely to trouble any communist regime arising in an underdeveloped country. Communist experience

in Eastern Europe and East Asia can thus be regarded as a
series of variations on themes struck some decades ago by
Soviet Russia.

The differences of opinion over the further development
of the revolution began to plague the party soon after the
beginning of the NEP. They were quite heated in the last
year of Lenin's life and became extremely bitter after his
death, which added the fuel of an intense power struggle to
the fire of ideological arguments. Not only opinions but personalities and ambitions, too, clashed head-on, and the conflict split the party into hardly reconcilable factions. By
"party" we mean that small group of Old Guard leaders who
as members of its highest policy-making and administrative
bodies were in actual command of the party. Even before
Lenin was dead, maneuvering began in this high command
to settle the succession problem. Interest centered on the role
and personality of Trotsky, who in the minds of many people outside and inside the party was the heir apparent. Although he had for many years opposed Lenin and his bolshevik faction and joined them only in the summer of 1917,
it was he who had been the chief tactician of the bolshevik
seizure of power, creator of the Red Army and main strategist of the civil war, savior of Leningrad, and second in
prestige only to Lenin himself. Abroad, it was customary to
mention Lenin and Trotsky in the same breath as the two-
man team ruling Soviet Russia. Within the party, however,
there were many leaders who well remembered Trotsky's
ancient conflicts with the bolsheviks and the comparatively
recent vintage of his party membership. To be sure, in join-
ing he had brought with him a bevy of friends who at once
became prominent leaders under Lenin and could support
Trotsky from positions of strength within the party. But
against this faithful cohort stood a broad stratum of old associates of the dead leader who deeply resented the new-
comer's prestige and power. Trotsky's own personality was
not designed to help him win his colleagues' favor. The
brilliance of his mind, his pen, and his oratory was matched
by great arrogance and tactlessness, by a certain inability to
deal with people and to recognize political constellations

within the party. As a political manipulator he was no match
for the old Leninist organizers. Finally, as architect of the
Red Army he could easily be regarded as or alleged to be a
potential Bonaparte, who would pervert the revolution while
saving it and make himself the dictator; and anything
Trotsky might have done to defend himself against this suspicion would only have increased it. Seeing this, he did nothing to cleanse himself of the Bonapartist taint. On the contrary, there is some evidence that he regarded himself as
Lenin's legitimate heir and promoted his candidacy for the
position of party chief, aided by some of his followers in the
party's high ranks. These moves evoked a systematic propaganda campaign in which the old Leninists, headed by G. E.
Zinoviev, Lenin's old-time companion and faithful shadow,
tried to stigmatize Trotsky as a menshevik. After these ideological preparations, Trotsky and those loyal to him were
demoted and isolated; and, while he was not denied access
to the centers of decision making (he remained in the Politburo until October 1926 and in the Central Committee for
a year after that), his vote in these organizations struck
against a solid wall of hostility. Meanwhile, the policy-making power of the party's administrative organs, from which
Trotsky and his followers were excluded, grew apace.

The next phase was a fight among the victors in the struggle against Trotsky, especially between Zinoviev (joined by
another old comrade of Lenin's, L. B. Kamenev) and the
party's General Secretary, J. V. Stalin. Zinoviev's political
strength was considerable. As chairman of the Executive
Committee of the Communist International, he was the
world's number-one communist. In addition to being a member of the Politburo, he was also boss of the important
Leningrad regional party organization, while the Moscow
organization was Kamenev's stronghold. In their fight against
the General Secretary, these two former associates of his
tried to pit the power, prestige, and the votes of their
satrapies against Stalin's growing control over the total party
machinery. This attempt was made at the fourteenth Party
Congress, the last congress to have exhaustive open debates
(December 1925). The attempt failed. The so-called Lenin-

grad opposition was voted down, and Zinoviev, Kamenev, and their supporters were removed from positions of authority and power.

This defeat was followed by a last-ditch effort in which Trotsky, Zinoviev, and their associates joined forces in a desperate attempt to regain their strength and influence in the party and to overthrow the party regime that had become entrenched. The Trotsky-Zinoviev opposition was a heterogeneous alliance of groups and personalities, which comprised old Leninists as well as the most prominent among those leaders who, like Trotsky, had joined Lenin in 1917; authoritarian and democratic bolsheviks; hard Marxists and soft Marxists; theoreticians and organization men. The bitter struggle which ensued between them and the Stalin faction (in which Bukharin was the outstanding theoretician) lasted for about six months in 1927 and rocked the party dangerously. Its outcome, Stalin's complete victory, was probably inevitable, because the whole strength of the party organization was in the hands of the General Secretary, who wielded it with considerable skill and cunning. Many historians date his dictatorship from the days of his victory over the Trotsky-Zinoviev opposition, and indeed his strength had now become unassailable. To be sure, while the rank and file membership of the party had been reduced to obedient yes men and while secretaries and administrators loyal to Stalin ran local and regional party organizations with an iron hand, the Central Committee, the Politburo, and other central party organizations still retained genuine decision-making power. But even there, Stalin could usually be certain of dependable majorities.

Once Stalin was well in control of the party, he adopted a great deal of the program of his left-wing critics—and as a consequence faced new opposition, this time from theoreticians like Bukharin and organization men like Tomsky and Rykov, who for various reasons were firmly committed to a program of caution and slow reform. This opposition fared little better than previous ones; within a comparatively brief period, its leaders were eliminated from positions of influence. Acknowledging that economic as well as political stagnation were major dangers facing the Soviet regime, Stalin now launched a program of rapid industrialization on the basis of a five-year plan—the most ambitious, not to say reckless, of the various plans elaborated by the party economists. Stalin himself later referred to the years of this first five-year plan as another revolution (adding that it was a revolution made from above); and rightly so, because not only did the five-year plans achieve revolutionary changes in the economic, social, political, and cultural fabric of Russia but these changes were initiated in truly revolutionary frenzy, which gripped the party and imparted its spirit to all fields of endeavor.

The plan for industrialization was carried out with utter disregard for considerations of economic balance or rationality, or for the demands of the consumer. Instead, it was executed as a desperate crash program. The Russian population again suffered lean years, with a drastic lowering of living standards, as every ounce of available energy—human as well as material—was pressed into service and pumped into investment. In agriculture, the new revolution brought with it a virtual civil war against the peasantry. The regime wanted to neutralize the peasants once and forever as a potential political force, wanted to subject them to economic, political, and cultural controls and pressures, and particularly wished to make sure that every year's harvest would reach the hungry mouths of the city dwellers. For without food and agricultural raw materials, the industrialization effort would be doomed. To secure these ends, the party decided to abolish private enterprise in farming and force the peasants into cooperative, or collective, farms, where they would be subject to all these controls, primarily because collective farms would not own the essential means of production—tractors and implements—but would have to rent them from government pools. Motor and repair shops were therefore in a position of control and could become centers not only for the economic exploitation of the farmers but also for their political control and education and for efforts to urbanize the farm population.

Peasant resistance to the attempt to "collectivize" them

was bitter and persistent, and the regime succeeded in over-coming it only through a virtual civil war, in which hundreds of thousands of peasants lost their lives, millions were rendered destitute, and the agricultural economy of the Soviet Union suffered damages that were not repaired until more than twenty years later. In the wake of collectivization, a disastrous famine killed millions of Soviet citizens.

For the first few years the industrialization was accompanied by a new radicalism in culture and educational affairs, a new stress on proletarian exclusiveness, but in other aspects Soviet Russia moved further away from socialist goals and methods. The workers, whose trade unions during the NEP had retained at least a modicum of bargaining and administrative power, were totally subjected to discipline under a new managerial system. Where formerly Russia's government and industry had been managed "collectively," that is, through administrative committees, a command principle was now instituted, whereby all agencies were to be run by single managers with full authority and responsibility. The country's administration was thus streamlined to resemble the organization and management of giant corporations in the Western world—a process through which the party itself had already gone some years before.

Two additional developments were required before Soviet Russia was transformed into the type of society it is today. I shall call one of these the cultural counterrevolution.* The other one is known as the Great Purge. The two phenomena are closely related to each other.

The origins and meaning of the Great Purge remain a matter of conjecture and controversy. The paranoid and vengeful personality of Stalin is as unsatisfactory an explanation as the totalitarian pattern of Soviet rule with its presumed need for an occasional personnel turnover through the means of a bloody housecleaning. We must take into consideration the tremendous difficulties faced by Stalin's regime in the 1930's. The reckless pace of industrialization

---

* The term has been suggested by my friend Robert V. Daniels.

and collectivization had led to serious bottlenecks and deficiencies in the national economy. In the party, the government, and the economy, serious morale problems were created by the arbitrariness with which impossible tasks were imposed on ill-trained personnel or inadequate facilities. In international affairs the Soviet Union began to face new grave threats from strong neighbors to the west and the east. It is plausible to assume that the victims of the Great Purge served, among other things, as scapegoats on whom all blame for these failures could be heaped. Furthermore, numerous party members may have been in a state of genuine panic and therefore quite receptive to what was alleged to be evidence of sabotage, treason, and the like. Most historians, finally, would point out that the cultural counter-revolution, the thorough bureaucratization of Russia, the decided turn away from revolutionary endeavors, and the entire trend of development in Soviet politics under Stalin's rule could not have been carried out successfully as long as the old bolsheviks were still alive who had helped make the revolution, who had been raised in a spirit of utopian radicalism and Marxist critique, and who would not have found it possible to adjust to Stalinist society without continually rebelling against it. The revolutionary generation, perhaps, was unfit for life in the society which the revolution had created.

Whatever the reasons, the fact is that between 1935 and 1938 the USSR became the stage for a veritable orgy of police activity, in which the party, the government apparatus, the economy, the armed forces, the schools and universities, and all the professions were decimated, especially in their higher ranks, from which vast numbers of personnel disappeared into the labor camps or execution dungeons of the secret police. In the Communist Party, nearly everyone who had ever disagreed with the dictator was physically eliminated; and the same fate befell countless officials within the party and outside of it who were denounced for, or suspected of, harboring dissent. As a result, the administrative body of Soviet society was decapitated; an entire generation of leaders fell victims to the purge and an entire generation of younger ones moved up to fill their places. Furthermore, we might say that the purge destroyed the Communist Party, although I know of no one who has expressed this fact so drastically. Nonetheless I believe it to be true. Not only did the Great Purge kill off or jail almost all those who had been members of the party before and during the revolution of 1917. In that sense, the party of Lenin certainly was destroyed. But in addition the place and function which the party had had in Soviet society was changed so drastically that we might speak of its destruction. In the first two decades of the Russian Revolution, the party had been the sovereign of the Soviet Union, to use an old-fashioned term. It had been in charge. It had acted as if it owned the country or as if it were administering it in the name of the working class. This undisputed sovereignty of the party was replaced, in the Great Purge, by the undisputed sovereignty of Josef Stalin. He made use of the party as one of the instruments of his rule; but he used it no more, and in practice assigned no greater importance to it, than the government administration or the political police. To be precise, Stalin's central organ of rule was his personal secretariat, which, even though it had close connections with the party and the police, was yet apart from them and above them, assigning them a secondary role.*

The cultural counterrevolution, or, as Timasheff called it, the Great Retreat, was a process of transformation consummated about the time of the Great Purge. Its outward manifestation was a decided return to traditionalism in education, art, social science, mores, and other elements that make up a society's cultural life. It included such developments as the reintroduction of military ranks and tsarist-style uniforms, the strengthening of the family and of the authority of both parents and teachers, and the abandonment of *avant-garde*

---

* We might recognize the justification for asserting that the party was destroyed in the following figures of the proportion of voting delegates at party congresses who were party members before 1921, that is, before the end of the civil war:

Seventeenth Congress (1934) .... 80.0 per cent
Eighteenth Congress (1939) .... 19.4 per cent

art styles in favor of the naive naturalism of what Hitler called "heroic art" and which in the USSR is called "socialist realism."

But if this was a *return* to traditionalism, from where did it return? The answer is, from Marxism. True, Marxism remained as the acknowledged creed of the Soviet state, hailed as the last word in social and natural science as well as philosophy, elevated to the status of official dogma. But only the words of Marx became dogma; essential elements of what he meant and what he wanted were abandoned. In returning to traditionalism in cultural and intellectual life, the Soviet regime rejected at least two major elements of Marxism. One was the dream of a society without alienation or (to eschew utopianism) without that surplus alienation which goes beyond the minimum of alienation required to keep a modern industrial economy operating,[4] a dream which had been kept very much alive in the period of the NEP and the first five-year plan. The regime that emerged in the mid-1930's seems to have come to the conclusion that the yearning for such a society, for the institutions and processes depicted in Lenin's *The State and Revolution,* would never, or not for a very long time, be satisfied, and that the yearning itself, therefore, was disturbing and disruptive. So it became subversive to talk about or ask for the withering away of the state, the disappearance of oppressive institutions and social or economic inequality. At the same time, Marxist doctrines or words were twisted in such a fashion as to create the impression that a major portion of the dreams of Marx and Engels had indeed come true. Socialism had been achieved. The class struggle had been abolished. The Soviet people were a happy people.

The assertion that socialism had been achieved implied the rejection of one other element of Marxism, namely, the use of social science for the purpose of analyzing social phenomena as the superstructure of exploitative economic systems. Marxism had not been only a dream of the future. It had also been critical of the past and the present; and it is by its very method and orientation a critical social theory. Soviet society, however, continued to incorporate intense alienation of all its citizens, which the Soviet Union became altogether unwilling to admit. Soviet theory has been reluctant to concede that its own society incorporates repression, domination, and exploitation. At most, it hints at remaining differences between the interests of the state and those of the individual. Being unwilling to admit these repressive features, it cannot, of course, justify them, as well it might be able to do. As a matter of fact, we might say that one of the main distinguishing features of Stalinist theory is this unwillingness to admit the necessity (in bolshevik terms) for repressive measures. Stalin and his comrades obviously did not dare take the people into their confidence about the hard road that lay ahead in the drive for rapid industrialization. I think that here lies the main difference between Stalin and Trotsky: the policies they advocated were similar; but the latter was honest about their harshness, whereas Stalinism sought to conceal it behind phrases to the effect that the Soviet world is the best of all possible worlds. Important among the ideological taboos resulting from this unwillingness to look reality in the face is the inability to admit that the isolation of the "proletarian" revolution in a backward peasant country was, from the point of view of original Marxism, a historical freak and, from the point of view of the proletarian world revolution, an unmitigated disaster. There was therefore even a marked reluctance to admit that tsarist Russia was a backward society in comparison with Western Europe. These ideological taboos have little to do with Marxism; on the contrary, they are in sharp contradiction to it. Marxist theory, in fact, has been thoroughly emasculated and converted into apologetics. Under Stalin, even though Marx and Engels were the prophets of Soviet society, their writings were available to Soviet readers only in expurgated editions; their earlier works particularly were either suppressed or explained away, for these works contain in the clearest form their critique of domination and their yearning for liberty. Entire concepts were eliminated from the storehouse of Marxist methods, because they might yield conclusions uncomfortable to the regime. Occasionally, Stalin even ventured to criticize some of their works openly; for instance, he denounced Engels for his hatred of tsarist Russia and his eagerness to see Western Europe united in a war to destroy that hated state.

The turn to traditionalism came to pervade all of Soviet culture. In the teaching of history, the preoccupation with class wars and economic developments and with the depressing features of tsarist Russia's past gave way to the old-fashioned kings-and-battles approach familiar to us from our own high-school texts; and the heroes no longer were the exploited masses but Russian emperors, generals, and conquerors of backward people in the Caucasus and Central Asia. Art turned into a weapon of mass propaganda, using the vehicle of popular style and expressing ideas designed to give cheer to the laboring masses. The idea of equality, which had inspired many of the deeds of the revolution and the civil war, now was denounced as a petty-bourgeois delusion; and henceforth in thought and in fact Soviet society came to lay stress on social differences, for the avowed purpose of providing incentives that had previously been considered unnecessary. By emphasizing differences of salary and rank, peak performance was encouraged, so that the Soviet population came under the sway of what Marcuse has called the "performance principle." To back up the system of rewards, police terror and concentration camps were provided, imposing stern sanctions on anyone not conforming to the regime's demands. Finally, as we have seen, a social theory was carefully designed not to unmask inequalities and alienation but to conceal them. Malfunctions, henceforth, were explained not as the symptoms of an ill social system (as Marx and Engels would have done) but as moral failings of individuals who were either weak and therefore had to be treated sternly or who were criminal conspirators who had to be eliminated. Or malfunctions were explained as unavoidable mechanical difficulties; for instance, Soviet medical theory recognizes almost no other cause of insanity but physiological deficiencies of the brain. In all these and many other fields, Soviet culture returned to the Victorian age.

With these developments, Soviet life was set for the next

two decades. In short, out of the purges, the first two five-year plans, the collectivization campaign, and the cultural counterrevolution, Stalinist society emerged. Soviet society acquired a certain stability for the first time. Henceforth, it might still undergo changes, but they would be less drastic in scope and less violent in form.

7

The Stalinist Theory of the State

• In this chapter, I shall summarize the self-image developed by Soviet ideology since it emerged in its Stalinist form. Again, despite the growing diversity among communist societies, the ideological preponderance of the USSR within the communist world was overwhelming in the formative period of most other communist polities. For this reason, the self-images developed by these other societies are but variations on the theme struck in this chapter. It should be read with this in mind.

According to official Soviet rhetoric, the USSR no longer is a proletarian dictatorship but has turned into a socialist state of toilers, in which exploitation and the class struggle have disappeared together with private property in the means of production. It is a state governed in accordance with a constitution which is more democratic than any other constitution past or present, because government is more truly representative of the people, and the rights of citizens are guaranteed more meaningfully than anywhere else.

After the completion of the second five-year plan, in the mid-thirties, the Soviet regime announced that the USSR had become a socialist society. It based this claim on the assertion that private enterprise had been eliminated completely with the abolition of the NEP and the collectivization of agriculture. Since production now proceeded according to a national plan presumably based on the needs of society rather than on the demands of the market—since, in other words, commodity production had been abolished—socialism was established by definition. This did not mean that the final goal of the communist movement had been reached. That final goal is communism, and party doctrine follows Lenin in making a careful distinction between socialism and communism. Communism is understood to incorporate the following features: an economy sufficiently productive to satisfy the material needs of all citizens and thus free them from material want; absolute equality of rewards, with the understanding that individuals will have different needs and different interests—equality of rewards then comes to mean the opportunity for every citizen freely to satisfy his own personal needs; universal rationality, or, as Soviet terminology expresses it, consciousness—a state in which all citizens have been raised to the level of consciousness hitherto attained only by the most advanced individuals, the vanguard; a universal collective conscience which persuades every citizen to work freely and cheerfully, and without expectation of reward, for the collective good—under communism, Lenin said, unrewarded work for the community will have become a habit. All these traits of communism imply that it is also without classes. All work will have become so mechanized that it will have turned into a routine everyone can perform. Or, perhaps, it will be so light a burden that people will be able to become skilled in many tasks. In any event, no longer will the division of labor divide men against men. In particular, all production will have become so mechanized or "automatized" that the differences between industry and agriculture, between city and country, will have been wiped out. Finally, under communism, institutions of domination will have become superfluous. Rule of men over men will have given way to the "administration of things" and to genuine collective self-government—the state will have withered away. Of all these features, voluntary work and equality of reward are singled out by Soviet doctrine as the principal ones; for communism is defined as a social order governed by the principle, "From each according to his ability; to each according to his need."

Socialism, in contrast, is the society which, once the capitalists have been expropriated, sets out to reach that final goal, communism, by means of economic growth and the education of the people for communism. By definition, therefore, this is a society in which abundance is not yet produced. But if there are wants or needs that remain unfilled, there is no equality of unfulfillment or misery. Since voluntary work for the common good has not yet become the habit of every healthy organism, incentives are still required to make people work. Incentives, however, imply a system of managed inequality, the exact amount of the rewards (in material goods, status, power, or other values) to be determined by the individual's performance or his value to the community. And so socialism is defined as that system which is functioning according to the principle, "From each according to his ability; to each according to his work."

The need for incentives (and, as we shall see, sanctions) gives this socialism some similarity with capitalist and pre-capitalist societies. While Soviet theory concedes this, it would stress the difference between the incentives in socialism and those operating in previous societies: socialist incentives, according to Soviet ideology, are more humane. Under feudalism, the main incentive was the knout—whoever did not perform to the satisfaction of the lord was whipped. Under capitalism, the main incentive was hunger—whoever did not compete successfully in the labor market starved to death. To be sure, the Soviet system also threatens its citizens with hunger if they do not pitch in; it has written this threat into its constitution, which contains the biblical words, "He who does not work, neither shall he eat," and makes them a guiding principle for Soviet society. At the same time, Soviet theory claims that the principal incentive under socialism is the expectation of greater reward, and, even more important, the desire for personal growth. Soviet citizens compete with each other not for the purpose of cutting each other's throats but in order to become more useful and more productive citizens. Soviet theory thus assumes a considerable amount of altruism, or, perhaps more correctly, of enlightened self-interest, because the expectation of reward is supported by the conviction that labor for the collectivity is labor for one's self. Since private property in the means of production has yielded to public ownership, the individual working for the government or the society is in fact working for himself, and the harder he works and the less reward he receives, the more quickly will he benefit from the general economic growth resulting from his and his fellow citizens' labor and deprivation. Thus, while rewarding those who produce above the general norm or who have scarce skills, the Soviet government expects its citizens in general to postpone gratification of their material needs for the sake of raising the common level of production.

Until the early 1930's, the Soviet regime tended to be apologetic about the resulting differences in reward and regard them as a temporary emergency measure. As a matter of fact, in the first years after the revolution, it had tried to foster equality as much as possible and especially to prevent party members and government officials from profiting materially from their positions of authority. While these measures to level society down to an equality of misery were never entirely successful, they worked within limits; and the rhetoric of equality prevailed for about fifteen years. Since then, Soviet theory has taken a more positive attitude toward differences in material reward and has denounced "equality mongering" as a petty-bourgeois deviation from, and a betrayal of, socialist ideas—as something hostile to Soviet socialism.

A very similar change in doctrine must be noted in a closely related problem—the differentiation in authority possessed by the citizens. Lenin's statement that after the revolution any female cook could take a turn at running the government was abandoned very quickly. But for a decade and a half after 1917 there was a cult of equality and a distrust of authority and rank, which may be explained in part by the fact that the individuals in positions of authority often were former tsarist officers or "bourgeois specialists" such as engineers and managers. To some extent, also, the cult of equality was a reaction against the age-old Russian tradition of rank consciousness, which had pervaded military and civilian life. One of the features of early Soviet administration, the custom of managing public agencies by committees, was clearly a result of this revulsion against authority as such. This egalitarianism, too, was now abandoned and denounced. It gave way to an authoritarian principle of individual leadership (*edinonachalie*), after Stalin announced that in Soviet society "cadres decide everything." The principle of hierarchy in command and authority was thus made part of the definition of socialism.[1]

Did the claim that socialism had been achieved imply that Soviet Russia had become a classless society? By no means. Classlessness is attributed only to the final stage, communism. Then did this mean that a class struggle was still raging in the socialist society? Again the answer is no. To be sure, two different classes are acknowledged to exist, classes that have different interests and different relations to the means of production. One of these is the working class (no longer called proletariat, because a proletariat is defined as the class exploited by capitalism); the other one is the peasantry. Out of both classes, who are said to be held together by a firm and friendly alliance, rises an additional group, not a class, but only a "layer." This is the intelligentsia, which in Soviet terminology denotes all who are not workers or peasants. That means all white-collar and professional people, from clerks and typists to movie stars, generals, and cabinet ministers. The existence of these classes (plus one stratum) is thus acknowledged, and hence the existence of different class interests and class consciousnesses. But a conflict of classes is not admitted. Soviet theory asserts that the interests of these classes do not conflict, that class harmony and class collaboration characterize Soviet socialist society. For even though there are differences, these differences are not as deep as class differences in capitalism, because no class owns the means of production. No class exploits another class. There is no leisure class; all Soviet citizens—workers, peasants, and intelligentsia—are "toilers."

There is yet another distinction Soviet theory makes

among its citizens. That is a distinction between the toilers on the one hand and the most advanced members of the working class, who make up the membership of the Communist Party, on the other. The party is considered the most advanced organization of Soviet society because it knows the real interests of the workers, speaks for them, leads them, and represents them in word and in deed. The party is credited with outstanding accomplishments. It has led the Soviet people to emancipation from feudal and capitalist oppression and it now provides guidance and supervision to Soviet citizens in all their endeavors. The membership of the party comprises the most conscious and advanced persons in every type of Soviet organization and in every walk of life. The party has always guided the Soviet people faultlessly, always accurately analyzing existing problems and situations, always correctly interpreting the interests of the people and finding the proper means toward the implementation of these interests. It has succeeded in this even though at times hostile elements have managed to worm themselves into the ranks of the party, even into very high places. Moreover, Marxism, which guides the party in its actions, is not easily mastered; and, while the party leadership has never wavered in the correct application of Marxist methods, even well-meaning members have at times deviated to the left or the right, succumbing either to the lure of antirevolutionary traitors or to the unproletarian influence of their own petty-bourgeois background. Whether or not such deviation is conscious, or willful, or based on evil intentions, objectively it makes the deviant member a counterrevolutionary. But the party has always saved its integrity by eliminating counterrevolutionaries. In recent years, it has been admitted further that in some matters even the party leadership went astray: under Stalin, it fell victim to the "cult of personality" and allowed the general secretary to arrogate excessive power to himself, in violation of the principle of collective leadership. This led to grave and dangerous mistakes; but, wherever possible, these mistakes have been corrected; and, wisened by the experience, the party will not fall into this error again. Soviet theory does not make it clear, however, what guarantees there are against the revival of the personality cult.

This, then, is the social structure of Soviet socialism, according to Soviet doctrine. It is a dynamic society, moving steadily toward all the transformations still required to bring about communism. The party expects to achieve this final goal within the foreseeable future. Several details of the process by which it expects to achieve it are worthy of our attention.

For one thing, Soviet doctrine asserts that the leap from socialism to communism will be made without a revolution. It will indeed be a leap, but it will be made as a result of gradual cumulative changes, and it will require neither the violent overthrow of an existing social order nor a system of domination. In Soviet socialist society, the superstructure does not lag behind the development of the forces of production, as it does in all other societies. It does not therefore get in the way of economic progress. On the contrary, it is a major agent of progress; and the last of the great Russian revolutions was the work of the Soviet government. This last revolution was the forcible elimination of kulaks and NEP men—the abolition of private enterprise; and it was a "revolution from above." Still, while the bolshevik revolution, according to Soviet theory, aligned the superstructure with the base, it still is a superstructure; and, as we know, this must disappear under full-fledged communism. Left-wing critics of the Stalin regime in the early 1920's postulated a "third revolution" which would have to remove the superstructure. Soviet theory, however, asserts that the superstructure will simply wither away after it has done its job fully.

Marxism in its original form incorporated a theory of lag; the relations of production and the superstructure of traditions, mores, institutions, and ideologies growing out of these relations lagged behind the development of productive forces and became an obstacle to further progress. In Soviet doctrine, this relationship has been reversed. Soviet theory concedes that there is some lag; for instance, the continued maintenance of some private property in farming and of cooperative private enterprise in various crafts is regarded as a hangover from the capitalist past which sooner or later must be removed in order to align the relations of production with the productive forces. But, in the main, consciousness as well as social relations, in Soviet socialism, are regarded as being ahead of the development of the forces of production and as instruments to help build them up. The party's main tool in this is the *state*, which therefore acquires positive value as a force of progress. Formerly, the state was seen as a product of class struggle. Now there is no class struggle, according to Soviet theory, even though a conflict of interests is still acknowledged, such as the conflict between the individual's "immediate" and his "real" interests. Some communists argued that therefore there was no justification for the state. But the party rejects this argument. We shall discuss the main grounds for this rejection below. Here we note only that the party justifies the state as an essential instrument for planning, organizing, and managing some of the transformations necessary to bring about the transition to communism, especially the growth of the forces of production. The state is the entrepreneur of socialism. By promoting production, it creates the preconditions for its own withering away. Soviet theory indignantly rejects the idea that the Soviet state might have become, or might in the future become, the instrument of rule for a privileged elite. Instead, it asserts (without being about to prove this except by tautological definitions) that the contradictions of Soviet society, including the clash between rich and poor, powerful and subordinate, will never entrench themselves and that the privileged elite expresses the common interest. While the capitalist state is the product of class antagonisms which it then helps to perpetuate, the Soviet state will resolve class antagonisms by increasing production.*

---

* Against this, a growing number of analysts assert that Soviet society, like all modern industrial societies, is bound to develop into a stratified class society in which the industrial managers will sooner or later obtain control because they control the essential means of production. Developed as early as 1918 by the Polish socialist Waclaw Machajski, this theme was later picked up

Additional agents of change and progress, according to Soviet doctrine, are *criticism and self-criticism*, as well as *socialist morality*—in short, the individual's intellectual awareness of his own and his fellow citizens' shortcomings, the free discussion of these failings in communal meetings and in media of mass communication, and the moral determination to overcome them and contribute to the best of one's ability, to be loyal and patriotic and confident of ultimate success. Failures in the Soviet system, poor performance of individuals or organizations, even criminality, neurosis, and insanity, according to Soviet theory, can usually be explained by the inadequate consciousness or insufficient morality of some members of society. What else could be their cause, since the system itself is beyond criticism? Moreover, Soviet psychology assumes that all people are basically equal —not to believe this would be to succumb to myths about race and heredity. But if all human beings are equally endowed with intellectual and physical potentialities, differences in performance can be explained only by differences in will and application.

One of the cornerstones of Soviet doctrine is the concept of *socialism in a single country*. We remember that the bolsheviks seized power in the firm expectation that the Russian Revolution would lead to proletarian revolutions in the entire civilized world. We have indicated why they expected this and why without world revolution their own success made little or no sense to them. In signing the Treaty of Brest Litovsk, the Soviet regime chose coexistence with capitalism; but it did so only in the belief that the world revolution was still developing and needed only a chance to "catch its breath." After the abortive German revolutions of 1921 and 1923 it became clear to many Soviet leaders that the world revolution was going to take its time. The Com-

---

by James Burnham, *The Managerial Revolution* (New York, 1941), and repeated, with slight modifications, by Georg Achminov, *Die Macht im Hintergrund* (Ulm, 1950) and Milovan Djilas, *The New Class* (New York, 1957). The thesis is related to the pessimistic theories of both Roberto Michels and Leon Trotsky about inevitable bureaucratic perversions of socialism.

munist International in its 1924 congress decided that world
capitalism had entered a period of stabilization and that the
world as a whole was in a transitional period between the
Russian Revolution and the world revolution, a period during
which the Soviet regime would have to coexist with the capitalist countries and find a *modus vivendi* with them.* Some
members of the party pointed out that in this case the revolution would have been in vain, a senseless and costly adventure likely to discredit the Marxist movement as a whole.
The Trotsky faction countered the doctrine of the stabilization of capitalism first by denying it and then by calling for
vigorous revolutionary action on a global scale. They argued
that the stabilization of capitalism was a passing phenomenon and that excessive attention paid to it amounted to opportunism and a betrayal of the revolution. Instead of adjust-
ing to the ephemeral prosperity and stability of the capitalist
world, the party should prepare for the new revolutionary
upheavals that would inevitably accompany the equally inevitable end of stabilization. Not only that, the party ought
to do its share to undermine capitalism and thus to promote
and speed up the development of a new revolutionary situation. Here we have the global aspect of Trotsky's theory of
"permanent revolution."

Against the arguments of the Trotsky faction the Stalin-
Bukharin faction developed its theory of socialism in one
country. They conceded that the revolution could never be
completed, nor any of its achievements be safe, before the
entire world (or a large portion of it) had become communist. But even though the achievements of the revolution
would not be safe as long as they remained isolated in one
country, this was no reason for despair. Even under such
limiting conditions, socialism could be built in a single country, even a backward country like Russia. And to deny this
possibility, they said, was defeatism and menshevik pusilla-

---

* Coexistence does not necessarily mean *peaceful* coexistence;
Lenin's theories also contain the idea of an inevitable clash between the "camps" of capitalism and socialism, and he described
the entire transition period between capitalism and socialism as
an era of world wars and revolutions.

nimity. To be cowed by economic conditions or to emphasize the immaturity of any society for socialism, they argued, was shallow determinism. For a bolshevik, social and economic conditions are not insurmountable obstacles but a spur to action. There is nothing that resolute action by the party cannot overcome.

With the victory of Stalin, the doctrine of socialism in a single country became party dogma, and with it the idea that a long transition period comes between the Russian Revolution and the completion of the world revolution. Two main implications were inherent in this: the recognition of *coexistence* as an inescapable necessity for the duration of the transition period, and the admission that socialism confined to one country (and a backward one at that) would look different from what the revolutionaries of 1917 had imagined and hoped it would look. These two implications are closely related to each other, the former being responsible for the latter. For it is a central point in Soviet theory to blame the exigencies of coexistence (termed "capitalist encirclement") for any disappointing features of Soviet socialism. In particular, capitalist encirclement is cited as the main reason why the state has not yet withered away, as a Marxist ought to have expected once he was told that exploitation and the class struggle had been abolished. Indeed, once the party had announced that socialism had been reached, there seem to have been queries by party members whether the state could now be expected to wither away. In answering with a decided "no," the party stressed capitalist encirclement, but also alleged that coexistence had its domestic equivalents too, in that some elements of Soviet society were still susceptible to insidious capitalist influence from outside. A strong state, including a mighty army and a police force, was thus required to keep capitalism at bay, and the stronger it was made, the more quickly and surely would it wither away.* While Soviet theory thus makes coexistence respon-

---

* Herbert Marcuse in *Soviet Marxism* (New York, 1958), pp. 51–55, rightly points out that this is a theory of containment: according to Soviet theory imperialism seeks to destroy the world revolution. He has shown that, despite modifications and reserva-

sible for repressive features of Soviet society, Marxists who are antagonistic to the USSR have argued that the repressive nature of Soviet society is responsible for coexistence. The revolution occurred first in a backward country not mature for socialism. Whether this is to be blamed on bolshevik adventurism or whether it was unavoidable is controversial. In any event, in a backward country only a sad caricature of socialism could be developed. This, it is argued, has so discredited revolutionary Marxism as a whole that it has perverted the normal course of history and enabled capitalism to entrench itself in the Western world, where true socialism might otherwise have been created after a proletarian revolution.

Soviet theory does not acknowledge the need to be apologetic about anything. True, the state has not yet withered away. But it is, after all, a most acceptable state, a constitutional democracy of a superior type, in which democracy is not just a phrase but a reality. Government by soviets, it is claimed, is the most ideal form of representative democracy because it gives the common man a better chance for direct control of, or participation in, the process of government than any other institution. Being a sensitive barometer of public opinion, Soviet government institutions allegedly do not require checks and balances or a division of powers. Soviet government is good government; and good government ought not to be curbed by such devices.

The Soviet constitution, it is claimed further, fulfills liberal ideals by being a federal constitution. The Union of Soviet Socialist Republics is a voluntary federation of free nations, each one of which is at liberty to determine its own national destiny, even to the point of seceding from the USSR. That in fact this destiny consists in merging with the other nations making up the Soviet Union is taken for granted by Soviet theory; and anyone actually advocating secession from the

---

tions in their theory, the actual strategy of world communism has always presupposed that the revolution in the West had little chance, and that communist action should always be on the defensive.

Union would at once be recognized as an enemy of proletarian internationalism, and dealt with accordingly. The liberties granted by the most democratic of all constitutions are meaningful only as long as they are not abused by the class enemy.

In addition to providing self-determination for all nations of Soviet society, the constitution of 1936, more amply than any other constitution, provides the individual citizens with basic rights. It grants not only the customary freedoms of speech, assembly, the press, and religious belief; it also outlaws discrimination based on sex, race, religion, or national origin. And, finally, it grants all citizens the right to employment, to an education, and to medical and other assistance in case of need. It thus complements political rights with social and economic rights.

Soviet theoreticians point out that, unlike all previous constitutions, the Soviet constitution also provides guarantees for these rights and thus makes them meaningful. What good is the capitalist freedom of the press to the workers who do not have the money to start a newspaper or run a television station? How valid is the freedom of assembly in societies where club houses or meeting halls are for hire or purchase only to those who are able to pay? In the USSR these and other rights and liberties are guaranteed by the fact that assembly halls and media of mass communication, as well as all the means of production, have been taken away from the capitalists and are now in the hands of the party and other organizations representing the will of the people, just as Soviet democracy is made truly representative by the fact that its informal processes, such as the nominations and selection of candidates for public office, are largely in the hands of the party, the trade unions, and other organizations expressing the interests of the toilers.

According to Soviet doctrine, the USSR is not only the most democratic state in the world, it is also the chief defender of democracy in international affairs. Lacking aggressive tendencies, the Soviet Union since its inception has consistently played a progressive role in world politics. Therefore it is supported loyally not only by almost all its own citizens but also by all truly class-conscious workers in the world.

In recent years, Soviet ideology has turned its attention to the problem of the transition from socialism to communism. We have noted that this was to take the form of a gradual, nonviolent transition. In his last essay, published shortly before the Nineteenth Congress of the party, Josef Stalin spelled out some of the preconditions for this transition. Communism would come within sight once the Soviet economy was able to raise real wages for the entire population to a specified level—and by extrapolating the rate of growth from records of Soviet productivity, economists could estimate that communism was still a few decades away. Further, Stalin postulated a major transformation of the collective farms before communism could be placed on the agenda, and a number of other conditions. On the basis of Stalin's calculations, the prospect of attaining communism in the near future receded. In retrospect, Stalin's conclusion can be interpreted as manifesting a conservative attitude. Stalin obviously meant to imply that any deviaton from his own methods of government would be premature; the time was not yet ripe for any major changes. His successors have, however, become more optimistic. Nikita Khrushchev has announced several times that Soviet society is now entering the stage of gradual transition from socialism to communism. In particular, he has asserted that the state has already begun to wither away, and to support this assertion he refers to various measures taken by his regime to decentralize administration, place some functions of government in the hands of neighborhood groups and other grass-roots agencies, and curb the powers of the political police. Khrushchev's successors have made similar statements, although they seem eager to play down the theme of the transition of communism.

Soviet ideologists have spent considerable effort on the elaboration of this thesis. In their writings, they stress the idea that in the future, life will be more communal and less individualistic than heretofore. Ongoing pilot projects heralding throughgoing reforms in administration, education, economic management, and other endeavors show that these writings, far from being speculative, are in fact blueprints of an impending transformation of the Soviet way of life. A milestone in this process of planning for communism was the adoption of a new party platform by the Twenty-second Congress of the Communist Party, in the fall of 1961.[2]

Here and there, in passing, we have noted differences between the Soviet theory of state and the spirit of Marxist thought. We have even ventured to state that Soviet theory is in decided opposition to the humanist ethics and the radical criticism inherent in Marxism. Soviet theoreticians would not, of course, agree with this. They would, rather, assert that the history of the Russian Revolution, the development of Soviet society, and the doctrines of Soviet ideology are all in full correspondence with Marxist ideas. To make Marxism fit Soviet history and ideology, it has been transformed, in the USSR, into a dogmatic philosophy bearing some striking similarities both to Thomist philosophy and to the scientific clichés of the Victorian age. Its more abstract branch, corresponding to what Western philosophers would call ontology, epistemology, logic, and the philosophy of science or nature, is called "dialectical materialism." The parts dealing with anthropology and psychology, ethics, aesthetics, and the philosophy of history are called "historical materialism." In both branches, a catechism of philosophical laws has been abstracted from the writings of Marx, Engels, Lenin, and Stalin, laws which are said to describe the nature of all phenomena, social as well as nonsocial, in the universe. This philosophy affirms the objective reality of all phenomena and characterizes this reality as capable of being known by man. It defines the substance of all reality as matter and ascribes to all material phenomena certain dynamic qualities, such as contradictoriness and motion, or change. Dialectical materialism further spells out the patterns of interrelationships between material phenomena, such as the multiple chain of causality relating all phenomena to each other, but especially the laws of motion of matter, or, as we might say, the morphology of change. As for historical materialism, it is a catechism of the most general assumptions and methods used by Marx, Engels, Lenin, and Stalin in describing and analyzing social phenomena.

Marx, and even more Engels, manifested positivistic tendencies amounting to a rejection of philosophy. Soviet philosophy opposes this positivistic attitude. It does not follow Engels in identifying philosophy with the method of natural and social science, nor restrict it to logic and the history of ideas. Instead, it recognizes philosophy as a branch of learning distinct from natural and social science, even though the boundaries between philosophy and science have never been defined satisfactorily. The result of this dualism is that scientific pursuits are, as it were, made subservient to, or brought into line with, philosophical dogma, in a fashion comparable to the manner in which the Church subordinates the rational pursuit of knowledge to the acceptance of revealed truth. In both cases, scientific findings are recognized as valid only as long as they do not conflict with the established dogma. In both cases, also, it is taken for granted that the independent, rational search for scientific truth cannot possibly come into conflict with the dogma.

Soviet theory expresses this relationship in somewhat oblique fashion by asserting that all science is, and must be, partisan, or in line with the spirit of the party. This conformance to the party's policies and beliefs is called *partii-nost'*. Its imposition on everyone engaged in intellectual pursuits is justified by the party in the following manner. All knowledge, they argue, is the reflection or expression of some class interest. In all fields of knowledge, therefore, there are feudal, bourgeois, petty-bourgeois, and proletarian schools. There cannot be any neutrality. Even those who believe they are neutral or who think that their fields of endeavor are far removed from politics will in fact ("objectively") reflect the point of view of one or another class. Now, Marx has shown, according to Soviet arguments, that the class consciousness of the proletariat is true consciousness, whereas the consciousness of all other classes is false, ideological. Only in the consciousness of the proletariat does class interest lead to the emergence of truth unvarnished and undistorted. It follows from this that in every field of knowledge the search for truth will be successful only as long as the scholar wholeheartedly adopts the point of view of the working class. And since this point of view is expressed best by the Communist Party, no scientific truth can stand which conflicts in any way with the party's views, the party line. Science, social as well as natural, including the purest research in physics, biology, or mathematics, must be pervaded with the spirit of *partiinost'*. In effect, this means that in any realm of knowledge where the party has expressed a definite opinion, it has been, until very recently, virtually impossible to engage in discussion with Soviet scholars, because, imbued with *partiinost'*, they could not deviate from the accepted line or even the accepted terminology and were obliged to label any disagreement with their views or their vocabulary as the ideology of the class enemy. Thus scientific truth could not (and perhaps still today cannot) be pursued freely, and truths conflicting with the party line are declared falsehoods. As a result, more than one branch of Soviet science has suffered lasting damage. But what we have said applies with particular force in the social sciences, where the party line has been refined and defined with so much precision that it seems to consist of inflexible magic formulas—a catechism or a litany which, according to Marcuse, does in fact function as magic; or, to say the least, social science is used for the purposes of public relations, and the principles of advertising are in eternal conflict with the search for truth. Where the inflexible formulas developed in social science are changed ever so slightly, we must always suspect changes in party policy or party views. Soviet ideology thus serves as an esoteric code of communications easily read by the initiated but decipherable also by the informed outsider.[3]

The transformation of theory into catechism is not, however, restricted to the social sciences but applies also in the more "remote" areas of knowledge and ideology. The reason for this is simple. If we are right in asserting that Soviet social theory serves mainly to obscure and veil the clash between the idea and the reality of socialism, if its dogmas are to pervert the ideals of liberty, equality, and brotherhood by affirming that socialism has been attained, then the ideals thus perverted or betrayed will tend to retreat into the "inner emigration" of seemingly remote and neutral areas—art, philosophy, and science. But here too they are dangerous to the regime, and the party has tried very hard to ferret them out. There is therefore no safe place for an inner emigration in the Soviet Union, at least not in the intellectual realm.

Lest this picture be considered one-sided and overdrawn, we should, perhaps, add two qualifications. First, despite the tendencies just described, there have been some branches of social science in which respectable scholarly work has always been done. Even when speaking of the Stalin period, therefore, we should not underestimate the ability of Soviet social scientists to engage in significant research. But a second point which concerns the erosion of dogma, or at least of dogmatic rigidity, in Soviet intellectual life is more important. We have already mentioned this loosening up, but we should add now that in recent months, the pace of this process seems to have speeded up considerably. If a few years ago we could say that the higher ranks of the party were allowed freedom of discussion (though not yet freedom of speech), it now appears that it is practiced far more widely and far more openly than Western scholars would have believed possible, even in recent years. In line with this, Soviet social science, too, may emerge from its subsidiary role as a mere exercise in public relations.

8

Stalinist Society and
Its Transformation

• Inevitably, my way of describing Soviet society would be different from that offered in the preceding chapter. It would doubtless be less sympathetic, even though it would represent an honest attempt to understand the reasons why it has developed into what it is. In presenting this attempt at describing Soviet society since the mid-1930's, I must apologize for the temerity of trying to condense such a complex and controversial theme into one brief chapter. This can be done only by omitting all detail and by overgeneralizing; hence the result can be no more than an interpretive essay in which every sentence is subject to challenge. *

I would begin my description of Stalinist society by classifying the Soviet Union as a relatively underdeveloped country engaged in a crash program to exploit its resources and outstrip the Western world in productivity and economic potential. It comprises a population of many languages, races,

---

* Since first writing this book, I have expanded the present chapter into an entire book, *The Soviet Political System* (New York, 1965). For another interesting attempt to describe Soviet society, see Zbigniew K. Brzezinski and Samuel P. Huntington, *Political Power, USA/USSR* (New York, 1964).

For a discussion of communist societies other than the Soviet Union, see Chapters 10 and 11.

religions, and cultures, which, one generation ago, consisted primarily of rural people, peasants or nomads, on a level of technology, literacy, and productivity below that of urban and industrial Europe and North America. These were people without a strong tradition of self-government, yet they were rebellious against their ruling elites. About thirty years ago the Communist Party ruling over these people decided to make an all-out effort to industrialize their country as rapidly as possible. Whether this was a decision which sooner or later had to be taken, regardless of who was in power or what motives guided him, is a highly controversial question and must be left unanswered here. In any event, the decision was taken.

To carry it out, the Soviet social system had to undergo a number of adjustments, and the party had to take certain broad measures. Industrialization of an undeveloped economy requires, first of all, the marshaling of all material and human resources, hence an austerity regime in which every available scrap of energy is expended for the construction effort and every ounce of material resource that can be diverted from consumption is invested. Rapid industrialization, in other words, calls for continued low living standards and forbids consumer sovereignty. This applies all the more to a revolutionary regime surrounded by hostile neighbors, who cannot be expected to help the industrialization effort by large-scale material and technical assistance or long-term credits. The Soviet Union was forced to pull itself out of the morass of backwardness by its own bootstraps. From all this it becomes clear that, secondly, industrialization under such circumstances can be accomplished only through central organization and strict discipline, including a managed system of rewards and sanctions. While centralized planning and organized inequality are not necessarily incompatible with political liberty and representative democracy, it is nonetheless obvious that the planners and managers themselves are likely to look at constitutional democracy as a luxury which a backward country in the process of rapid industrialization cannot afford. And, if we look at the ruthlessness of the Soviet regime and at the starkness of the material austerity it imposed on its population, we have to conclude that such measures could have been carried out only by a powerful dictatorship ruling against the will of the people.

Forced saving and political dictatorship alone, however, are not sufficient. One more measure is required to achieve industrialization in a backward country; that is the training of the population for life in the machine age. Americans ought to be familiar with the adjustments this transformation in the way of life requires, with the difficulty of shedding traditions, beliefs, and behavior patterns that have become dysfunctional in the machine age. We all know the helplessness of the country hick stranded in the big city, the small-town folks' stubborn resistance against, and resentment of, the ways of the metropolis. We know the pains of adjustment in the style of life that are being suffered as America transforms herself from a country of farmers and petty merchants into a modern industrial and corporate giant. These pains of acculturation are intensified many times when a country like Russia engages in a crash program of industrialization. They are intensified because Soviet Russia has attempted to do in one generation what America has been doing for the last 150 years, and because the cultural level from which most of Russia started was even more remote from the way of life of the atomic age than was the society of Jefferson or Jackson. Lenin, for one, was aware of the magnitude and rapidity of the transformation he wished to bring about and fittingly called it a cultural revolution. In my opinion, this cultural revolution is the most difficult of all the tasks which the Russian Communist Party has set itself.

Power Structure

In describing the social relationships that have grown out of these problems, let us begin by a summary of the power structure in Soviet society. In his book on the process of politics in the United States, David Truman distinguishes between two major types of government existing in the modern world, constitutional government and corporate government. In describing the latter, he is concerned primarily with the manner in which such associations as business corporations and organized interest groups manage their affairs. But I believe we can easily apply his model to the Soviet Union as a whole. Some of its key features include the differentiation between the functions of the owner and the manager; the hierarchic command system of decision making, which must be contrasted to responsible and representative government; the bureaucratic (rather than democratic) division of powers; and the servile and subject status of the lower ranks, for whom final recourse against the commands of the organization lies only outside that organization. One of the principal differences between a Western corporation and the USSR therefore lies in the fact that the aggrieved employee of a Western corporation can quit the organization more readily than a Soviet citizen, who in most cases has no possibility whatsoever of escaping from his society; and, short of quitting, the employee can appeal to authorities outside his corporation. Despite this and other major differences, I think it is useful to compare the USSR to a giant corporate enterprise, in order to understand some of its structural features.

It is difficult to define the owners of USSR, Incorporated, just as it is difficult to define precisely who owns General Motors. Certainly some own it more than others; or we might say that the quality of ownership varies with the quantity. Ownership of a few shares entitles one to a small share of the profits, while ownership of a substantial portfolio carries with it the right to sit on the Board of Directors, which hires and fires the managers and sets policies for the corporation. If we are right in saying that, for practical purposes, the Communist Party might be said to own the Soviet Union, we have to understand that the ownership functions of the rank-and-file party member are no more meaningful than those of Aunt Lucy, who owns a share of AT&T. Let me add at once that the Communist Party does not have legal title to the USSR and does not claim it. Ownership, however, may be defined not only in legal but also in sociological terms. In the latter case, ownership is established as soon as individuals or groups behave *as if they owned* an enterprise. And the Communist Party of the Soviet Union, especially its "Board of Directors," certainly does so behave. It treats the country as if it were its property. To use a traditional term of political science, the party acts as the *sovereign* in the Soviet Union—and, historically as well as philosophically, the concepts of sovereignty and property are virtually synonymous. To be sure, just as in the Western corporation ownership and management functions are tending more and more to be united in the same persons, so in the enterprise USSR, Incorporated, party members and managers (such as government officials) are often the same persons. And yet, a significant number of party members function solely as party administrators. They are the inner core of the party, the *aktiv*, as it is called in the Soviet Union, whose most successful members form the majority of such policy-making directorates as the Central Committee, the Secretariat, and the Politburo. If we speak of the party as the sovereign owner of the USSR, then, it seems, we must mean particularly the party *aktiv*, a ruling elite about whose size, composition, and informal structure we have only the sketchiest information. It, too, is meant by the Soviet citizen when he talks about "the party."

The party itself is much larger than its active core, for it includes the millions of members who are active professionally in other pursuits, and whose party membership is therefore in the nature of additional duty. The size and character of this membership has fluctuated. Today it comprises roughly ten million, or 4 per cent of the population (or roughly 8 per cent of the population of voting age). It is today a *cadre party*, which means that its members are selected from those citizens who occupy positions of respect, responsibility, and authority in all the many professions or pursuits to which Soviet citizens may be devoted. One might be tempted to say that the party recruits those members of Soviet society who in our society would become members of country clubs, although the criterion for selection is not wealth but managerial or technical responsibility. Like membership in a country club, party membership is at times an indispensable help in furthering an individual's career or even a precondition for various sensitive or responsible assignments. Unlike country-club membership, however, it does not promote the pursuit of golf, swimming, dancing, or other diversions. Instead, it tends to become an arduous and onerous additional duty. Party members are expected to be active in the various party activities; they are supposed to educate themselves further in the history and ideology of the party; and, finally, they are assumed to lead exemplary lives as model citizens.[1]

As the sovereign owner of Soviet society, the party (in its highest organizations) not only makes the basic decisions of public policy; on all its levels of organization it also sees to it that these decisions are carried out. It concerns itself, furthermore, with the selection and assignment of the top managers in all fields of endeavor and, finally, strives to propagate its views among the population. We might compare the individual party member to the information and education officer in our armed forces, who is supposed to inform the men about current world affairs to tell them "what they are fighting for" or "whom they are fighting against." In addition, the party acts as the cheerleader of Soviet society, who through rallies, demonstrations, and publicity of various kinds seeks to build enthusiasm and morale. In everything that is done in Soviet society, the party claims to represent the people, to act in their name and in their behalf and for their benefit. Such claims cannot, of course, be proven and will be self-evident only to those who are already convinced. Among the population of the Soviet Union, there doubtless are people so convinced, and also people who are not. The evidence suggests that various members of Soviet society admire the party, or tolerate it as a necessary evil, or hate it with all their heart. The gulf between the party and the people seems to be deepest in rural areas and among the national minorities. In the countryside, the Communist Party at times appears like an army of occupation or a militant church *in partibus infidelium*, while in Central Asia, Buriat-Mongolia, and other minority areas it assumes some of the aspects of a colonial administration (although there are significant differences between the "colonialism" of the Soviet Union and that of Western nations).

The organization of the party is well adapted to its various tasks. Apart from the strong predominance of centralistic tendencies and the absence of any meaningful democratic procedures, the most notable feature is the mixture of territorial with functional principles of organization. On the higher levels, the party is subdivided into regional, provincial, local, and similar territorial organizations, all of which, together with the all-Union headquarters in Moscow, have usually had staff organizations dealing with the functional divisions of Soviet life and activities—the economy, the armed forces, education, art, youth activities, national minorities, and the like. At the grass-roots level, however, the territorial principle is abandoned for the functional one: with few exceptions, the party primary organizations (which have evolved from the conspiratorial cells of prerevolutionary days) are formed within economic or administrative organizations, such as workshops, farms, scientific institutes, army units, or government offices. The party unit thus formed takes charge, as it were, of the organization, regards it as "its own," and functions as a representative of the sovereign. The party primary organization is composed only of members of the parent body—a committee of it, in a sense; and it does act as some sort of steering committee. But, even though formed only of men and women who work in the organization, it is in reality the *direct* representative of the entire party.

I deliberately stress the word *direct*. For, after all, the ministry, or the regional planning and executive organization (*Sovnarkhoz*), and also the bank, the public attorney, and other supervisory or command organizations including the political police—all represent the party, however indirectly. All nonparty organizations in the USSR are, in effect, departments or divisions of the over-all enterprise, USSR, Incorporated.

Any Soviet organization, economic, administrative, cultural, military, or what not, is subjected to the party through numerous command or supervisory channels at one and the same time; and Soviet society can therefore be seen as an administrative maze of parallel hierarchies. We may speak of the trinity of party, government, and police as the main pillars of this structure; or, looking at the economic enterprise, we may see that trinity dissolve into a multiplicity of legal, financial, economic, political, and police hierarchies, which may be working in harmony or may be vying with each other for control or jurisdiction. Whether separately or jointly, however, they all impose their particular tasks on the managers and lower personnel of the given unit.

Chief among the party's agencies in managing the country is the government, which includes not only most of the legislative, administrative, judicial, military, and penal institutions that are part of all modern governments, but also the entire economy, all educational and scientific pursuits, health services, and even entertainment and cultural endeavors. Certain processes of this government can be studied more easily than others and are therefore better known. Not known at all among Western students of the Soviet way of life is the legislative process. The constitution notwithstanding, policy decisions taking the form of laws, regulations, or decrees are discussed, formulated, and adopted behind closed doors, and we have only the scantiest information even concerning who discusses them, what the procedures are, and so forth. It is clear, however, that the major task which the enterprise USSR, Incorporated, has set itself is the task of production, or better, of rapid economic growth. In Soviet rhetoric, the task is defined as one of catching up with, and outstripping, the USA in production and productivity.[2]

The major political decisions for the managers of the enterprise during any one period are therefore the production plan and its supplementary decisions. Supplementary directives include financial plans, raw materials, utilization plans, labor plans, and others. The shaping of all these and the major production plans is a complex and continual operation based on information regarding available resources and skills, on experience regarding past performance, and on the political decision regarding priorities in production. The execution of the plan is the responsibility of the Council of Ministers, which used to include production ministries, just as a corporation includes production divisions, but which has recently delegated a great amount of work in administering and even shaping production plans to regional planning organizations. Through various channels, the commands of the Council of Ministers are conveyed to the principal economic units, the factories or enterprises, and, in modified fashion, the state farms and collective farms.

In accordance with the principle of individual managerial responsibility, the Soviet enterprise is given a certain degree of autonomy, even to the point of making it a juridical person. It is set up to resemble a business firm, with its own capital and cash resources. It deals with other enterprises of the Soviet economy through the means of contracts; and where there are contracts, there is a system of laws governing contractual relationships, and a court system to enforce them. Unlike a Western firm, however, the Soviet enterprise in its various activities of buying, selling, hiring, pricing, and production planning is subjected to the plan and to the controls of its numerous superior agencies. And yet, restricted as his discretion is, the director of a Soviet firm is responsible not only for adherence to the various plans, laws, and directives specifying permissible ranges of the use of materials, labor, credit, and the like; his firm is also supposed to operate at a profit; and, most of all, it is to meet or outstrip the production goals handed down from the planning authorities. Under such multiple pressures, with high rewards offered for outstanding performance and severe sanctions imposed for a poor showing, the Soviet production manager has become part of a rat race very similar to that in which his American colleague is engaged. Similar conditions, moreover, are imposed on responsible personnel in noneconomic fields—physicians, artists, teachers, scholars, administrators, and even members of the working class itself. The rat race is as all-pervasive in Soviet society as it is in America.

In the Soviet Union, it is caused by a coincidence of various factors. For one thing, the party asks all citizens, high and low, to work their very hardest and give their very best. The rule of this performance principle, as Marcuse calls it, is enforced not only by pitting fellow citizens and rival organizations against each other in managed competition but also by manipulating rewards in such a fashion that only peak performance is rewarded adequately. Secondly, the rat race is a function of the multiplicity of authorities imposing often conflicting standards of behavior on the administrator. Whatever a Soviet manager does, he is often forced to violate some standards in order to satisfy others, because taken together all the commands he has been given are impossible to carry out. While at first glance the result of this is inefficiency and chaos, it may nonetheless be a very satisfactory and efficient method of management for the party. Through its many agencies, it enforces its standards selectively and therefore wields a complex administrative machinery that is very sensitive to subtle changes in policy. Such changes need not be announced formally but can be signaled by a slight shift in the selective enforcement of multiple standards. The party enjoys not only the possibility of manipulating the society but also the privilege of not having to contradict itself, while the lower managerial personnel take all the risk. They are struck with sanctions when shifts occur.[3]

Finally, the rat race in the Soviet Union is aggravated by the personal insecurity of the superiors, who are compelled to engage in struggles for jurisdiction, control, and authority. The subordinate administrator therefore must not only follow all directives given him but also beware of excessively close connections with a superior official who is going to be a loser. Much is written in the Western world about the ramifications of this kind of power struggle in the Soviet elite. But we know next to nothing concrete about it. All we can say with some degree of certainty is that the development of Soviet Russia into a modern industrial society has brought with it tendencies of unmeasurable strength toward the differentiation of special groups within the power elite, tendencies similar to those characterizing Western societies. Such groups, to which we can attribute different and conflicting interests, are based on loyalty to leaders, commitment to diverging policies, fields of professional specialization, or identification with particular regions or localities. In the concrete, these various interests doubtless overlap and conflict with each other, any one individual being a member of many identifiable groups. Without doubt, also, the resulting tendencies toward the development of some sort of pluralism are held in check by the strong bonds of joint interests which all members of the Soviet power elite have in common when they face the outside world and their own population. Moreover, we shall see below that some of the tendencies toward pluralism may have been checked, at least for the time being, by the Communist Party's resuming that sovereign position in Soviet society which it might be said to have lost between 1938 and 1953.*

---

* The detection of rival interest groups among the Soviet power elite and the analysis of jurisdictional struggles between them or between the Kremlin's leading personalities is a favorite pastime of Western scholars, journalists, and intelligence personnel. The methods employed by these "kremlinologists" are subject to very serious challenge. Painstaking and patient record keeping of the known facts concerning the careers of high bureaucrats, as exemplified by the works of John A. Armstrong, Boris Meissner, and T. H. Rigby, to name only some scholars in this field, will yield some rewards when used with great caution (see Boris Meissner and John Reshetar, eds., *The Communist Party of the Soviet Union,* New York, 1956; John A. Armstrong, *The Soviet Bureaucratic Elite,* New York, 1959; and T. H. Rigby, "Crypto-Politics," in *Survey,* No. 50, January 1964). Equally diligent probing into the esoteric code of communication used by the communist world can be crowned with considerable success, as proven by Myron Rush, *The Rise of Khrushchev* (Washington, 1958). Most statements made in the West about politics within communist countries are based, however, on irresponsible speculation about group loyalties and faction formation within the communist hierarchy. Some kremlinologists have such a thorough acquaintance with all the available information and gossip about the communist world that even their speculations should be listened to with respect, even if they seem to be unsupported by concrete evidence. Such a writer is the late Boris I. Nicolaevsky, whose shrewd guesses have recently been collected in his *Power and the Soviet Elite* (New York, 1965). For other examples of kremlinology on a relatively high level, see Robert Conquest,

Types of Social Control

Most Western political scientists would without hesitation
describe the USSR as a totalitarian society. What the word
totalitarianism means precisely is not at all clear. It came
into vogue in the Western world after World War II, when
the unspeakable inhumanities of the Nazi regime became a
matter of public record. The term carries with it the notion
of a regime's utter disregard of the dignity, feelings, and interests of its citizens. It reeks of the arbitrary and bloody
police state, evokes nocturnal arrests and the concentration
camp. Since then, some not very successful attempts have
been made to refine the concept and to portray totalitarianism as a unique phenomenon of our century. One of these
attempts consists of the enumeration of certain essential
features which together make up the totalitarian syndrome.
When I use the term, I am thinking primarily of a society
which attempts to control its citizens totally, a regime in
which not the slightest degree of autonomy is conceded to
individuals or groups, whatever their endeavor may be, a
government which regards every human activity or pursuit
as a matter of public policy. In this sense, the Soviet Union
comes closer to the totalitarian model than any other modern
society, although, with due allowance for technological differences, it can be argued that many societies of the past
were governed according to similar totalitarian principles
and manifested most if not all the essential traits of the
totalitarian syndrome.

The term "totalitarianism" came into use in the English-
speaking world only after World War II. Previously it had
been used with pride by the German national socialists to
describe the organizational principle of their party and state.
After the defeat of Germany, the limitless brutality of the Hit-

---

Power and Politics in the USSR (London, 1961); Roger Pethy-
bridge, *A Key to Soviet Politics* (New York, 1962); Myron Rush,
Political Succession in the USSR (New York, 1965); and Wolfgang Leonhard, *The Kremlin Since Stalin* translated by Elizabeth
Wiskemann (New York, 1962).

ler regime, which then became common knowledge, begged to be described by a new term, and totalitarianism came to be used for the purpose of describing what was thought of as a completely new form of government and social organization. With the shift of attention from German fascism to Russian communism, the term came in handy as an ideological tool of the cold war. In due time, scholars made serious attempts to define totalitarianism. One of the most useful definitions has been offered by Carl J. Friedrich and Zbigniew K. Brzezinski, in their *Totalitarian Dictatorship and Autocracy* (second edition revised by Friedrich, New York, 1966).

No author using the term claims that any existing political system conforms in every detail to such "models" of this new form of government. Also, any claim that communist states inevitably are totalitarian must deal with the fact that these political systems do not always conform to the model even in some apparently crucial features; or if they incorporated these features in the past, they no longer do so. If one does not wish to dispense with the concept of totalitarianism altogether, one could argue that totalitarianism is likely to be no more than one specific phase of communist systems, or that there are different types of totalitarianism. For instance, one could differentiate one type of totalitarianism which is typical of communist societies in the crash program phase of industrialization—the Stalinist phase—which is characterized by police terror, superhuman work assignments, minimal rewards for most of the population, the ruthless eradication of preexisting groups and traditions, and the use of human beings as an expendable resource. In passing, one must then point out that many or most of these features were characteristic also of the early decades of industrialism in the allegedly democratic Western countries. Another type of totalitarianism could then be associated with fully industrialized modern societies. It is marked by the bureaucratization of all endeavors, by the powerlessness of the individual, by the rule of irresponsible elites wielding modern means of mass communication, creeping conformism, anti-intellectualism, and similar features which have been present, more or less strongly, in the contemporary Western world, in both fascist and constitutional regimes, and that also characterize much of public life in the communist world.

My own preference has been for the former solution, according to which totalitarianism, if indeed it can be described in such a manner that social scientists agree on the definition, probably is the political framework of the crash program phase of communist development. If this is acceptable, how then should one characterize the Soviet and other communist systems after the threshold of industrialization has been crossed, the system settles down into a comparatively stable mold, and the methods and instruments of totalitarian rule are, by and large, dismantled?

My answer would be that in the crash program phase, and even more so afterwards, communist societies in their structure and functioning closely resemble those large, complex administrative organizations which we call bureaucracies. Public life in the Soviet Union, in Eastern Europe, and also in the People's Republic of China generally goes on within a framework of formal institutions, informal groupings, and processes that strikingly resemble those of large bureaucracies in other parts of the world. Hence communist societies share with modern bureaucracies the managerial problems and irrationalities, and the various modes of individual adjustment to these problems tend to be similar and the personality types arising in them are apt to be alike. In short, communist societies can be defined as modern bureaucracies writ large —i.e., societies in which the managerial forms and patterns characterizing business corporations, public institutions, army posts and battle ships, large governmental agencies, and the like are extended to the management of the entire society. *

---

* For an elaboration of this thesis, see Alfred G. Meyer, *The Soviet Political System* (New York, 1965). The thesis is echoed by Franz Schurmann in his *Ideology and Organization in Communist China* (Berkeley, Calif., 1966); also in Zbigniew K. Brzezinski, "The Soviet Political System: Transformation or Degeneration," in *Problems of Communism*, vol. XV (January–February 1966), pp. 1–15 and John A. Armstrong, "Sources of Administrative Behavior: Some Soviet and Western European Comparisons," in *American Political Science Review*, vol. LIX, No. 3 (September 1965), pp. 643–655. See also my introductory chapter to

The totalitarian and the bureaucratic models of Stalinist and post-Stalinist society may well be complementary rather than mutually exclusive. Again, I, for one, would argue that the totalitarian model applies primarily to the Stalinist phase and that the bureaucratic model may well apply to both phases, in which case totalitarianism would be a *variant* of the bureaucratic political system. Whatever model we may prefer, however, to describe the Soviet Union since the mid-1930's, most scholars would agree that there is little if anything in the lives and activities of Soviet citizens which the party does not regard as a matter of public policy and seek to manage or control—political activities; economic and professional performance; education and employment; both the production and enjoyment of entertainment, art, and all leisure activities; family life; ideas and beliefs, and even emotions, or at least their outward manifestations. In the eyes of many students, therefore, the Soviet system of government is characterized primarily by the universal urge to *control*, which they tend to derive from an insatiable urge to dominate; and this urge, in turn, is explained in many different ways. In their writings, the attempt to establish total control at times becomes the very essence of the Soviet way of life, subsuming all other motives and relationships; and communist theory, too, is reduced to an organizational scheme designed to establish universal controls.[4]

Such a one-sided theory must be supplemented by additional explanations. A partial explanation lies in the fact that the economic goals of Soviet society (as defined by its power elite, to be sure) require a good deal of centralized planning and control. The relationship between economic goals and political systems, once the prime interest of students in political economy, has not in recent times received the attention it deserves. But it does seem clear that economic systems can be classified according to the goals to which they give priority, such as economic growth, equitable distribution (welfare

Harry Shaffer (ed.), *The Communist World* (New York, 1967), and my article, "The Comparative Study of Communist Political Systems," in *Slavic Review*, vol. XXVI, No. 1 (March 1967), pp. 3-12.

state), the preservation of property rights, the most rational allocation of resources, and perhaps others. If it is true that to every one of these goals a specific political structure is best suited, then undoubtedly centralization rather than decentralization, command rather than democracy, austerity rather than consumer sovereignty, seem to be designed to achieve rapid economic growth; and perhaps we might expect the attainment of this goal to open the way for a certain mellowing of the Soviet political system, a thesis expounded in recent years by Isaac Deutscher and some others.[5]

In subscribing to such a hypothesis, we need not be so naive as to suppose that the mellowing of the Soviet social system inevitably spells the emergence of constitutional democracy. Although such a development should not, perhaps, be dismissed as impossible, it seems far more likely, at this time, to assume that Soviet society will increasingly be characterized by a complex, pluralistic structure of interlocking bureaucratic hierarchies, perpetually straining under conflicting centralist and centrifugal tendencies, a unity containing ever increasing diversity. Again, in visualizing these trends of development, the model I have in mind is that of the giant Western corporation.

I should like to point out again, in this connection, that economic growth, or, more precisely, the rapid industrialization of a backward country, requires not only heavy capital investment and hence consumer austerity, which has to be forced upon people, not only centralized management, planning, and control of the economic machinery, not only hard work from every citizen, from each according to his ability; it also requires that cultural revolution which Lenin demanded as early as 1922. And it is my belief that the exigencies of this concerted effort to transform a vast nation's entire way of life are as much responsible for Soviet totalitarianism as any other factor we have named. To be sure, Lenin said that the Soviet government must attempt to "build socialism" with the human material it found available in Russia. In fact, however, once the program of industrialization was started in earnest, the party tried to create the "new Soviet man," an individual well fitted to help in the effort to build and run a modern industrial establishment, a man equipped to live according to the rhythm of the machine rather than the rhythm of nature.

The methods used by the Soviet regime to control its population for these ends can be grouped in four main categories: rewards, sanctions, education, and organization.

Rewards. Chief among the rewards is organized inequality, according to the motto, "To each according to his work." In the USSR, the entire society is, as it were, earning piece-rate wages, sharply graded, with regressive taxation accenting the differences. Soviet society has been made rank conscious, for the rewards for top performance include deference made visible by uniforms, badges, titles, and similar tokens of status.

Equally important are the material benefits granted to all citizens regardless of performance. The USSR is a welfare state, in the sense that it strives to eliminate the most grievous hardships caused by disaster, disease, and old age, and tries to raise the material level of living for all. The regime has at last begun to convince many of its citizens that the collective effort will result in material benefits for each individual, that unselfish work for little reward may therefore be no more than the rational pursuit of each individual's self-interest. Evidence of graft and high living among the power elite contradict this theory; but a majority of the population may nonetheless have accepted it. The steady improvement in the living standards, especially the improvement in social services such as education, medical help, and old-age security, have acted as powerful arguments in this direction. So also have the indications (of which most Soviet citizens are aware) that at last the USSR is showing herself capable of catching up with the West in industrial production and scientific achievement. The Soviet citizen is beginning to feel that he is a partner, albeit a lowly one, in a growing and successful enterprise. Several Western observers who have spent some time in the USSR seem prepared to say that this sentiment is particularly strong among the Soviet working class and that it leads to considerable job satisfaction. The Soviet worker genuinely seems to believe that he

is working for himself, not just for his weekly pay enve-
lope.

In addition, Soviet society is expanding, and the demand
for talented and skilled personnel in every field seems insatiable. It is therefore a society with plenty of room at the
top, not the very top perhaps, but certainly room in the top
layer of experts and managers. Professionally, the USSR is a
society wide open for young people with physical or intellectual endowment who are willing to work hard. Awareness
of this undoubtedly attaches many of the younger generation
to the regime.

Sanctions. Societies and cultures have not only different
hierarchies of values but also different conceptions of the
seriousness of deviant behavior. In modern societies, these
conceptions are expressed by criminal law. Criminal law in
the Soviet Union is designed to inflict harsh punishment on
those citizens who refuse to contribute to the social construction effort in the prescribed manner.

Conformity to party standards is enforced, furthermore,
by the extralegal terror of the political police. The aim of
organized terror in the Soviet system is not so much to punish
malperformance as to *prevent* heresy, dissent, or actions hostile to the regime. This is accomplished by keeping a continual check on all citizens' activities, associations, and
environmental influences and by punishing those individuals
or groups who on the bases of these influences can be expected to have open or latent tendencies toward disloyalty.
Jerzy Gliksman has called this function of the terror "prophylactic justice." But even though this appears to be a very apt
description of one of the tasks performed by the political
police, it neglects another, equally important one, which is
that of serving as the eyes and ears of the regime in continually gauging the moods of the population. The secret
police, in other words, functions as a public-opinion polling
institution and in this fashion also helps to maintain controls.
An incidental result of "prophylactic justice" was the use of
prison labor on a very large scale in work projects for which,
because of their difficulty or hazards or inhuman living conditions, it would have been hard to find volunteers. This

notorious labor-camp system has been important in Soviet society since the early 1930's but has declined in recent years. Whether its decline is attributable to awareness that prison labor is inefficient is a matter of speculation. It could more simply be explained as a natural result of the marked decrease in the party's reliance on terror as a means of controlling the population. The party may no longer consider such drastic methods necessary; or else its leaders may have come to the conclusion that terror is too costly and too dangerous a means of control.

In recent years, the Soviet regime has experimented with sanctions wielded by peer groups of colleagues or neighbors, who are empowered to mete out summary punishment to persons unwilling to conform to Soviet standards of work or behavior. While this practice grossly violates Western notions of due process, the party has hailed it as one of the proofs that the state has begun to wither away.

Even if there were no terror whatsoever, the fact that the Soviet state is virtually the sole employer and educator makes all citizens highly dependent on the authorities and doubtless acts as an effective sanction against deviant behavior. The effectiveness of this hold of the monopolistic employer on the citizens may increase as the Soviet economy manages to replace human labor with automatic machines. Some observers of the Soviet scene already see the specter of technological unemployment looming over the horizon. So far, this seems to be mostly speculation.

Education. Little needs to be said about education in the USSR. Entirely in the hands of the government, it is both a means of inculcating Soviet values and the party outlook in the younger generation and a method of structuring the labor supply and of screening personnel in all branches of activity. To the individual Soviet citizen, the educational system is a valuable social service provided without charge, which gives him an opportunity to move upward in the social scale, if he is not screened out by the very stiff selection process. What proportion of young citizens are aware that a strong bias distorts the information they receive; how many of them feel that *partiinost'* comes into conflict with science; or how many of them resent the tutelage exercised over their minds by the party—these are questions we cannot answer on the basis of available information.

Education is not confined to schools and universities. In the Soviet Union, as everywhere else, the media of mass communications—the press, radio, television—also function as educational institutions. Moreover, in the USSR, the entertainment media, too, have been made vehicles of the party's educational effort, and so have all other forms of communication, even literature and art, which are promoted and tolerated only as long as they carry the party's message to the masses. Whatever he may hear, see, or read, the Soviet citizen is thus likely to receive messages sent to him by the party with the aim of making a more loyal and cooperative, a more "conscious," citizen of him. In short, all communications media in Soviet society serve the purpose of frantic and relentless indoctrination designed to make all citizens accept fully and genuinely the values and goals of the political leadership. We have already indicated that, on the whole, the party has been quite successful in thus socializing its citizens.

Organization. Whatever the success of this unending and inescapable educational effort, it could be achieved only because all media of communication, from schools to billboards, from the press to opera houses, are directly or indirectly in the hands of the party. The party ensures the success of its many efforts at indoctrination, control, and management by wielding control over all the organizations within which the individuals carry on their various activities.

In modern industrial societies everywhere fewer and fewer functions are carried out by the isolated individual. Instead, the functions of society are performed by organizations and associations, both formal and informal. The founder of Russian communism, Lenin, was one of the first men to realize the political implications of this fact. He seems to have realized that an elite dominating the many organizations within which men play their social roles could dominate the members. Organizations, said Lenin, are transmission belts transferring to all members the impetus given by the power behind the organization. Organization is the tool by which men can be manipulated.*

Accordingly, the party in the USSR has attempted to get hold of all organizations and associations, formal and informal, constituting the society. It has done this with so much success that the entire network of organizations and associations in the Soviet Union is a huge and complex system of what we might call party front organizations. The process by which this organizational mastery of society was achieved is akin to the *Gleichschaltung* of German society undertaken by the national socialists after coming to power. It is essentially a dual operation. The first step is the destruction of all existing organizations and associations which are not agencies of the party, from rival parties through professional associations to youth organizations and stamp collectors' clubs. In the Soviet Union, much of this was accomplished in the period of war communism; but the process was not completed until about fifteen years after the revolution. Once it has been accomplished, a new network of organizations can be created by the party, in which all key positions are filled by party members subject to party directives and discipline. The result of this reorganization (which began long before the destruction of the old social structure was completed) will be that many seemingly spontaneous activities are in fact carried out under the planning, supervision, and control of the party. This, far more than nighttime arrests and labor camps, is the essence of Soviet totalitarianism.

Strains and Tensions

I have called the Soviet system a successful and growing enterprise, and I am sure that most observers would agree with me in this judgment. Our awareness of the successes which Soviet communism has had in maintaining and strengthening its economic system and social fabric must not, however, cause us to neglect the strains in Soviet society, of which we can list only the most important here.

---

* See Chapter 4.

A very substantial amount of strain inherent in Soviet society is the result of (mostly latent) hostility and resistance shown to the regime by the peasants. On a mass scale, open resistance was offered last at the time of forced collectivization, over thirty years ago. Since then, the peasantry has, most of the time, submitted to the regime. But it has done so passively and sullenly. It has, despite its submissive attitude, resisted both the party's attempt to press a maximum of agricultural produce from the *kolkhoz* system and the effort to educate and urbanize the peasant, wean him away from religious beliefs and make a conscious communist of him. The political education and the cultural revolution have not been spectacularly successful in the Soviet countryside. This should not astonish us; for, after all, the very meaning of the cultural revolution was to stamp out the peasant way of life. It is the peasant who is least adapted to the machine age and its compelling rhythm; he who is most bound by religion and tradition; and he, too, who more fervently than any other class yearns for private property.[6]

What applies to the peasant applies with even greater emphasis to many of Soviet Russia's national minorities. Not only are most of them overwhelmingly agricultural in their occupation; some of them lived on an even more primitive level of civilization than the Russian peasant, so that the attempt to educate them to communism implies an even more thorough break with their traditional way of life. In addition, the attempt to make the USSR into a homogeneous industrial society necessarily led to the imposition of the Russian language as an all-Soviet *lingua franca* and to the encroachment of Russian personnel and Russian ways on the minority areas. Finally, tendencies toward political independence or autonomy have been stamped out ruthlessly wherever they appeared, often as a direct result of the cultural revolution. All this makes some of the minority areas centers of latent discontent and gives the party administrators something of the character of colonial officials. And yet, while there is some justification for comparing Soviet rule in Asia with colonialism, it must be pointed out that this colonial character of Soviet administration is bound to be a passing phenomenon, for the USSR is doing its utmost to industrialize the minority areas and integrate and absorb the minority peoples as quickly as possible.

The latent hostility against the regime is even greater in those areas which, like the former Baltic republics, are populated by minorities proud of their Western culture, who used to regard Russians as uncultured barbarians but must now learn to live as minorities within Communist Russia.

If the passive resistance shown by peasants, religious believers, and national minorities is a hangover from the pre-Soviet past, other loci of actual or potential discontent are the products of communist rule and industrial development. Foremost, and most general, among these is the silent resistance of large parts of the population against the sometimes impossible demands made on all individuals by the regime. This resistance takes many forms—apathy, alcoholism, and other forms of flight into deviant behavior, such as imitating Western styles of appearance or entertainment, and escape into illness, imagined, simulated, and even self-inflicted—but only rarely takes the more organized form of the strike, although occasionally one does hear about strikes in the Soviet Union. In the case of the responsible administrator, impossible or conflicting demands are countered by numerous evasive devices that seem to make a mockery of central planning and orderly, lawful procedure. Among virtually all citizens, it takes the form of a latent, but nonetheless persistent, dissatisfaction with the material austerity imposed on them by the regime, or, to put it differently, of consumer pressure for more adequate housing, clothing, food supplies, social services, and a general rise in the standard of living. Even though this consumer pressure does not take organized forms, the Soviet regime apparently shows a modicum of sensitivity to it.

Secondly, tension is created by the apparently growing resistance of professional experts in many fields against the eternal supervision and control by the party and the police. Soviet society, in other words, is not free of that conflict between professional and political considerations which plagues decision makers in other societies also. But in the Soviet Union this conflict is rarely allowed to come into the open; indeed, its very existence is denied because no possibility of conflict between professional and political considerations is acknowledged. Still, we receive increasing indications that economists, scientists, engineers, artists, lawyers, or professional soldiers make attempts to pit their own views against those of the party or simply to assert their professional autonomy. However feeble, this pressure amounts to a yearning for freedom of thought; and since the party has sought to incorporate all and any branches of knowledge into the ideology of Soviet Marxism, it is also a yearning for freedom to interpret or reinterpret Soviet dogmas. At times, the perpetual pressure for this freedom is carried even into such sensitive and openly political subjects as Marxist philosophy, history, or constitutional law; and the recent preoccupation of the party leaders with the struggle against "revisionism" is in actual fact nothing else than an attempt to curb freedom of thought in these areas.

Revisionism, so-called, is dangerous to the party because any reinterpretation of Soviet dogmas might cause any number of Soviet intellectuals to pay renewed attention to certain elements of original Marxism which the party regards as inconvenient. Marxism is a liberational system of ideas. Again and again Marx stressed his absolute opposition to all social systems in which man is abused, dominated, exploited, or humiliated by his fellow men. This system of ideas has remained the Holy Writ in a society that incorporates domination and exploitation. It should not astonish us, therefore, that Marxist thought has a tremendous explosive potential, which every once in awhile is realized in individual Soviet citizens. That is why the party strives to maintain a tight monopoly on the right to interpret the Holy Writ and has transformed it into a dogmatic catechism designed to serve conservative functions. And yet, there are ever-recurrent tendencies to go back to the spirit of Marx, to criticize existing institutions in the name of Marxism and to press for the realization of the ideals it incorporates. These tendencies are the essence of what party ideologists call revisionism.

In the most general fashion, the strains within post-Stalinist communism (at least in the USSR and Eastern Europe) might be explained as follows: Communist societies are revolutionary societies. This means that they seek to destroy a preexisting social system and substitute a new one. The destruction begins with the fall of the previously established political order and the ascent to power of the Communist Party. The party then attempts to undermine and destroy the social structure and culture patterns associated with the old order and to replace them with an entirely new social and political system. The destructive task is difficult and painful, and it is never quite complete; some vestiges of the previous social order remain. The task of system-building is even more difficult and, because this difficulty makes the communist regime insecure and impatient, it resorts to Stalinist methods to speed up the process. After some decades of false starts, general chaos, and much waste of material and human resources, however, the party succeeds in establishing a relatively viable new social order. In doing so it creates, among other things, a new social structure and a new political culture—neatly reversing the relationship between social base and political superstructure which Marx had taken for granted. Marx had assumed that the social order gives rise to a political system, not the other way around. In time, however, the newly created social structure and political culture establish and strengthen themselves and, having done so, begin to be seen by the political leaders as a reality with which they have to reckon and to which they have to adjust. The substructure thus begins to assert a measure of sovereignty. Some process like this began in the USSR a few years after the end of World War II.

Postwar Developments and Trends

World War II strained every fiber of the Soviet social fabric. The population at large, the armed forces, and perhaps even the party, were unprepared for the German attack, and there was a good deal of demoralization. In the first few weeks, vast areas of territory and hundreds of thousands of troops were lost to the enemy. In some regions, particularly in the Ukraine and the Northern Caucasus, many greeted the German troops as liberators from the communist yoke, only to be disillusioned cruelly by the unspeakable barbarity of German rule in Russia.[7] As everyone knows, the war ended in the defeat of the Germans. But the Soviet Union bore the major brunt of it, and deep scars remained for many years. Millions of men had been lost, other millions maimed for life; countless villages, towns, and cities were razed; the grand effort toward rapid industrialization must have suffered serious setbacks affecting particularly the standard of living of the population.

During the war, the Soviet regime made a concerted effort to gain or maintain the loyalty of the entire population. For this purpose, the party de-emphasized specifically communist themes in its propaganda and stressed instead the ideas of patriotism. This war was to be a war for the defense of the native land rather than for the defense of communism. In line with this attempt to appeal to all Soviet people, the party opened its ranks to those who had distinguished themselves in battle; it tacitly tolerated peasant encroachments on collective farm property; it demonstratively made its peace with the Church; and by its alliance with the Western democracies it consciously or unconsciously instilled in many Soviet citizens the hope that after the war Soviet Russia would continue to collaborate with the democratic countries and that a more relaxed and a more prosperous life was in store for them.[8]

To curb these hopes, the party decided, once the war had been won, to return to the sternest methods of economic, political, and ideological reconstruction. The party ranks were purged of many who had recently been admitted. Rigid consumer austerity and work discipline were enforced once more, and all ideas about ideological compromises or about future collaboration with the noncommunist West were driven out of the heads of intellectuals with an iron broom. The ensuing campaign to purify Soviet doctrine and eliminate all deviators is often referred to as the *zhdanovshchina*, because Andrei Zhdanov, the head of the Leningrad regional party organization and a member of the Politburo, acted as its chief spokesman and inquisitor. But even after his death his policies were continued. As a matter of fact, the political atmosphere inside the country became even more tense in the late forties and early fifties, as additional deviators or presumed deviators were ferreted out, both in Russia and in the countries of Eastern Europe. By 1952 it appeared very much as if another major purge was being prepared in the highest levels of the party which would engulf Soviet society in a new reign of acute terror. Before these obvious preparations could bear fruit, however, the dictator of the country, Josef Stalin, died, in March 1953.

His death brought to the surface, at least temporarily, currents that had been hidden under the crust of his rule. One of these currents was the rivalry at the very top of the leadership group, possibly symbolizing a clash of group interests extending into the subordinate administrative layers. One of its first manifestations was the unsuccessful attempt by the police chief Beria to seize power. It was followed by signs of a sharp rivalry between economic planners and managers, on the one hand, and the party *aktiv,* on the other; in this *aktiv* the balance of power seems to have lain in the provincial and regional party secretaries. Furthermore, there were some unsuccessful efforts by a few generals to make their weight felt in politics. The temporary rise and reign of N. S. Khrushchev seemed to signify the recovery of a sovereign position in Soviet society by the highest leadership of the Communist Party, and the regaining of a role which the party had lost after 1938. In any event, the professional party administrators on the highest level appear to have regained the sovereign position within Soviet society which they had lost after 1938. Still, in the long run, the pluralistic tendencies within the Soviet power elite seem to have a good chance of corroding the sovereignty of the party, however slowly.[9]

A second current which came more into the open after Stalin's death was the yearning for professional autonomy and freedom of thought on the part of the educated. This yearning was expressed, albeit timidly, in many forms.

There were ventures into new themes and a rejection of stereotyped formulas in novel writing and other forms of art. There were more open and more controversial discussions than previously about the relation between Marxism and various sciences. There was, and still is, a continual effort to reinterpret the history of the party and of Soviet society, with the result that Stalin has been denounced for having committed some mistakes; the great purges have been re-evaluated, and some of its victims have been rehabilitated. All in all, there were efforts in almost every field of activity and learning to release the intellectual ferment; and these efforts appear still to be going on, even though the party has repeatedly tried to bottle up the ferment. Here, too, the long-range trend is likely to favor the gradual corrosion of Marx-ist-Leninist dogmas and the growth of similarities between Soviet and American thinking and social processes. Already Soviet economists are employing Western planning concepts and are openly challenging the validity of basic Marxist ideas; while Soviet military strategists have, since 1955, re-jected Stalinist dogmas in favor of Western principles of warfare. Similar processes of transformation are going on in many fields of endeavor.[10]

Since Stalin's death there has also been some relaxation of discipline, domination, and austerity. After the fall of Beria, the police was deprived of some of its arbitrary authority. Some of the "correctional labor" camps were dissolved. At-tempts were made to bridge the social gap between the peo-ple and the rulers and also to draw the common man of So-viet society a little more into public life. While in the last years of Stalin's rule Soviet society was almost hermetically sealed off from all contacts with the non-Soviet world, the flow of communication between Soviet citizens and the out-side resumed in the mid-1950's, through Western tourists, cultural exchanges, scientific collaboration, and the like.

Furthermore, the present-day Soviet regime is marked by a significant decrease in the feverishness of indoctrination. Since much of the party ideology has been internalized by a sizable portion of the population, it has become like Sun-day sermons or Fourth of July oratory. It is repeated cere-

moniously and in stereotyped form for the purpose of upholding the regime's legitimacy, but it serves less and less as
a guide to action. In fact, indoctrination, like police terror,
is becoming a superfluous part of Soviet political behavior.
Finally, a new party statute was adopted in the fall of 1961
which makes some initial concessions to the pressure for
greater freedom of discussion and greater security of the individual party members.[11]

If these measures showed that the regime was more confident of success and of the loyalty of the people, it had
good reasons. Not only had the USSR emerged as one of the
two major world powers, whose leader was received in the
White House, it had gained this world stature by spectacular
military and scientific advances which few Westerners would
have predicted ten years ago. Unlike the economic growth
under the first and second five-year plans, progress was now
accompanied by a rapid and steady rise in the standard of
living for the entire population, and because of all this, vast
masses of Soviet citizens must have gained greater confidence that they were part of a useful enterprise and that it
would be to their self-interest to collaborate to the best of
their ability. For the first time since the revolution of 1917,
the regime seemed able to keep some of its promises.

9

The Communist International, 1919–1943

• When the Russian bolsheviks seized power in 1917, they firmly expected that their deed would spark proletarian revolutions in the advanced countries of Western Europe. As a matter of fact, most of them thought that without worldwide revolution the establishment of a communist regime in a country like Russia made no sense whatever. Socialism, in their minds, presupposed a high stage of industrial development and a numerous, politically mature working class that could use this industrial establishment in rational fashion so as to ensure material plenty for all. In any society not coming up to these conditions, the erection of a socialist government was thought to be a premature and dangerous adventure. Either the socialist party would be overthrown very quickly, running the risk of total annihilation by the victorious counterrevolution; or, if against all odds it maintained itself in power, it could do so only by catering to the interests of a population not yet receptive to a Marxist program; the proletarian regime would turn into a sad caricature of itself and greatly discredit the whole Marxist movement.

And yet the bolsheviks seized power. Compelled by the traditions of their own movement to do nothing that did not correspond to Marxist prognoses or could not be fitted into Marxist programs of action, their leaders had to assume that the world revolution was around the corner and that the productive potential of a socialist Europe would secure the gains made by the revolution in Russia. Not all bolshevik leaders shared this confidence—those who did not hotly argued against seizing power—but those who did must not be regarded necessarily as utopian dreamers or reckless adventurers. On the contrary, there were many indications in 1917 that Europe was on the brink of revolution. A disastrous war had ruined her economies and shaken her regimes. Troops in France, Italy, and Germany had mutinied. Grave political unrest had made itself felt despite wartime censorship and emergency military rule. Where such indications were absent, their own theory told the men around Lenin that a revolution *had* to be in the making as a result of the war. And that this would be a proletarian revolution ushering in socialism, they all took for granted, just as Marx and Engels on the eve of 1848 had taken for granted that the coming revolution would inevitably be transformed into a proletarian one.

The bolshevik hopes were disappointed. The Russian Revolution remained isolated and, only a few months after the October uprising, had to adjust to the disappointing need for coexistence with capitalism by signing a peace treaty with Imperial Germany. To be sure, in signing this document, Lenin and his associates thought that they were only buying time sufficient for the world revolution to catch its breath. But the short breather extended to decades, and the very same arguments which had rationalized coexistence for but a little while came to sanction it for a long period. Rationalizing coexistence, however, meant rationalizing the pursuit of a policy devised for the purpose of securing the survival of the Soviet state. Coexistence therefore meant the emergence of a Soviet national interest or *raison d'état*, the pursuit of which was said to coincide with the interests of the proletarian world revolution.[1]

Still, by opting for coexistence, the Russian communists had not meant to abandon the cause of the world revolution. On the contrary, they signed their peace treaty with a capitalist power only so that the revolution might be given a chance to get under way. The war was still going on, after all, and in their eyes the world was still on the very brink of proletarian revolution. And indeed, even when the military conflict ended in November of 1918, the vehement economic, social, and political disturbances ensuing in the wake of the war lasted for another five years, keeping alive the most ambitious communist hopes.

During the war, Lenin had demanded that a new International be formed to replace the Second International, that world-wide federation of socialist parties which the war had destroyed. He had been exasperated by the leaders of these parties when with little hesitation they decided to support the war effort of their governments and thereby showed that national loyalty was stronger than their feeling of solidarity with the proletarians of all countries. In Lenin's eyes, they were traitors to the cause of the proletarian revolution, and he was determined not to be associated with them any longer. A revival of an international organization of working-class parties there must be, but definitely without any of the leaders who in his opinion had no place in, and could not contribute anything to, the party of the international proletariat. There were many socialist leaders who like Lenin regretted the collapse of international working-class solidarity and who joined him in criticizing the leaders of the European socialist parties; and yet many of them were hesitant to perpetuate the gulf that had opened between revolutionaries and moderates. Instead, they were eager to repair solidarity by trying to resurrect the international organization that had crumbled in 1914. Lenin's scorn of these people was as vehement as his hatred of the moderates.

Early in 1919 a congress of radical socialists assembled in Moscow to create the new International Lenin had demanded. The time seemed propitious. True, the Spartacus uprising in Germany had just been drowned in blood. But Hungary and Bavaria were in the hands of communist governments. Revolts against Western rule seemed to be brewing in the Near and Far East. All of Europe was in the throes of a violent postwar crisis. Still, the parties or factions represented, or purporting to be represented, at the founding congress were as yet without substantial following or even organization. Some delegates were extremely hesitant to help create an international socialist organization designed for the express purpose of keeping out the majority of socialist leaders and organizations. They would have preferred a renewal of the old International. But Lenin was eager to go ahead precisely because he wanted to anticipate and forestall the revival of the Second International. He wanted to face international socialism with a *fait accompli* and thus force all socialists to take sides, either with the new international or against it. The statutes of the new organization, adopted by the Second Congress, in 1920, were designed to enforce this compulsion to choose by imposing conditions on every would-be member party designed to antagonize and eliminate all those desiring a compromise—the famous twenty-one conditions. In addition, these statutes had the effect of imposing Lenin's principles of organization on every member party and on the Third International as a whole. Moreover, since that organization was designed to facilitate the exercise of leadership or command over a disciplined political machine, the imposition of Leninist organization also spelled the imposition of Leninist (or Russian) policies on the Third International, since quite naturally the Russian communists, with their prestige as successful revolutionaries, dominated the top command of the International from the very beginning. The many communist parties which came into life after the creation of the International, and also the even more numerous auxiliary organizations in all the world, in this fashion became appendages of the Russian *apparat*, in organization as well as in policy.

From its very beginning up to its dissolution, the policies of the Communist International were confused by the ambiguity of its main aims. Ostensibly, its objective was to promote proletarian revolution everywhere and, as an auxiliary move, to promote colonial revolutions in areas dominated by Western powers. But the pursuit of this goal was complicated by the fact that all communist parties were also expected to support the national interests of the USSR; and these interests were not always easy to reconcile with the presumed interests of revolution making. In fact, the evidence strongly suggests that, at least in Europe, where the USSR tried very hard to coexist with the leading capitalist nations, the efforts of the Communist International and those of the Soviet Commissariat for Foreign Affairs eternally embarrassed and frustrated and negated each other. Western communists could not but be aware of the baneful influence of Soviet national interests over the policies of their parties. Nor were they entirely happy that Russia was the country which became the pathbreaker and model for the development of a proletarian revolution. This raw and uncouth land of illiterate peasants, governed with a mixture of inefficiency and oriental ruthlessness that repelled many visitors, was not really a very suitable advertising sign for Marxist communism—certainly not in the first two or three decades of its existence. On the contrary, it was in many ways a source of embarrassment for Western communists. Meanwhile, Western diplomats and bourgeois politicians, compelled by various reasons to seek friendly relations with the Soviet Union, could not, in their turn, help being aware (even if they had not been reminded constantly by their constituents) that Moscow was not only the capital of a state with which it was necessary to coexist but also the headquarters and planning center of an international revolutionary movement aiming at the overthrow of all bourgeois governments.

In Asia, the incompatibility between Soviet foreign policy and the activities of the Communist International was not nearly so pronounced. In China, Afghanistan, Persia, and Turkey, Moscow was dealing with revolutionary regimes seeking to emancipate their countries from Western domination. Colonial revolution could be fitted into the policies of Soviet foreign relations as well as into the policies of world communism. And yet, on closer examination, difficulties abounded in this area of the world too. While communist theory sought to convert the colonial revolution into an ally and an auxiliary force of the Western proletarian revolution, strategies to promote this end had not been elaborated and were a matter of keen controversy. Questions concerning the aims that ought to be promoted in colonial revolutions and the objectives that ought to be set, the forces with which communist parties ought to, or might, ally themselves, the nature of such alliances and the very meaningfulness of communist parties in countries where no industrial proletariat existed—these and many similar problems faced the strategists of the Communist International. Many different methods were tried: occasional attempts to spread communism by force of arms; the founding of communist parties, which then sought a mass basis among the urban workers, the peasants, or even national and religious minorities, and which were ever prone to be dismayed by Moscow's orders to ally themselves with other revolutionary parties. Furthermore, in order to aid the colonial revolution, Moscow (and it is not always clear whether Asian policy emanated from the International or from the Soviet Foreign Office) at times supported popular revolutionary parties or leaders (such as the Kuomintang or Kemal), anti-Western princes (such as Reza Pahlevi in Iran and Amanullah Khan in Afghanistan), or even feudal lords like Ibn Saud, as long as they were actively opposing the West (meaning especially Britain). Here too, therefore, considerations of foreign policy and revolution making came into conflict with each other, to the eventual detriment of both.

A further difficulty besetting the policies of the Comintern was the result of overcentralization. The International had been organized in the image of the Russian Communist Party not only because its kind of organization made it into a centralized, disciplined striking organization. That pattern of organization was rationalized further by the assumption that the working classes everywhere are basically alike. When Marx and Engels in the *Communist Manifesto* said that the proletarians have no fatherland, they presupposed an international solidarity of workers who in their living conditions and problems, their thinking and their political goals, were more like each other than like the capitalists in their own countries. In short, Marx and Engels assumed that capitalism, fundamentally, was the same everywhere. Hence the possibility of an international, united proletarian movement. Lenin and his comrades subscribed to these views; and the

Third International was organized so as to serve as the united, centralized Communist Party of all proletarians everywhere.

On a very high level of abstraction, the view of the workers of the world having certain problems and interests in common may have been defensible. But, concretely (and that means also politically), it was a mistake. The working class of each country could, rather, be expected to have problems of its own and to fight its own capitalists with weapons and strategies attuned to its own special conditions. If this is accepted, it will be clear that overcentralization and its corollary, the imposition of a unified policy line on the International, were a serious blunder which must have wrecked the chances of many a revolution.

The programs and strategies of the various member parties were thus fitted to the Procrustean bed of the Comintern's world-wide party line. Resistance to any of the more disastrous decisions which this procedure imposed on the various parties was stifled and punished as a serious breach of discipline. Communist parties were ill equipped, therefore, to accommodate leaders who thought for themselves or who thought that conditions in their own countries demanded a special course of action. The rapid turnover of leaders in the bolshevik party from its very beginnings therefore came to be a characteristic feature of the Communist International as well. The situation was not at all improved by the fact that disputes over policy were often intertwined with, or affected by, the struggle for power raging among the leaders. More specifically, conflicts within the Third International were closely tied to the bitter fights within the Russian party and were decided by the outcome of these fights, so that personnel turnover within the various member parties faithfully mirrored the personnel changes in the Russian party. In many ways, the cards were stacked against the Comintern's becoming an effective promoter of any rational policy.

After all I have said, it should not astonish anyone that the Third International was one gigantic failure. It did not succeed in creating a single proletarian dictatorship or communist regime. Nor did it manage to preserve and strengthen many of the strong communist parties that had been created in the years after World War I, although some of these parties survived World War II or even emerged from it more numerous and influential than ever before. Finally, the Comintern must be considered a dismal failure in its efforts to shield the Soviet Union and promote its national interests. I shall try to support these generalizations by a brief survey of the history of the International.

In the first years after World War I, valuable time was lost in gathering experience and organizing. The creation of the Comintern required vigorous efforts to persuade all like-minded socialist leaders to split off from the more moderate parties to which they had belonged and to found communist parties conforming in organization and policy to the Russian model. Some of the member parties started out as small, insignificant sects. Others acquired a mass following fairly quickly, especially the Communist Party of Germany (KPD), which soon became and for some years remained the center of the International's hopes. The new parties were as yet unsure of their goals and methods. In their sporadic attempts at promoting proletarian revolutions and seizing power they placed great reliance on organizers and leaders sent by Moscow, usually Russian or Hungarian comrades whose experience in real revolutions gave them tremendous prestige. Nonetheless, the first attempts at revolution were handled in amateurish fashion and ended in failure, as did the desperate attempt, made in 1920, at exporting revolution at bayonet point by conquering Poland. In the wake of these failures came not only the first purge of disobedient leaders but also the first major switch in the policy line of the Communist International: after the abortive communist revolution in Germany in 1921, the International abandoned such reckless adventures, decided that the major danger to the working-class movement lay in right-wing authoritarianism, and consequently adopted the policy of the "United Front" with the moderate socialists. In line with this policy, communist parties were enjoined to offer collaboration to moderate socialists, ostensibly for the purpose of safeguarding democratic institutions and workers' rights, but in reality with the aim of infiltrating socialist parties and more particularly trade unions. In China, which together with Germany was the main focus of Comintern hopes in these years, the new policy led to the alliance and actual merger of the Chinese Communist Party with the Kuomintang—a step which at the time was hailed with enthusiasm, though in the end it brought only disaster to the Chinese communists.

In Europe the policy of the United Front came to naught for several reasons. For one thing, the moderate socialists were generally in no mood to ally themselves with communist parties, especially since the communists themselves were frank enough to admit their desire to destroy or swallow up the moderates. Secondly, as the aftermath of World War I came to a dramatic climax, it seems that the rank-and-file membership of the communist parties became impatient with the moderate and cautious defensive policy which the United Front implied. While political and economic chaos engulfed Europe, the high command of the International and the leaders of the European parties were divided; and the top decision makers hesitated. In the end, an attempt to unleash revolution in Germany, which was finally made in October of 1923, was bungled and ended in disaster. Changes of personnel and policy followed as a matter of course.[2]

Following the debacle of the "German October" in 1923, the Communist International settled down to the serious work of consolidating its substantial gains in Western and Central Europe. It found it possible to elaborate greatly its network of auxiliary organizations set up to organize and educate different groups in the population of the capitalist countries. A great deal of energy was spent also in the recurrent fights against opposing factions and, once the major oppositions had been eliminated, in making personnel changes which brought to the top disciplinarians and obedient spokesmen of the Kremlin, organization men who could not be expected to make any trouble. This change of personnel was called the "bolshevization" of the Comintern.

For serious revolution making, the time did not seem pro-

pitious. In Europe and in the New World, this was a period
of "normalcy" and prosperity, which brought with it a flow-
ering of constitutional democracy and middle-class culture.
Sporadic outbursts of labor trouble, as for instance the British General Strike of 1926, did not yield any benefits to the
communist parties. In Asia, national revolutions continued
to break out. But in India, China, the Dutch East Indies,
and elsewhere the communist parties did not succeed in
playing major roles in these revolutions. To be sure, the
Indian Congress Party contained a left wing headed by
Jawaharlal Nehru which found a good deal of inspiration in
communist ideas; and similar intellectual currents were alive
in other colonial countries. But they did not yield benefit to
the communist parties. In China, the happy merger of the
party with the revolutionary Kuomintang was forcibly dissolved in 1926. "Comrade" Chiang Kai-shek, officially still
affiliated with the Comintern, decimated the ranks of the
Chinese Communist Party by a bloody purge and destroyed
communist hopes for years to come. The years of prosperity
ended with the Communist International better organized
than ever—strong parties and a widely ramified network of
auxiliary organizations, all of them in the hands of "safe"
leaders. Although the period had not brought any more tan-
gible political success, the spokesmen of international communism were confident that new trouble was brewing for
the capitalist world and that the years of prosperity were
coming to an end. From the coming depression, which they
predicted accurately, the communist world expected the development of a new revolutionary situation that would take
global proportions.

The Great Depression predicted by the Comintern came
in 1929. It hit the capitalist world cruelly, ruined its economy, created mass unemployment and misery. It brought
with it a general turn toward political radicalism, which in
Eastern Europe, Germany, and France destroyed democratic
constitutionalism. It was a time of profound crisis in the
capitalist countries from which the Communist International
might have benefited, but did not. The general shortcomings
of the Third International go far in explaining this. But

some additional reasons must be mentioned. First of all, the Great Depression coincided with the first and second five-years plans in the Soviet Union, a time when Russia was busy with her own problems and her leaders were unwilling to trouble themselves with international complications. Revolution making was as far is it could be from the minds of the men in Moscow, who had plenty on their hands in trying to industrialize their country and control their population. The International in this period made a good deal of radical noise; but this was primarily to hide its actual policy of isolationism.

The radical rhetoric was a function of the new policy line adopted by the International at this time, a policy of uncompromising leftism. It should by now have become clear that one of the major problems of communist policy making has always been to define the attitude of the party to other socialist parties. Just as the communist is ambivalent in his appraisal of the working class itself, at times being confident that the proletariat has become "conscious," at times despairing over its lack of consciousness, so his judgment changes about parties which, like his own, purport to speak for the workers. To be sure, the Comintern was founded with the specific purpose of making the gulf between communists and social democrats unbridgeable. Lenin's own loathing of moderate socialism and its representatives was shared by his followers. And even when the International expressed the desire for an alliance between the two parties, the understanding was that the communists sought to support the socialists "as the noose supports the man who is being hanged." And yet, the actual policies of the Third International toward the moderate socialists were subject to considerable modifications. Whenever the Comintern was convinced that its very existence (or that of the USSR) was threatened by conservative or reactionary forces, it formed a defensive alliance with left-of-center liberals or moderate socialists, an alliance formed ostensibly to preserve constitutional democracy and the liberties associated with it. But its basic hostility toward the social democrats would break through in full force particularly in periods when a revolutionary situation was believed to be developing. At such times, a communist had to be on guard against the socialists, because in his opinion they were, after all, only the left wing of the bourgeoisie, and they could be expected to betray the revolution. When the time for great decisions draws near, it is always the unreliable ally who becomes the most dangerous enemy and must be unmasked and opposed.

And so, when the Western world was staggering under the blows of the economic crisis, when constitutional democracy was eroded by radicalism of the right and the left, the communist parties concentrated their fire on the socialist parties. As a result, the Comintern achieved partial success: "bourgeois democracy" in much of Continental Europe was destroyed. But the communist parties did not manage to take the second step which they had hoped and expected to take—to grab the power from the tottering capitalists. Instead, right-wing authoritarian regimes took over wherever constitutional democracy could not manage to maintain itself. These regimes came to power partly in the name of militant anticommunism; and once they were in power they usually proceeded to stamp out communism, together with the remnants of socialism and democratic liberalism. As a result, the most important communist parties outside the Soviet Union, together with some lesser ones, were destroyed almost completely. The vast political machinery of the Third International, built up with blood and tears and tremendous resources, was destroyed in one terrible blow.

Nor was the movement any more successful in the colonies and underdeveloped areas. In China, Comintern agents or Chinese leaders obedient to the commands of Moscow made futile attempts to stir up the urban masses. They were defeated by the lethargy of the workers, by the Kuomintang, and by the Japanese invasion of Manchuria. Meanwhile, a little-known communist warlord, Mao Tse-tung, while paying lip service to Comintern instructions, silently began to build up the strength of the party on the basis of an overwhelmingly rural following—a proletarian party without a proletariat. In the northwestern part of China and also behind the lines of the Japanese (after they had occupied portions of China proper), substantial rural areas came under the authority of this Communist Party, so that, gradually and without attracting much notice in Comintern circles, the nucleus of a veritable communist republic developed.

A major reversal in policy was undertaken in 1935, not only as a result of the defeats we have just discussed, but more directly because of new international developments. By this time it had become apparent that the Great Depression and the ensuing political crises would not lead to proletarian revolutions. Instead, they had produced fascist and authoritarian regimes which were not only militantly anticommunist but also militantly aggressive in international relations. The Soviet Union felt itself threatened by the clear and present danger of German and Japanese attacks. More than ever her leaders were concentrating their attention on the problems of economic and military growth and on instilling unquestioning loyalty and discipline into her population. But they also tried to secure themselves through action in the international arena.

From the beginning, the foreign policy of the USSR relied primarily, though not exclusively, on the device frequently used by powers that are weak and feel themselves threatened —this device is to seek allies among other weak, threatened, or dissatisfied powers, so as to confront the major powers with a protective alliance of the underdogs. The underdogs, or have-not powers with whom Soviet Russia cultivated mutually fruitful relations on this basis, included Germany, Italy, Japan, China, Iran, and Turkey. It should be noted that this policy was altogether unrelated to the real pursuits of the Communist International. If anything, these pursuits were in conflict with Soviet attempts to cement its alliances with the underdogs of the capitalist world of nations.

Now, in 1935, for the first time the policies of the International were geared immediately to the Soviet's policy of alliances. Alarmed by the military threat of German and Japanese power, Moscow's satellite parties adopted the policy of the Popular Front. Communist parties everywhere sought to ally themselves with, or even give unrewarded support to, any political group or government ready to resist fascism, national socialism, or other forms of government regarded as direct threats to the Soviet Union.

To be sure, attempts were made to use Popular Front arrangements or alliances for the purpose of weaning the masses away from moderate programs, to build up communist strength by taking command over socialist or liberal groups of one sort or another and thus to prepare for proletarian revolution. As a consequence, a good deal of ill feeling and distrust arose between the communist parties and the groups they sought to use or abuse. But, in general, the International and its affiliated parties tended to tone down their specifically communist aims and programs. The communist parties at least ostensibly transformed themselves into the left wing of liberal and moderate socialist parties. They came out as defenders of due process and constitutional government and, in international affairs, of collective security. The USSR entered the League of Nations, which for years it had denounced as the victors' club of the big imperialist states, and the Soviet spokesman, Maxim Litvinov, acquired the reputation of being the staunchest defender of global democracy. The Soviet government and its satellite parties went to great pains to persuade the world that the USSR itself was a thoroughly democratic country governed on the basis of a liberal constitution. In his interview with Roy Howard, in 1936, Stalin rejected the allegation that he or his government was interested in promoting world communism. How much of this line, if any, was deliberate deception is impossible to say. At least to some extent, the attempt to mobilize the forces of democracy against fascism and the like was made by Moscow with the expectation that it would fail (and would thereby reveal the hypocrisy of liberal democracy). Doubtless many communists preached liberal ideals only in order to show that under capitalism these ideals cannot be fulfilled. Perhaps Litvinov's disarmament proposals and communist attempts to safeguard civil liberties and constitutional democracy were similarly motivated. But the first impetus for these attempts undoubtedly came from the threats of aggression facing the USSR.[3]

In pursuit of the Popular Front policy, communist programs were not only toned down. Actually there were cases in which deliberate steps were taken to prevent or sabotage revolutions. In China, for instance, the Popular Front policy compelled the communists to ally themselves with their archenemy, Chiang Kai-shek, against Japan and even to save his life and liberty after he had fallen into their hands through the kidnaping at Sian in 1936. The Chinese communists did so only with the greatest reluctance, many of them doubtless feeling that Moscow was betraying them. In Spain, the party faced a dilemma—either to support and promote the working-class revolution that had begun, and thereby endanger the war effort, or deliberately to postpone and stamp out the revolution for the purpose of winning the civil war. Without hesitation the party chose the latter course and lost both the war and the revolution.[4] In the United States, the Popular Front policy caused the party to support the New Deal, even though they had at first denounced it as a semifascist attempt to save capitalism from certain collapse.

It should also be remembered that the years of the Popular Front coincided with the Great Purge in the Soviet Union. The Western world was being challenged to defend constitutional democracy just at the time when police terror was celebrating bloody orgies in the USSR. This was, moreover, a period of national frenzy and intense xenophobia in Russia, and, whether by accident or design, foreign nationals were hit with especial ferocity by the purges. The Soviet Union, by this time, was the refuge of great numbers of foreign communists who had fled from political persecution in their own countries. These colonies or foreign communist leaders were decimated by the Great Purge, which virtually wiped out several communist parties. The work left unfinished by the Gestapo or similar institutions in Poland, Hungary, and other states was thus completed by the NKVD. Meanwhile, the entire purge orgy, with its open and secret trials, its fantastic confessions, had a chilling effect on many people in Western countries in sympathy with communism and so jeopardized the success of the Popular Front policy.[5]

In the end, the Popular Front policy turned out to be as much of a failure as all previous Comintern policies. The communist parties did not succeed in making lasting alliances with any socialist parties, although numerous left-wing groups and associations in the Western democracies came under the influence of their new communist members (who had joined in obedience to Popular Front policy directives) and often voiced the party line. That line consisted in warnings against fascism, praises for liberal democracy, and assertions that the USSR in its domestic and foreign policies was the only country which consistently followed and promoted the ideals and precepts of liberal democracy, while in the Western democracies these ideals were being betrayed or in danger of being betrayed. Although some of these notions attained considerable popularity among intellectuals in England, France, the United States, and a few other countries between 1935 and 1938, the Communist International was unable to make these ideas pay off: the Western democracies did not yield to the prodding given them by Moscow and by their own left-of-center circles to resist German, Italian, or Japanese aggression. Instead, they followed the paths of "nonintervention" and "appeasement," which in the end led to the Munich pact of 1938. This pact marked the complete and utter failure of the Popular Front. Once again the Third International had miscalculated disastrously.[6]

From this point on, it was a moribund organization. In response to Munich, the USSR signed a treaty of friendship with the Third Reich in August of 1939, dismaying and rebuffing sympathizers and fellow travelers in the West and also many party members, who had supported the USSR and the party as the staunchest bastions against fascist aggression. As England and France girded their loins to fight at last against Nazi Germany, the Communist International advised its followers that the new war was an imperialist war—a family quarrel between imperialist nations and of no concern to the party of the proletariat. Instead, the workers were urged to sabotage the war effort, to resist emergency controls and the imposition of wartime hardships, and to desert from the armed forces. The small number of people who heeded this call attested to the lack of influence any of the communist parties had among the masses.[7]

The final reversal of Comintern policies was a natural consequence of Hitler's attack on the USSR in June of 1941. The Communist International automatically resumed the slogans of the Popular Front, this time with renewed vigor and with changes in emphasis. No longer was it necessary to goad the Western democracies into resistance to national socialism. Their will to resist was now assured; and, if it needed to be revived occasionally, this was accomplished far more advantageously by the Soviet government, now allied with the democracies, than by the communist parties. These parties had only one more function left—to persuade their followers that the only task for faithful communists now was to support the allied war effort. Workers in the West were to forget their grievances against capitalists. They were to do their best and make no demands. Racial, religious, or national minorities feeling the sting of discrimination were to shelve their complaints for the duration of the war and forget about their aims to gain equality. Rebellious nationalists in the colonies were to forget or postpone their demands for freedom and self-government and give their full support to the governments they had always been told to regard as their oppressors. Communist resistance groups in countries occupied by the enemy were urged to merge with, and even subject themselves to, noncommunist resistance forces, to give up their identity and goals so as not to jeopardize the war effort or embarrass the Soviet Union.[8]

It is obvious that instructions of this nature had not the slightest similarity to communist programs. Moreover, the USSR apparently regarded the very existence of the International as an embarrassment and a hindrance. In its efforts to cement the wartime alliance with the Western democracies, which Moscow considered essential for the successful defense of the Soviet Union, the Kremlin did not wish to remind its allies that it had once been the headquarters of the world revolution. That world revolution was not, for the time being, on the agenda. Consequently, without ceremony or fanfare, without even the pretense of going through elaborate formal procedures, the little side show or, as Stalin is reputed to have called the Communist International contemptuously, the "little shop" quietly closed its books and folded its tents. The year was 1943. It is ironic and perhaps significant that the international organization of communist parties was dissolved precisely at the time when for the first time since 1917 the international communist movement was about to achieve important gains. The battle of Stalingrad was the turning point of the war and of the history of the world in our century. The Soviet Union began to emerge as a major world power.[9]

Equally important was the fact that a number of communist parties, working with greater independence from Moscow (because the war prevented communications and control), managed, *because* of this absence of control, to make important gains in size and influence. As a result of World War II and because of the demise of the Comintern, communism for the first time became an important world force.

It might be argued that some credit for this new success should be given to the Comintern and its Russian leadership, including Stalin. After all, it was this leadership which first built a world-wide communist movement and it was its emissaries and agents who provided foreign communists with knowledge of revolutionary techniques. Against this, I submit that communist parties would have been created in many parts of the world in any event, and more spontaneously, even without the help of the Comintern. Indeed, they would most probably have been more closely attuned to their own political systems and would therefore have been more successful. Moreover, inventiveness in revolutionary techniques is no Russian monopoly, and we can safely assume that revolutionary leaders throughout the world would have acquired the necessary know-how without instructors from Moscow. The fact remains that wherever the Comintern remained in control, communist revolutions inevitably failed. The gains which communism made after World War II were achieved despite the weight of Comintern history, and despite Stalin's leadership.

10

World Communism since World War II

• We live today in the most revolutionary of all ages. Major social transformations are going on in our lifetime which are more profound, more rapid, and more extensive than anything the history of mankind has seen. This revolution of our time is manifested in scientific, technological, political, and cultural changes which by far transcend the topic of this little volume. But we can single out several changes that are directly related to the development of world communism since World War II.

One of these changes is the emergence of the Soviet Union as a world power, by virtue of her industrial growth, her scientific achievements, her military victories, and her political successes. Further, the international communist movement, too, acquired new strength, partly because it was now backed up by a strong power that could make its weight felt in world affairs, but much more because various communist parties managed to operate in much greater independence from Moscow. Not only did international communism acquire new strength; its methods, too, underwent significant changes. For one thing, now that Soviet Russia was able to take the initiative in international affairs and the outcome of the war presented opportunities for moving into power vacua, the Kremlin was given a chance to ex-

pand the area of Soviet domination by military and diplo-
matic rather than by political means—a rather curious
method of making "revolution." With the exception of Yugoslavia, and perhaps one should add Czechoslovakia, the
communist governments of Eastern Europe were created
from the outside, as it were, with the local communist parties
serving as little more than auxiliary forces. I propose to call
the events in Eastern Europe "contrived revolutions."

The growing importance of communist parties in various
parts of the world was a direct consequence of the war.
Throughout Europe the war caused vast destruction, economic disruption, massive social dislocation, and political
instability. In this situation, communist parties became influential, not so much because they tend to thrive on instability and misery—that is probably only a half-truth—but
because of their political record during the war. Wherever
German occupation forces appeared, resistance movements
came into being—guerrilla forces trying to harass German
troops, sabotage German communications, or prepare for
setting up governments of liberation. Communists took a
very active part in these resistance movements, being prepared for such warfare because of their underground experience and their political schooling. In many countries, they
distinguished themselves by competent leadership and heroic deeds. In Eastern Europe, especially in Poland and Yugoslavia, communist resistance forces fought bitterly against
both the German and Italian occupation troops, and the
puppet regimes installed by the occupiers, and against noncommunist guerrilla units, whereas in the West the general
pattern was a merger of all resistance forces under unified
command, so that communists fought together with people
of many other political orientations. Throughout the occupied territories, the communist parties derived considerable
prestige from their activities, which after the war they managed to translate into political power, at least for a while. In
Western Europe and Greece they did not hold on to this
power because of American and British interference, or
partly because of it; in Eastern Europe, their independence
of thought and action was almost totally curtailed by the

sovereign presence of the Soviet Union. Still, although in the long run communist parties lost out throughout Europe, in the immediate postwar period they were recognized as respectable parties, whose representatives were entitled to share government responsibility.

In all areas occupied by Japan in East and Southeast Asia, very similar successes were won on the basis of participation and leadership in the resistance forces, and in many of these areas, the guerrilla activity meant the emergence of the Communist Party as a fully organized political force. Since in many of these areas, instead of orderly government revolutionary civil war followed the defeat of the Japanese, political power often also meant the emergence of the Communist Party as a military force. Like the resistance movements of Europe, these guerrilla armies—communists and noncommunists alike—received some military support from the Western Allies during the war, and in some cases the collapse of the Japanese forces enriched their weapons supplies significantly.

Foremost, however, the war spurred the colonial revolution to unprecedented intensity, and, with it, the strong push of all the poorer nations for liberation from their underprivileged positions. If I have called ours the most revolutionary age of all history, I should assert also that the most spectacular element in this revolution of our time is the rise of the underdeveloped nations. When we study social sciences, we usually study the history, politics, and economics of Western Europe and North America. Our view of the world for centuries has been highly ethnocentric—and rightly so, for the nations of Asia, Africa, and Latin America did not count. However populous, they were negligible because of their political, economic, and military weakness. They were objects of exploitation or domination, either as colonies or as dependencies or satellites. The white man ruled these countries through unbelievably arrogant and arbitrary colonial administrators, military or civilian. Neither these officials nor the builders and traders and overseers who represented Western business were always the highest representatives of European civilization; on the contrary, service in the white man's underdeveloped dependencies often was sought by highly unattractive personalities, people who, as Hannah Arendt has put it, had become superfluous in their own societies.

The West, however, brought not only domination by tactless, stupid, or ruthless colonial officials, not only new forms of economic exploitation for native labor; it also brought blessings: material wealth through the implantation of Western industrial enterprises, valuable technical and administrative skills for a small elite of cooperative natives. For those blessings, the people of Asia, Africa, and Latin America are not, as a rule, grateful to the West. On the contrary, one legacy of colonialism and dependency is an unbounded hatred of the white man, who is remembered as the arrogant intruder, the tyrant, the barbarian, who disrupted and destroyed the traditional way of life and even claims gratitude for it.

Whatever the natives' attitude toward the West, there is one other thing which the white man's rule has brought to their countries; and that is revolution. Wherever they appeared, Western administration and Western commerce and industry disrupted old-established cultures, uprooting entire social classes. Christian missionaries meanwhile acquainted the natives with the idea of brotherly love, while Western educators sought to propagate democracy, free enterprise, nationalism, and socialism. With this education, the natives in underdeveloped and dependent countries were given various directions for solving the problems which the encroachment of the West had created for them. The lesson was that the colonial nations might improve their lot by applying Western ideas and ideals to their own societies.

The need for drastic action, for revolutionary transformation, which is felt by political leaders in underdeveloped areas is given its sense of urgency by the material misery of these countries. It has by now become common knowledge in the Western world that roughly two-thirds of the world's population exist on a level so low Americans cannot even imagine it. The picture is a composite of starvation, disease, infant deaths, and short life spans on a gigantic scale, and in view of the population explosion which aggravates this misery there are no easy solutions. It might be argued that there is nonetheless no reason for the political leaders in Asia and Africa to become excited over the low standard of living in their countries, since, after all, this has been their condition for centuries. While this may indeed be true, there is one significant change: The world has today become a single political community. The various countries, industrial or preindustrial, no longer can lead a separate existence but become more and more aware of each other. Americans and Western Europeans, with their high standard of life, have become fellow citizens in this world community with starving Indians, disease-ridden Africans, and belabored South American peons, who therefore assume the character of underprivileged classes. Individuals in these classes may be illiterate and ignorant, and uninterested in sweeping political changes; but their spokesmen and manipulators are well aware of the unbelievable gap between the wealthy and the poor in this world community.

The solution most of these leaders advocate is westernization, that is, the adoption of the Western industrial way of life, the building of industries and cities, the training of the population for life and work in this environment, and the willingness to learn from Western experience in government and administration. Westernization, as advocated by revolutionary leaders in underdeveloped countries, must be seen as an act of revolt both against the old way of life and its representatives in the old ruling classes and cliques and against the West itself; for westernization is not only designed to modernize undeveloped countries and promote economic growth; it is also seen as a means of liberation and emancipation.

But what has all this to do with the development of communism? Merely because the colonial revolution is so clearly directed against the white man, we should not be so foolish as to characterize it offhandedly as a communist conspiracy. On the contrary, some of these revolutions would have happened earlier or been more successful had Moscow been more encouraging and cooperative, or more intelligent in its leadership. Indeed, in the eyes of many Asian or African leaders, communist countries have as much potential as exploiters and oppressors as the former colonial masters or imperialist bosses. Despite these reservations, communist nations may be desirable as partners in economic construction for newly established regimes. Beyond that, the Soviet, Chinese, and Cuban experiences are studied by many revolutionary leaders in underdeveloped areas and may exert a strong influence upon them. In their eyes, these countries were the first underdeveloped nations that emancipated themselves from Western influence and either have succeeded in overcoming or are promising to overcome their economic backwardness by a concerted effort of industrialization. When growth rates in the communist world are contrasted with the business cycle in free-enterprise societies, or with growth rates in India, Ghana, or other countries on a comparative level of development, the Soviet Union and China may become models for development, models that are the more meaningful because ideals of democracy, individual freedom, and due process are not deeply rooted in many former colonial areas, especially where colonial administrations have mocked them for decades; or they may be considered luxuries which a backward nation cannot afford. Instead, the avowed elitism of the communist movement may appeal to revolutionary leaders in hierarchically ruled countries. In addition, communist theory has features which make it well suited to inspire such leaders. It is a sweeping theory of salvation and damnation likely to make converts in violently disturbed societies and in times of dramatic revolutionary upheavals. It is at least overtly an optimistic theory, which asserts that progress is possible—again something which seems almost deliberately designed to appeal to nations emerging from preindustrialism. Moreover, in advocating the machine age, although rebelling against Western capitalism, communist thought very precisely expresses the ambivalent attitude toward the West of people who wish to westernize even while ridding themselves of Western rule. Finally, and perhaps most significantly, communist theory, in its ideas about imperialism, incorporates a systematic theory of underdevelopment, and it is the first and perhaps even

the only theory which has attempted to describe systematically the genesis and problems of underdevelopment. The
communists thereby have established a virtual monopoly on
explaining the underdeveloped nations to themselves; hence
the curious and slightly disturbing phenomenon that spokesmen of such nations, however violently anticommunist they
be, almost inevitably use the language of Lenin when they
begin to talk about the economic problems of their countries.
In this fashion, then, the disintegration of Western influence
is at least indirectly related to the growth of communist
strength since World War II.

The Cold War

The political context within which the revolution of our
time has been going on, or with which it is inextricably connected, is the cold war. This is the conflict between the two
major powers that emerged from the Second World War,
between the two alliance systems these powers headed, and
between the ideologies and social systems to which they are
more or less strongly committed. It must be pointed out at
once that the cold war is not and was not a one-sided defensive struggle of a peace-loving camp against a conspiratorial, aggressive troublemaker, though zealots on both sides
like to present it as such. In reality it is the result of defen-
siveness and aggressiveness, of good will, hard-nosed Machiavellian game-playing, and sheer paranoia on both sides.
Even if all the political leaders involved in it had had the
best intentions and the clearest reasoning power, the cold
war might nonetheless have raged simply because bipolarity,
that is, a situation in which two superpowers dominate the
global political community, almost inevitably leads to conflict between them. I point out the two-sided responsibility
for political developments after World War II although in
the context of this book the total picture cannot be presented. Instead, I shall concentrate, rather one-sidedly, on
the communist activities which form part of the cold war.

As early as 1943, once it had become apparent that the
war was about to be won, some party members in the Soviet

Union were told confidentially that, after the defeat of Germany, the next enemy would be the United States. Simultaneously, among the guerrilla forces of the resistance groups, some communist leaders doubtless prepared themselves ideologically and politically for the power struggles that would inevitably come in their own countries after liberation. Similarly, of course, some American diplomats warned the Roosevelt administration that undoubtedly the coming victory over Germany and Japan would be followed by a bitter struggle with the Soviet Union over the shaping of the postwar world. Still, for several years after Stalingrad, and indeed well into the postwar period, the Kremlin appeared reluctant to let any hostility against the West come into the open. Stalin apparently believed for a number of years that he could ill afford to antagonize his former ally, the United States. That is the most plausible explanation of the fact that in this period he repeatedly discouraged and hindered the attempts made by communist parties in Yugoslavia, France, China, and elsewhere to shift from a strategy of wartime alliance with "bourgeois" forces to one of open opposition and revolution. It may also be (and it is rather plausible to argue) that Stalin had long ago ceased to care for the promotion of communist revolutions unless he himself, or his direct subordinates, could plan and supervise them. Thus, while communist parties outside of direct Soviet control were forced to collaborate with groups whom in reality they wished to dislodge (Stalin did not succeed in forcing all communist parties to adopt this line), Soviet activity in the conquered or liberated countries of Eastern Europe seemed designed primarily to ensure the establishment there of docile regimes. More and more, Western scholars are beginning to assert that here too Stalin deliberately prevented or perverted genuine communist revolutions that might have occurred without such interference.

The Soviet advance into Eastern Europe began in September 1939, when on the basis of her recent agreement with the Third Reich the USSR annexed the eastern half of Poland. Supported by the same treaty, she added the three Baltic republics as well as parts of Finland and Rumania the

following year. All these territories were lost again to the
Germans in 1941, but Moscow kept claiming a legal right
to them; and her new allies in the West did not consider it
opportune to challenge these claims openly. Moreover, the
wartime governments of Britain and the United States considered themselves so dependent on continued Soviet cooperation that in their agreements with Stalin they conceded
to him overriding influence in all of Eastern Europe except
Greece. Provisions guaranteeing the independence and democratic nature of the postwar regimes to be set up in Eastern
Europe were left deliberately vague. In effect, therefore, the
Western powers allotted or sold these countries to the Russians; they thought at the time that such a deal was inevitable.

If Stalin was thus given a fairly free hand in transforming
Eastern Europe according to the Soviet image, the local
communist parties were aided by a number of additional
circumstances. Their record in the resistance movements
gave them prestige and a claim to a share in power. The old
ruling classes had been decimated by the occupation or stig-
matized as collaborationists; their parties had dwindled or
were outlawed; their property had been taken over by the
Germans and, after liberation, was often retained by the
new governments as being enemy property. Many people
in Balkanized Eastern Europe, moreover, were weary of
bloody conflict between national minorities, and some of
them may have been impressed with the Soviet solution of
this problem. In some of the Eastern European countries,
finally, age-old feelings of brotherhood for the Russians had
been reawakened and could be exploited by the communists.
There were thus, in spite of widespread hatred or fear of
the Russians or of communism, many factors which predis-
posed many people in this area to accept socialism and collaborate with the communists. Nonetheless, the transformation of Eastern Europe into a set of purely communist regimes had to be done by a combination of stealth and force,
utilizing all the advantages which the communists possessed
by virtue of the Soviet army's presence. The transformation
was, on the whole, well managed and was accomplished in

less than four years. By the spring of 1948, all governments
in Eastern Europe were in essence communist dictatorships.
Although formally these regimes were governed by parties
with a broader following and a more diffuse ideology than
communist parties, for practical purposes these coalition parties were full-fledged communist parties. By means of thorough purges and other less bloody maneuvers, Stalin managed to place every one of these parties under the command
of men absolutely loyal and obedient to him, little Stalins
themselves, who faithfully followed every cue Moscow gave
them and ruthlessly enforced their commands through means
of government tested in the USSR. Party dictatorship, police
terror, forced collectivization, economic centralization, consumer austerity, and the strictest control of all human activities came to characterize the regimes of Eastern Europe,
while, in turn, Moscow maintained its own control over them
by a variety of methods. In the ten years following the end
of World War II, communist government in Eastern Europe
resulted in rapid industrial growth and equally rapid social
dislocation—a scrambling of society which, in the short run,
gave rise to tremendous tensions and dissatisfactions, especially among the urban workers and intellectuals, but which,
in the long run, was doubtless designed to make communist
government more acceptable to these nations. The undeni-
able success of the regimes in transforming their countries
in the Soviet image and raising them to the level of industrial nations was marred, however, by several factors: Soviet economic exploitation robbed them of much of the fruits
of their labor and, in fact, may have retarded industrial development; economic growth was perverted by strong strivings for autarky, which were encouraged by the Kremlin;
and, finally, these strivings for self-sufficiency were part of
a surprising amount of national antagonism between the various Eastern European regimes.

Once again it should be stressed that these regimes did
not conform to the hopes of the native communist leadership and were not really created by them. They were created by the Russians for purely Russian purposes. Their
establishment increased the military, political, and economic

strength of the Soviet Union; and if the interests of the Soviet Union are identified with those of world communism
as a whole, then the entire communist world was strengthened. From the point of view of the countries transformed,
the establishment of these client regimes undoubtedly was
deplorable: if these were revolutions, they were revolutions
gone astray, skewed in their development by outside interference. And, because such imposed regimes, whatever their
achievements, cannot ever govern benignly, one could argue
that the Sovietization of Eastern Europe, on the whole,
served to discredit the communist cause in the eyes of the
world.

Among the communist leaders who acquired power in
Eastern Europe after the war, there were many who, despite
their devotion to the movement and to Soviet Russia as its
center, were hopeful that some of the harshest features of
the Soviet way of life might be avoided in their own countries. The low living standard and the unyielding dictatorship of the communist bosses, the reign of the police and the
general disregard for the happiness of individuals and
groups, the lack of intellectual freedom and the hermetic
isolation of Soviet citizens from the outside world—these
and other features were explained as necessary consequences
of Russia's backwardness. In countries like Czechoslovakia,
Poland, Hungary, and East Germany, where an industrial
base already existed, where the old ruling class had been
wiped out or discredited, and where socialism was generally accepted as inevitable if not desirable, many native
communists sincerely believed that something like a democratic or at least more humane type of communism could
be developed and that the Soviet pattern of development
need not necessarily be followed in all its details. In short, the
Kremlin's effort to force the Eastern European regimes to
adopt Stalinist methods of "building socialism" came into
conflict with the obvious fact that the nations of that area
lived under circumstances differing from those in the USSR.
They lived by different intellectual traditions and on different levels of economic and social development. These differences were acknowledged, at least temporarily, even by

the Kremlin high command and found reflection in various doctrinal adjustments. For instance, the communist regimes of Eastern Europe were not designated as soviet republics and, for the time being, refrained from describing themselves as dictatorships of the proletariat. Instead, they called themselves "people's democracies," and the official explanation of this new term in the communist catechism made clear that the establishment of people's democracies spelled a coalition of parties and classes some of which were still features of the capitalist past; moreover, the fact that the countries of Eastern Europe were not incorporated in the Soviet Union was an explicit concession to the strength of nationalism in that area. Despite such doctrinal adjustments, however, the actual governing of the Eastern European countries was more similar to the Soviet pattern than was acceptable to many of their political leaders, including some communists.

It is ironic that the man who became the spokesman for such protest views was the one Eastern European leader who harbored the greatest reservations about them. Marshal Tito, the ruler of Yugoslavia, was the most loyal Stalinist of all the postwar leaders of Eastern Europe and the least sympathetic to the "revisionist" views of some of his colleagues in neighboring countries. Circumstances, however, caused him to quarrel with his colleagues in Moscow, and when he stood his ground, he unexpectedly found himself labeled a heretic and an outcast from the communist fold, a traitor to the revolution and an agent of imperialism. Once in this position, he was bound, though only very gradually and cautiously, to justify his status ideologically. Consequently, his regime began to express systematically some of the disappointed hopes of Eastern European communists. Moreover, many communists in Western countries seem to have been inspired by the notion of communism without some of the most obnoxious features of Soviet rule—an autonomous, polycentric, humane, perhaps even democratic communism. The stirrings in Eastern Europe and the successful resistance to Moscow of Tito were thus echoed by lively debates and a good deal of soul searching among communists and their sympathizers in Western Europe and North America, who now envisaged a non-Russian alternative to Stalinism.

In Eastern Europe, the yearning for more moderate methods was without doubt based primarily on an awareness of the sharp tensions and dissatisfactions created by communist policies. The aim of the "revisionists" was to ease the tensions and alleviate the dissatisfaction. Very likely the tougher-minded "Stalinists" who won over them temporarily were just as much aware of the underlying difficulties. But, instead of giving way to popular sentiment, they doubtless hoped to overcome these difficulties by suppressing them and thus all the more rapidly transforming society in the communist image. In other words, they were intent upon allaying dissatisfaction and unrest through industrialization and collectivization. Eastern European communism thus found itself engaged in the same great debate which shook the Russian Communist Party during the period of the New Economic Policy.

This time, the conflict was solved, for the time being, with the help of the Kremlin. While it may have seemed implausible at the time to assume that Eastern European revisionist ideas constituted a threat to the Soviet Union, Stalin took vigorous action to suppress all such notions. He may have had any or all of the following reasons for his intolerance. He may have realized more clearly than Western observers that these ideas could produce open rebellions such as those which occurred in Germany, Czechoslovakia, Poland, and Hungary in 1953 and 1956. He may also have worried about the impact which the development of some sort of democratic communism anywhere might have had on his own Russian population: if the Poles and the Czechs had been granted more freedom and a higher standard of living, the Soviet people might have demanded the same. In addition, distrust of autonomy and the urge to control and coordinate is endemic in the communist system of government. It so happened, moreover, that unorthodox ideas of this kind were particularly popular among communists who had fought in resistance movements in their own countries or who had spent the war years in exile in the West. The Russians, apparently, did not trust such communists and sought to replace them by faithful organization men who had spent the war years and perhaps more in the Soviet Union, who may even have weathered the great purges of the 1930's and were known as loyal and safe. The principal reason, however, which compelled Stalin to suppress the revisionists was the fact that he did not care to permit the people of Poland, Czechoslovakia, and other countries possessing an industrial base to benefit from this higher economic development. Instead, he wanted to divert a maximal share of the products of these countries to the USSR, for the sake of reconstructing his own ravaged country and raising the living standard of his own population. This policy implied the drastic imposition of an austerity regime in the Eastern European satellites, together with pressures for harsh work discipline and totalitarian conformity, dashing the hopes for autonomy and democratic communism.

In short, not only were the "revolutions" which brought communism to Eastern Europe contrived by outside intervention; they also did not establish regimes which were able to bring about social reforms appropriate for these countries. Nevertheless, heretical beliefs and hopes never did perish among the communists of Eastern Europe. And in subsequent years, their heresy was to present the Soviet Union with grave political problems, with which we shall deal further below.

Moscow's fight against the heresy of revisionism began in earnest before the defection of Tito (1947), though it became a bloody purge only in subsequent years. The creation of the Communist Information Bureau (Cominform) in 1947 appears to have been a move toward keeping the parties of Eastern Europe and those of France and Italy in line. In other ways, too, Moscow put its foreign comrades on notice that the conflict with the former allies, especially with the United States, had broken into the open. The purge of Earl Browder from leadership of the American Communist Party (he too had advocated a sort of autonomous communism) is as much part of this development as the denunciation of

the Soviet economist Varga, who had attempted to demon-
strate that the American economy would survive the difficulties of converting to peacetime production; or the fight
against "rootless cosmopolitans" among Soviet intellectuals,
who dared to maintain contact with their Western colleagues
or even to acknowledge that Western achievements in science or art merited any attention whatsoever. The cold war
was on in earnest. From the point of view of the communist world—or perhaps one should say from the point of
view of Stalin—it was primarily an anti-American political
operation. America was regarded as the principal troublemaker in world affairs, the heir of imperialism, and the center
of a world-wide conspiracy to involve mankind in a new war.
The capitalists of Wall Street were seen as the wirepullers
making reactionary politicians all over the world dance
obediently. To oppose this conspiracy to dominate or destroy
the world and annihilate the constructive gains of Soviet socialism, Moscow appealed to numerous forces and groups
that might be alarmed into opposing America. In Asia, the
USSR gave open or silent support to communist parties and
military units, such as the armies of Mao Tse-tung, Ho Chi-
minh, and North Korea, and the guerrilla troops of Malaya.
Precisely how much support they received from Moscow is
obscure and has become controversial; it is possible that,
in the heat of the cold war, Western scholars and statesmen
grossly overestimated the help and encouragement Stalin
gave to these and other communist forces in Asia and
grossly misunderstood Soviet spokesmen when they tried to
make their attitude clear. Moscow's caution or even hesitancy
in supporting Asian communism was, indeed, masked by a
great deal of tough talk; yet the tough language was directed
not only against the West, but also against revolutionary
movements in various parts of the world, particularly against
any force not completely subject to Soviet control. Such
revolutionary movements, and all proponents of the idea of
a "third force" standing outside the cold war, were denounced on the principle that "whoever is not uncondition-
ally with us is against us." In effect, this spirit of exclusivism

allowed the Kremlin to sound tough and at the same time keep out of many revolutionary stirrings, whether intentionally or unintentionally is not clear. At the same time, the Soviet Union as well as the entire world communist movement showed themselves very eager to enlist noncommunist support for defensive or diversionary operations, such as the so-called peace campaign and the demand for disarmament, especially in the field of atomic weapons (where the United States, until the early 1950's, still enjoyed a monopoly).[1] In the name of such issues, war-weary people in all countries and from all walks of life were urged to join the protest against atomic armament, the cold war, and American domination in world affairs. Meanwhile, many people in the West watched the ongoing world revolution with concern and regarded it as Moscow-inspired and Moscow-led. Some people tended to make monolithic communism responsible for everything we had not planned, had not foreseen, and did not like. Again, we will not know for a long time how much (if at all) the leadership in Moscow was involved in many of the turbulent events of this period. This applies even to those events most important to the recent history of communism: the victory of the communists in the century-old Chinese revolution, the Korean War, the wars in Malaya and Indochina, and the revolution in Cuba.

The balance sheet of the first seven or eight postwar years shows some spectacular successes and some important failures for communism. In addition to Eastern Europe and North Korea, the whole of continental China had been added to the communist bloc, and the northern half of Vietnam was added some years later. The Korean War, however, had ended in a draw, and in Europe there had been setbacks. The defection of Yugoslavia had created a serious gap in the phalanx of Eastern European satellite governments, the communist parties of Italy and France had been eliminated from the coalition governments they had entered after the war. Berlin remained a Western outpost and a thorn in the flesh of the East German communist rulers. On a world-wide scale, the United States committed herself with some determination to the policy of "holding the line" and organized her allies in a number of defensive blocs that created a ring of military bases around the entire communist world. At least for a short period, the front lines hardened.

Stalin's death in March 1953 brought with it a slight relaxation of tension. The "breaking of the ice" (usually translated as the "thaw") noted by Soviet intellectuals made itself felt also in international affairs: while still stressing the basic incompatibility between capitalist and communist goals and methods, the leaders of the communist world gave new stress to the themes of peaceful coexistence, constructive competition, and an easing of tensions. Within the communist camp, Moscow showed some toleration of revisionist or autonomist heresies in Eastern Europe; in these countries, too, doctrinal discipline was relaxed somewhat, and the Eastern European regimes were allowed to experiment with administrative or economic methods hitherto prohibited. The emergence of a communist China had already made it necessary for Moscow to make allowances for differences in method and ideology, if only by implication; for with Mao Tse-tung and Chou En-lai men had come to power who were the equals, not the subordinates or creatures, of the rulers in Moscow. By 1955, Moscow had extended the principle that socialist development may take different forms to Yugoslavia. The dissolution of the already moribund Cominform in 1956 was merely a symbol of this rapprochement between Moscow and Belgrade.

About the reasons for this relaxation we can only speculate. It may be that Stalin's lieutenants, insecure in their leaderless position, wished to secure the loyalty of their constituents. Some students think they can detect in prerevolutionary Russian history a recurrent pattern of relaxation and concessions after the death of each tsar, and they place the policies following Stalin's death in this pattern. Others argue that the new leaders were so preoccupied with the struggle for power among themselves that they could not exert as tight a control over Soviet society as the late dictator, and that the reimposition of such control had to wait until a new dictator had installed himself. Again, there is some indication that the new leaders had convinced themselves that Stalin's ruthlessness and inflexibility had led to a stalemate, and that the governing of the more mature society which Russia had become called for more enlightened methods. Some Kremlin leaders undoubtedly were swayed by the logic of atomic and nuclear warfare, which demands accommodation and compromise and makes truculence a suicidal attitude. Finally, after Stalin's death the Eastern European regimes began to be troubled by a good deal of restiveness and disorder. Beginning with more and more open expressions of discontent and disillusionment by hitherto loyal communists, this widespread restiveness at times erupted into open uprising—a spontaneous revolt in East Germany in June 1953, which was sparked by a workers' demonstration and had to be put down by Soviet military forces; a serious strike during the same year in Plzeň, Czechoslovakia; the Poznań riots in the summer of 1956 and the general ferment following these disorders; the subsequent defiance shown by the Polish communists to the Soviet emissaries after the reinstatement of the "revisionist" Gomulka as party chief; and, finally, the Hungarian uprising of October 1956. These acts of defiance not only contradicted the conviction current among most scholars that there was no possibility of revolt against communist totalitarianism; they also demonstrated to the Eastern European communists the shakiness of their regimes. For the people who had led all these revolts, at least in the beginnings, had been either workers—the class considered most loyal and reliable by the communists—or Communist Party members and leaders, who had encouraged the expression of criticism and prepared political changes. This certainly was the case in both Poland and Hungary. In both countries the party leadership was openly divided, and the advocates of reform and relaxation defeated the "conservative" Stalinists. In Poland they were able to make their victory stick, win a number of concessions from the Russians, rid themselves of some of the leaders whom Moscow had imposed on them, and institute several reforms in their own country designed to satisfy or appease the peasantry, the Church, small independent businessmen, or the population as a whole. Very

similar measures were begun by the Hungarian regime, but
the reform movement got out of hand and turned into open
revolution, which was then bloodily suppressed by Soviet
troops. Both before and after this dramatic event, almost all
of Eastern Europe's communist regimes, in varying degrees,
relieved their citizens of some of the pressures previously
imposed on them; and the USSR, in turn, appears to have
made economic concessions to its satellites.

While the unrest in Eastern Europe may have been one of
the causes for the post-Stalin relaxation of pressure, the
brutal suppression of the Hungarian uprising seemed to mark
the end of a period of concessions and to usher in a new
period of aggressiveness in domestic and international affairs. Yet, in the long run, domestic and international pressures for relaxation and sweeping reforms turned out to be
stronger, as we shall see. Before turning to them, however,
we must pay some attention to the successes of communist
parties in China and adjoining areas.

The victory of the Chinese Communist Party over the
regime of Chiang Kai-shek in 1949 was the culmination of
revolutionary disturbances that had troubled the vast empire
of China for more than a hundred years, disturbances which
had been provoked by a great variety of problems much too
complex to mention within the framework of this slender
study. The immediate cause of the communist victory was
the collapse of the Kuomintang government, which had become corrupt, ineffective, and unpopular. The communist
revolution took different forms from that of Russia: large
areas of China had for years been under communist rule, so
that in fact two Chinese states existed side by side, each with
its own government and army, at times collaborating with
each other in an uneasy and suspicious coalition against the
Japanese, but on the whole considering each other mortal
enemies. The revolution consisted mainly in the conquest of
the rapidly disintegrating Kuomintang state by the communist armies, the population of the former observing the conquest with hostility, indifference, relief, or enthusiasm. Not
only did the revolution take different forms; because of the

long-protracted civil war, it also was carried out by very different methods: an army led by communist political leaders would secure a base area in the countryside from which it would direct nationwide guerilla operations. Self-contained guerrilla units, obtaining their weapons, supplies, and food primarily from the enemy and from the local village population, would merge imperceptibly with the local population and strike at the government forces at night, from ambush, only to melt away in the day. Loyalty to the revolutionary army would be created by a mixture of terror and reforms, including the distribution of landlords' holdings and the successful elimination of corruption. In time, the entire countryside would be under communist control, first at night, and later also in the daytime; and only in the last phase of the revolutionary war would the operations be extended to the cities as well. These methods are quite different from those employed by the Russian bolsheviks, and imposed on all communist parties by the Third International. This is the strategy of Maoism; and Moscow never approved of it. From the point of view of the Russian communists, this was a travesty on Marxism and Leninism; and it is indeed questionable whether it has very much in common with the thinking and the plans of Marx or Engels. Yet it was successful in China, and it has been tried since, with varying degrees of success, by communist-led movements in other parts of Asia, and also, in fact, by noncommunist rebels, such as the Cuban guerrilla forces led by Fidel Castro. For revolutionary movements in underdeveloped countries throughout the world, Mao's methods have become the focus of considerable interest.

Once in control of the vast Chinese subcontinent, the government of the newly established People's Republic of China quickly organized itself on lines similar to the Soviet state and instituted sweeping social changes designed to weaken or destroy big capitalism, both domestic and foreign, and landlord control. By these measures the regime tried to attract mass support among workers, peasants, and intellectuals, establish firm control over the economy, destroy hostile classes, emancipate the economy from foreign control and ownership, and try to rehabilitate a productive system gutted by years of occupation and war.

At the same time, some of the methods of the Chinese Communist Party were quite different from those applied in Russia. The chief difference at first was the party's attempt to collaborate with elements of the former ruling classes, thus to mitigate class warfare and to eradicate capitalism by nonviolent methods. In order to rationalize these differences, Chinese communists had to redefine the concept of the dictatorship of the proletariat and the idea of the best road toward socialism. These unorthodox innovations were, willy-nilly, tolerated even by Stalin.

By 1953, the government of Mao Tse-tung was sufficiently confident to launch its first five-year plan, which was to carry the economic transformation of the country a significant step further. While the first years of communist rule had eliminated landlords and absentee capitalists, the first five-year plan was to prepare the way for the collectivization of agriculture and the total socialization of industry and handicraft. China thus tried to copy the rapid transformations undergone by the Soviet economy, but in far less time, even though the base from which China started was infinitely more backward than the Russian economy of 1917. The Chinese leaders claimed that this faster rate of revolutionary transformation was made possible by generous Soviet aid and by the more advanced state of modern technology. By the fall of 1956, the outlines of the second five-year plan began to take shape. It was formally adopted in early 1957 and began to be implemented in 1958. Its goal was to drive the Chinese economy and society into the "Great Leap Forward" to industrialism and socialism. Production goals were set which seemed fantastically high to Western economists, and some of which did in fact prove to be unrealistic. Methods of organization and management were applied which in centralization and unyielding collectivism outstripped anything that had been undertaken by Soviet society; and the Mao regime even claimed that China might virtually skip some of the stages of development which had marked the history of the USSR. The most spectacular of these social experiments was the transformation of agriculture from an individual peasant system to a thoroughly collective system and the concomitant merger of agricultural pursuit with industrial construction. Unlike the Soviet *kolkhoz,* the Chinese commune makes not the slightest concessions to individualism or to family traditions. Instead, it is an attempt to apply the organizational form of the labor gang or the drill platoon not only to farming operations, large-scale construction work, and other primary economic pursuits but also to all possible human activities, including housing, feeding, education, and recreation. Here was the utter militarization of life in the intensity demanded for the working class in Plato's utopia. Vast masses of people organized into disciplined labor armies were deployed in building dams and other waterworks, roads, railroads, and entire industrial enterprises, so that the Chinese people seem to be building much of their new industrial base in bucket-brigade fashion, with legions of unskilled manual labor. These people's communes were to combine all administrative and economic functions; and the party therefore claimed that they were leading directly to the withering away of the state. More generally, Mao and his comrades asserted that the Great Leap Forward and the establishment of people's communes should be regarded as a direct step into communism; and one implication was that China might reach that happy stage before the USSR.

Today, the Great Leap Forward is generally assessed as having been a failure. For several years after initiation of the plan, China's economic goals were revised downward—an obvious admission that they had been unrealistic. In addition, some of the most drastic features of communal life in the people's communes were mitigated. It is now apparent that the Chinese economy faces seemingly unsurmountable difficulties. Although some significant advances have been made, and although China has managed to join the ranks of the nuclear powers, at the time of this writing China is in a state of acute crisis—economic and hence, also political. The outward manifestation of this crisis is the so-called "Cultural Revolution," which might be described as a violent nationwide debate within the ruling elite over the path that the Chinese Revolution is to take henceforth. We shall come back to the Cultural Revolution in Chapter 11.

11

Contemporary Communism: Unity and Diversity

• If the word "communism" ever had a precise meaning (and it probably never did), it is rapidly becoming meaningless because it connotes too many different things. Within the last decade, diversity, disunity, and fast-growing mutual hostility have come to characterize the communist world. Only a few years ago, the popular image of communism prevailing in the Western world was that of an undifferentiated, unified bloc. The stereotype used to describe communism was a well defined and uniform monolith. Communist ideology was regarded by many as an elaborate matrix of ideas, a sharply outlined political blueprint, a firm operational code yielding school solutions to all those initiated in it. Even today, many people still speak of it as a master plan for world domination executed by an elite of diabolically cunning intelligence; they think of all communist policies as flowing directly from this operational code and therefore as consistent and unambiguous.

These images and stereotypes are now widely recognized as false. Communism means a wide range of social systems, political institutions, economic policies, revolutionary strategies, and ideological outlooks. In each of these areas of life and thought there is growing diversity and increasingly bitter conflict. Hence there are now different schools of communism; and, as we get attuned to the differences between these various schools, we may also begin to notice the similarities between some of them and various noncommunist societies, political movements, or ideologies. Communism must today be studied on a comparative basis, meaning, first, that different communist schools and systems must be compared and contrasted with each other, and, second, that the study of communist systems must be more fully integrated with the study of comparable noncommunist systems and ways of life.

The onset of this disintegration process need not have astonished any knowledgeable student of communism in any part of the world. But its speed and its impact have taken most people by surprise. What accounts for this quick development of differences and hostilities among the adherents of Marxism-Leninism?

A number of factors can be adduced as partial answers to this question. One of them is the so-called de-Stalinization, the attempt made by Soviet leaders since 1953 to dissociate themselves from some of the worst crimes, cruelties, and crudities of Stalin's rule by subjecting his policies, views, and personality to criticism, sometimes sharp, sometimes guarded. Even without troubling to list the milestones in this continuing effort to redefine Stalin's place in history, we can measure the devastating effect this criticism has had in destroying the unity of the communist world: if Stalin was fallible after all, the status of the Communist Party of the Soviet Union as the undisputed leader of the communist world could no longer be maintained. Communist parties would henceforth speak to each other a little more on the basis of equality and mutual accommodation.

As a result, other factors producing disunity came to the fore with renewed vigor. One of them was the strong pressure within communist societies outside the USSR to "go their own way" toward socialism, that is, to pursue policies and fashion institutions more in tune with the social systems and the cultural traditions of their respective countries and more closely responding to their national interests than the carbon copy regimes imposed upon them in the "contrived" revolutions which Stalin and his Soviet bureaucrats had engineered in Eastern Europe. With Stalin gone and his very image tarnished, communist states felt freer to begin solving their own problems without feeling apologetic, without facing the charge that they were heretics within the communist camp.

Similarly, communist parties not in power have shown increasing tendencies to resent the overcentralized direction given by Moscow under Stalin and to defy the global party line he imposed, according to which communists everywhere had to interpret current affairs in uniform fashion and to pursue uniform policies. Recognizing that such centralization and uniformity are suicidal, communist parties everywhere have striven to adjust their views and policies to conform to the political environment within which they operate. Communist parties tried to become integrated in national patterns of politics; this alone could assure them at least some successes, but it leads to the development of differences between them.

The process is slow and proceeds at uneven rates. In most communist parties, it is a matter of bitter controversy, which is yet another factor of disunity and diversity. Controversy, once considered intolerable and unthinkable in communist parties, has now become the rule rather than the exception. In many countries it takes the form of two or more parties, all claiming to pursue the true Marxist-Leninist path, existing side by side in sharp competition with each other, and differing markedly in their views and policies. The reason for the controversies and splits is not only the disappearance of Stalin, who acted something like an acknowledged pope of communism; even more so it is the open enmity that has broken out between the two major communist powers, the USSR and China. (I shall discuss some of the main reasons for this hostility later in this chapter.) There are now two major centers of communist rule, plus some minor ones. Throughout the world, these two centers compete for the allegiance of communists and seek to compel them to choose sides. Disagreement and discussion have thus been forced on communist parties everywhere, at least

on those not in power, but on most others as well, albeit in
more hidden form. Since knowledge and insight have a
better chance of emerging from discussion than from enforced unanimity, as disagreement forces people to think,
the long-range result of the enmity between Peking and
Moscow may be an intellectual or ideological reinvigoration
of communism in many parts of the world.

In stressing the irretrievable destruction of the unity of the
communist world, I do not, of course, wish to deny that all
communists, whatever their denomination, have some things
in common. They share one Holy Writ and one set of founding fathers—Marx, Engels, and Lenin—although they interpret them differently and fight over who should be included among the most loyal disciples. They are tied
together by shared traditions, shared experiences, a shared
vocabulary, and shared views on certain fundamental things
concerning the nature of the contemporary world. They all
see the world in terms of Lenin's theory of imperialism.
They all agree in identifying the United States as the major
imperialist power, heading a bloc of capitalist states that,
allied with the most reactionary tyrants in underdeveloped
countries, are fighting, with the utmost ruthlessness, a desperate rear guard action to preserve their political and economic investments in dependent areas against the onslaught
of native democracy. They all believe that in order to divert
the people's attention from capitalist misrule and exploitation, the imperialists without cease use their favorite device,
that of slandering communism and blaming it for all evils in
the world. Under the pretext of being threatened by communism, the imperialists, or the warmongers among them, are
preparing for war against the socialist countries, mobilizing
their populations, and perverting bourgeois democracy into
the open dictatorship of the garrison state. Meanwhile, out
of selfish commercial and evil political motives, the cultural
heritage of the West has been squandered, yielding to the
barbarism of nonobjective painting, Coca-Cola, and rock-
and-roll, to the reign of gangsters and the preoccupation
with sex. This, in brief, would be a summary of the way in

which communists everywhere would tend to describe the Western world.

If these views were the only bond between all communists, however, the bond would not be strong. For there are millions of people outside the communist camp who hold similar opinions; and within the communist world there are sharp conflicts over the details of this image, as well as over the practical implications. One of these conflicts concerns the aggressiveness of the imperialist world; related to it are discussions about the possibility of peaceful coexistence, the nature of the noncommitted countries, and numerous other matters.

As for the imperialist powers, communists take their aggressiveness and viciousness for granted, on the basis of both experience and doctrine. More generally, communists since Lenin have assumed the inevitability of world wars, as long as capitalism was not destroyed or weakened significantly. Again, this is based on the more general conviction that rival social systems cannot exist side by side for long periods without one destroying the other, and that no basic political problems are ever solved without the application of violence. In recent years, however, these doctrines have been challenged seriously, against stiff opposition from the more doctrinaire or radical quarters. Communist leaders in Russia, Poland, Yugoslavia and other countries have pointed out that the capitalist world is no monolithic bloc, but is rent by disputes and dissent, one of the issues being the widespread yearning for peace. High-ranking communist statesmen have asserted that among the leaders of the imperialist world there are reasonable people with whom one can negotiate and discover matters of common interest. Since about 1960, Soviet leaders have renounced the Leninist doctrine that war is inevitable. They now assert that they can curb imperialist aggression by their nuclear deterrent and that therefore war can be prevented. Moreover, they claim that war *must* be prevented, because they recognize it as unmitigated disaster. The nuclear bomb, they say, does not distinguish between capitalists and socialists, but wipes them all out. Even limited wars, they claim, should be prevented, because they are likely to turn into major ones. In short, the policy announced by the USSR now holds that there is no alternative to peace. Meanwhile other communist leaders have gone further by deploring the cold war, working toward bilateral disengagement, or even moving toward a position of neutrality in the cold war. All of these efforts to work for coexistence as a permanent state are, in turn, roundly opposed by communist leaders in China and her clients among communist nations or communist parties. They insist on upholding Lenin's doctrine that war is inevitable and that lasting coexistence means betraying the cause of the revolution. From the point of view of revolutionary Marxism-Leninism, Mao Tse-tung and his friends may well be right. The coexistence policy advanced by their antagonists is based on the argument that the communist camp can now relax a bit because the enemy is licked sufficiently and can now be contained. It happens that this is the position adopted by the Russian mensheviks vis-à-vis tsarist autocracy after the revolution of 1905. Russian (not to mention Yugoslav, Polish, or Hungarian) communism has thus become the heir of the mensheviks and is fought by Mao and his friends with the same arguments Lenin used fifty years ago. The one faction stresses lasting coexistence and the inevitability of gradual gains, the other insists on the continuation of the class struggle in its sharpest form and on a global scale.

The positions taken by the various protagonists in this running debate are obscured by a deliberately confusing vocabulary, in which peace is declared to be a form of warfare, and political-economic coexistence is declared to have no bearing on the fact that "ideologically we will never coexist." It is obvious that the "doves" in the communist world are hard-pressed for arguments to prove that they have not given up their basic aim of creating a world-wide communist commonwealth. The "doves" in all political systems tend to be on the defensive, because their antagonists, and perhaps their own consciences as well, tend to impugn their political loyalty. Hence they must conceal their peaceful policies behind warlike rhetoric. Or, as the "hawks" would say, they must detract from their cowardice and treason by promising easy successes through cautious behavior.

The success promised by the "doves" of communism, indeed, may not be easy, but they do promise it. Against the Maoist insistence that violence alone decides the most important political questions, the European branch of communism (if by this term we can lump together opinions now prevailing in the communist parties of Italy, Finland, Yugoslavia, Poland, and the USSR, to name only a few) maintains that communism can be brought about in many parts of the world without open revolutionary struggle. Again, the arguments of the two extremes remind us of the ancient debates between mensheviks and bolsheviks, or between social democrats and communists.

The commitment to (relatively) peaceful politics within the framework of democratic constitutions or the given political system in general is particularly strong in some of the communist parties of Western Europe and North America. The tendency can be explained by divergent causes. In the Anglo-Saxon countries, it probably reflects the despair of the leadership over the failure of their parties to make any impact whatever on the existing systems. These parties are small, insignificant, and impotent little sects; and some of their leaders appear to think that they might have a chance to become more than that if they change their ideology and policies to conform more to their environment. In countries like Italy, Finland, and France, on the other hand, the urge to adjust to the prevailing system may be due to the success these parties have had; in these countries they are relatively strong. They manage to hold on to a significant portion of the electorate. They have at times participated in government coalitions or may expect to be asked to do so in the near future. They have, moreover, tasted the fruits of many lesser offices. These parties have therefore moved in the direction of becoming patronage parties interested, among other things, in the immediate benefits of political office for their functionaries. Their mass strength, typically, is rooted in part of the trade-union movement. But this, together with the experience of holding local and regional political offices, has given these parties a preoccupation with bread-and-butter questions which Lenin condemned as "trade-unionist." In addition, the communists have to compete with other socialist parties for the allegiance of workers, school teachers, farmers, and other voters; and this competition has tended to drive them further and further to the right in their policy statements.

These Western communist parties, in short, concentrate on issues and goals that have little to do with communism. They are thus being assimilated to the domestic political scene, being tamed and absorbed. They fight within the present social and economic system, not against it. Typically, they try hard to identify themselves with national revolutionary traditions, with the national political and ideological heritage; their spokesmen are beginning to sound like old nineteenth-century radicals, or, in the United States, like spokesmen of the New Deal. To be sure, they roundly criticize the existing regimes and predict their overthrow either by proletarian revolutions or by defeat in elections. They receive the votes of citizens who feel they are getting an unfair deal and want to protest against the established order. Communist parties of the Italian type have become protest parties, but this very function militates against revolution. By protesting, by threatening with the doom of revolution, they obviate the necessity of seriously preparing such a revolution. Being the permanent opposition, they only perpetuate the permanent disfranchisement of the workers and the poor peasants, a political relationship which in countries like France and Italy has itself become traditional. In most cases, the communist parties of Europe have become the heirs or successors of the once powerful (and yet ineffectual) social-democratic movement, which by now is a shadow of its former self. Their avowed policy is to defend the exploited, to save democracy, and to prevent a third world war—a clear commitment to a "menshevik" minimum program. Their method is the United Front with other left-of-center groups, an alliance which in reality is impossible as long as the political system functions tolerably well, and unnecessary when it does not. Besides this, the communist parties have the eternal function of acting as shield, salesman, and possibly intelligence agent of Soviet Russia and other communist states; and where there are other socialist parties, the communists cannot be distinguished from them by greater revolutionary fervor but only by their unquestioning loyalty to the USSR or their more rigid, jargonlike vocabulary. Even this loyalty has now become shaky. Since Moscow is no longer the unchallenged headquarters of world communism, Western communist parties have quietly or openly espoused the principle of polycentrism, of which one implication is that the interests of any one socialist country are not necessarily identical with the interests of the proletarian movement everywhere. Still, communists, even of the Italian type, tend to feel a residue of political kinship with all countries ruled by communist parties. For this reason, crises in the entire movement are often provoked by unpopular or embarrassing action taken by Moscow or other leading countries of the socialist bloc, such as the armed intervention in Hungary in 1956.

The trade-unionist character of the Western communist parties not only implies a conflict between theory and practice; it also spells a profound difference in the personnel and following of various communist parties. And yet, the difference between the Italian and the Czech communist, to name two at random, would be even greater if the Italian party were truly radical and revolutionary, if its goal were the liberation of the workers rather than their better accommodation within the existing system. For were radical criticism and the idea of liberty alive in the Western communist parties, it would be difficult for their followers to identify their fate with that of the Soviet Union to the extent they have done in the past. Conversely, it is precisely because they learned to be subservient to Moscow that the Western communist leaders could accommodate themselves to the opportunism and trade unionism, the patronage seeking and lack of radicalism they have shown since the war.

Indeed, the really profound difference is not between an

Italian and a Czech communist, but between both of these on the one hand and the revolutionary communist of the Maoist type on the other. Whereas the European communist seems to be striving for a share in the power wielded by the bourgeoisie, the Maoist seems more interested in destroying that power. While the former expresses a desire to perfect constitutional democracy because he hopes this will benefit the party of the poor, the latter has faith only in the force of arms. The former strives to be a party politician; the latter, a guerrilla commander. The politician may secretly or openly sympathize with the guerrilla and may tell himself that, in some primitive countries, he too would go into the hills or the jungle to join communist partisans. But the only feelings which the guerrilla leader can have for the political tactician are envy and contempt. The difference between the two types of communists, therefore, is as deep as that between the NAACP and the Black Nationalists, to give the American reader a familiar example; and these are fundamental differences indeed. Despite their common allegiance to the doctrines of Marxism-Leninism, they are worlds apart because their interpretation of these doctrines ranges from the antirevolutionary menshevism of a Togliatti to the Maoist insistence on civil war as the only means of coming to power.

The precise position of any one leader within the range of opinions is not always easy to define. For instance, the Communist Party of Indonesia, before it was exterminated in 1966, cast its lot with the Chinese; yet in practice it seemed content to play a weak auxiliary role of support within a coalition regime. Many other parties are deeply split; in some countries two or more communist parties fight each other; and not all of them will call themselves communist parties, because in some cases that name appears preempted by one of the contending factions. More confusing yet, the Maoist strategy and views are shared by some parties, movements, or individuals that do not even claim to be orthodox Marxist-Leninists. For instance, Fidel Castro and his partisans came to power in Cuba by pursuing revolutionary tactics very similar to those employed by the Chinese,

Malayan, Philippine, and Vietnamese communist movements. Yet he did not at that time call himself either a communist or a Marxist, and the Cuban Communist Party, as well as the labor unions allied with it, did not support him. Similarly, the late Franz Fanon, whose *The Wretched of the Earth* is one of the ablest and most militant manifestoes of a bloody rebellion against imperialism, is customarily regarded as a spokesman of African nationalism rather than of communism of the Maoist school. Yet with some changes in terminology his program could easily be reconciled with that of Chinese communism.

Disagreements among communists over the nature of the contemporary world and over the best method of coming to power are related to equally sharp controversies, theoretical and practical, about the nature of the socialist states already established. Is there a "proper" road to socialism? If so, who is treading it—Russia, China, Yugoslavia, Cuba? If there are several roads, are there any essential features all communist systems should have in common? Are there limits to polycentrism? Is there anything that can or ought to be done to halt or slow down the inevitable process making communist systems more and more different from, and strangers to, each other?

The old Stalinist pattern was to enforce uniformity of methods, institutions, and doctrines throughout the socialist camp. Stalin's aim, as indicated above, was to suppress Eastern European communists who demanded the right to travel their own road toward socialism. Today, this effort has broken down, and a number of different types of communist governments have come to coexist. Let us briefly survey the Yugoslav, the Polish, and the Chinese variants, with some general observations about other Eastern European regimes. We shall begin with Yugoslavia.

Titoism can be reduced to a few simple formulas. It contains, first of all, the insistence that every country must go its own way toward socialism, the belief that local conditions and customs must be taken into consideration in mapping communist strategy both before and after the assumption of power. With this demand for an autonomous communism,

Tito, consciously or not, went back to ideas advanced in the 1920's by Bukharin, who, in turn, tried to justify them by reference to some of Lenin's ideas. The implication is that communist policies should be free from rigid coordination by Moscow. From this, Titoism developed the idea that in foreign policy as well a communist country should pursue its own aims rather than act as a Soviet satellite. In the beginning, the assumption was that, however independent of Moscow it might be, Yugoslav foreign policy should not be directed against the USSR. The autonomists assumed a compatibility of the interests of all socialist states. Immediately after the war, many Eastern European communist leaders seem to have felt likewise; the independent foreign-policy schemes of Dimitrov in Bulgaria, or the conflicts between the German Democratic Republic, on the one hand, and Poland and Czechoslovakia, on the other, could not otherwise be explained or justified. From this, however, it is only a small step to neutralism; and both Tito and his more orthodox colleagues in other Eastern European countries have at times declared themselves uninterested in the conflict between the USSR and the Western powers. The Yugoslav communists have wavered on this. At the time of writing, they are committed to a neutralist position, sometimes referred to as "national communism." At the time of the Hungarian uprising of 1956, they supported the Soviet intervention on the ground that socialism had to be saved from counterrevolution, thus indicating that, in a pinch, they could make only one choice between Soviet domination and the abandonment of socialism.

Titoism, furthermore, turned its attention to the Soviet Union and criticized Soviet communism as a perversion or distortion of the founding father's (Lenin's) intentions. Here Tito and his followers went back to the view first expressed by Trotsky that the Russian Revolution had gone wrong by producing a top-heavy bureaucratic machine, the members of which had turned into a privileged, exploitative ruling class running the Soviet state for its own interests and betraying the interests of the workers, Russian as well as foreign. Like Trotsky, Tito and his spokesmen explained this perversion by the fact that the revolution was victorious in a backward country which was not ripe for socialism. At the same time, having been a faithful product of the Stalinist system himself, Tito for many years was obviously reluctant to dwell on this theme but was compelled to do so by the logic of the position in which he had been placed. His reluctance becomes all the more meaningful when we realize that some of his closest associates later turned these same criticisms against his own regime.

Finally, Titoism developed social-democratic tendencies, implying that in Eastern Europe socialism could be constructed in a more democratic and more humane manner, through a regime which would give greater opportunities for meaningful participation and greater material benefits to the people. The Yugoslav communists have extended ownership and limited managerial authority to workers' councils and have decentralized economic planning and management. They have decollectivized agriculture and tried to raise productivity by giving incentives and encouraging cooperative ventures. They have revised the criminal code and written a constitution which diverges from the pattern of the Eastern European regimes. With increasing boldness, they have made efforts to democratize the entire political machinery of the nation. In 1966, they began to place serious limitations on the powers of the political police. In the same year, they signed an agreement with the Vatican ending more than two decades of conflict with the Catholic Church. Finally, they have even denied the necessity for a Communist Party and have changed not only its name but also its status and functions within the political system. In short, Yugoslavia under the communist regime, especially in the last few years, has made serious attempts to establish a democratic form of communism, and it has gone much further in this direction than any other communist regime so far. Denison Rusinow, an American scholar with long experience in Yugoslavia, goes so far as to call its system "laissez-faire communism."

Other Eastern European countries under communist rule have not gone as far as Yugoslavia in repudiating the Soviet model; but a good deal of diversity has nonetheless developed. The ebb and flow of these changes is much too complicated to be summarized here. But we have already seen that the imposition of Stalinist uniformity on the Eastern European allies created difficulties and that after Stalin's death there was a growing trend toward allowing room for variation of methods and institutions, as long, at least, as the Soviet bloc could be kept intact. These trends toward diversity were given a boost by the denunciation of Stalin which Khrushchev made in February 1956 at the Twentieth Congress of the Communist Party of the Soviet Union. This de-Stalinization, of which the famous speech was only the culmination, not only raised painful ideological questions of how to explain Stalin's excesses and how to make sure such abuses would not be repeated; it also led to the repudiation of the great purges of the 1930's and the rehabilitation of many men who had been cast out then and later. The revision of both theory and practice was further promoted by internal unrest and, in Poland, by sensational revelations of a former police officer, J. Swiatlo. By 1956, the communist parties of Hungary and Poland were in acute crises, as orthodox Stalinists fought bitterly against reformers, with rank-and-file communists as well as other citizens pressing for even further concessions, and the military supporting the forces of reform. In Hungary, this crisis brought to power a reformist communist, Imre Nagy, who went furthest in putting the domestic interests of his regime above the imperatives of Soviet policy. The reforms turned into a revolt against Soviet domination, which was crushed by Soviet troops.

In Poland, the victory of the reformists over the conservative Stalinist faction brought significant changes, some of which have endured. The first wave of revolt against the old methods of government brought with it sweeping reforms: the removal of Soviet military advisors; a broad amnesty for political prisoners, and the curbing of the police; the rehabilitation of civil servants who had been dismissed; the cessation of the jamming of Western broadcasts; limited debate in the national parliament (*Sejm*); and a curious alliance between the Communist Party and the Catholic Church. In the economic life of the country, the reforms made an end of collectivization and brought some decentralization of economic planning and management. Workers' councils were given some recognition, and the workers for a while were even given the right to strike. In the fields of trade and craft and light industry, private enterprise was permitted to reestablish itself; and the regime accepted credits granted by Western governments. In the field of culture and intellectual activities, there was a spontaneous growth of independent clubs, discussion circles, newspapers, and journals; free speech and free criticism, even of political affairs, flourished for a while; the universities were given a great deal of self-government, and in some fields thoroughly un-Marxist opinions were once again discussed; contacts with the West were established with a good deal of enthusiasm; and even the Church was readmitted to the schools for the purpose of giving religious instruction.

Since this first outburst of noncommunist activities and opinions, the party under Gomulka's leadership has steered a cautious and wavering course between the extremes of total indoctrination or control and total permissiveness. Many times the party has reimposed curbs on intellectual discussions and organizations, and in other matters as well, the Stalinist pattern of life, which never fully took hold, is still asserting itself against the urge for its complete abolition. Slow, gradual moves have been made to return centralization to the economy and to curb workers' control. The relationship between the party and the Church has at times been more problematic than in 1957. At the same time, collectivization has not been pressed on the peasantry. Free enterprise is still tolerated in trade and crafts, although perhaps only grudgingly. In local government, a good deal of autonomy still exists, and the citizens' participation has not been robbed of all meaning. Noncommunist parties still have their representatives in the *Sejm*, and this national parliament is not altogether a rubber stamp. Its committees do some meaningful work; and even the right of interpellation remains. The Polish press, although more controlled by the party than in

1956, for several years was livelier and less dogmatic than the press in other communist countries; in the universities, the social sciences are still pursuing inquiries that would be altogether impossible if the party enforced its orthodoxies. Within the party, revisionist critics may be removed from office or they may even be permitted to resign from the party, but they have not, as a rule, been jailed or transformed into social pariahs. In fact, pluralistic tendencies are quite obvious within the party itself. Lest the picture presented here appear too rosy, let me add that the party nonetheless asserts its control, that censorship continues to function, and that assertions of intellectual independence or deviancy are made with great caution.

Until a few years ago, even this cautious liberalism made Poland appear as a maverick within the socialist camp. Today this is no longer true, because in very recent years similar tendencies have made themselves felt in Hungary, Czechoslovakia, and the German Democratic Republic, so much so that despite the defeat of the 1956 uprising, Hungary today may be less "Stalinist," less rigid, less authoritarian, and more liberal than any other communist regime except Yugoslavia. But bold reforms have also been begun in Czechoslovakia and the German Democratic Republic. Whichever country may be in the lead in the process of liberalization, it is clear that it is not Poland; the Poles have by now been left far behind. The whole picture is complicated when an international dimension is added: I am thinking of the difficulties of generalizing about the case of Rumania, a communist regime which is, on the whole, less "revisionist" in its policies than some of its neighbors, but which is economically independent enough to defy the Soviet Union, playing a role within the East European alliance which one might call Gaullist.

Throughout the European communist countries, Albania excepted but the Soviet Union included, three distinct currents of doctrine and practice have developed. There is a dogmatic wing sometimes called "left," sometimes "conservative," whose leaders are suspicious or fearful of even the slightest deviations from established (Stalinist) patterns.

Against them stand "revisionists" or reformers who plead for what might be called a more liberal course in domestic as well as foreign policy. Finally, there are those who play the role of mediators between the two extremes, supporting sometimes one, sometimes the other side. These various groups, it seems, are now present within almost every Communist Party and government. They may represent, alternately, the faction in power or the opposition. It is therefore impossible to place any one of the communist regimes clearly in one or the other of these rather vague categories. The trend seems to favor the reformers, despite the serious setbacks they have suffered. One thing only is clear: endeavors to preserve uniformity within the bloc are a thing of the past. This becomes all the clearer when we realize that even before Stalin's death these endeavors had been frustrated by the success of the Chinese communists, who completed their conquest of the Chinese mainland in 1950.

To generalize about the nature of the regime in the People's Republic of China in a short space is a reckless undertaking, all the more so because of the scarcity of reliable information available to us. Of all the communist states existing today, China is the least accessible to Western scholarship, and only partly because we have deliberately denied ourselves access to it. Because of the resulting scarcity of hard and fast information, we are tempted to speculate about the meaning of obscure and chaotic happenings. We engage in this speculation with the help of theories and models the validity of which is not subject to easy verification. One such model all too readily suggests itself: It is to draw analogies between developments in China and the past history of older communist states, especially the Soviet Union. I, for one, suspect that, in the final analysis, the differences between these two societies will be considered more important than the similarities.

Still, similarities undeniably do exist. Today, almost a decade since the abortive Great Leap Forward, Chinese communism still bears strong resemblance to the Soviet way of life of the early 1930's—the period of the first and second five-year plans, when the USSR had not yet settled in its comparatively stable Stalinist mold, but was still engaged in the most primitive accumulation of an industrial base. This phase was marked by a crusading militancy stressing the class war character of all social change. The party in this period sought to mobilize the masses by relying exclusively on terror and indoctrination. Force and fear, faith and enthusiasm, were the predominant motives of cooperation, whereas consumption patterns were marked by stark austerity. All material rewards were to be postponed to another day, when the country might afford its citizens the benefits of industrialization. In Russia, the party became convinced fairly soon that terror and indoctrination must be supplemented by material incentives through a system of rewards; and managed inequality became a central feature of mature Stalinism. The Chinese party, however, has apparently been eager to try mobilizing its citizens without the use of mass terror. The police state methods we tend to associate with the Stalinist style of government have not been nearly so prominent in Mao's rule. The Chinese party has shown itself to be even more reluctant to cater to material wants. It has made consistent efforts to preserve at least the appearance of general equality in living standards and seems very eager to resist all trends toward social stratification. Furthermore, Mao and some of his leaders apparently wish to prevent the growth of bureaucratic patterns of management. On all these counts, the Communist Party of China appears to be in the hands of doctrinal purists, who may have learned the lessons offered them by the experience of Soviet society. Their pronouncements often have a decidedly Trotskyite flavor, and quite logically so; for Trotsky, after all, was the inspirer of the crash program of industrialization with all of its hardships, and at the same time was the sharpest critic of the bureaucratic and stratified society that emerged in the mid-1930's.

Nevertheless, Western observers have for some years noted a countervailing trend: Despite their manifest reluctance to do so, the Chinese rulers, too, employ material incentives; some of their economic planners think in terms of the "rationality" familiar to their colleagues in other countries, and the bureaucratization of the society seems to be developing apace. Just as I like to compare the Soviet Union to a giant Western corporation, so a recent book on China systematically compares that country to General Motors and describes its party as a managerial system, notwithstanding its reluctance to fall into the routines of the classical "Weberian" model.[1] Western observers seem agreed in regarding the fantastic upheavals of the current "cultural revolution" as a manifestation of the conflict between these two tendencies. In other words, the question behind the struggles going on in China is whether industrial growth and general modernization can be achieved with enthusiasm alone or whether it requires bureaucratic management and the use of material incentives. For China, this is a most decisive crossroads; hence the bitterness of this conflict in which behavior patterns have manifested themselves which remind the scholar of the period of the great purges in the Soviet Union. However, that analogy, too, should be used only with the utmost caution.

With regard to world affairs, another comparison between Soviet Russia and the Chinese People's Republic suggests itself: Just as the USSR, between 1928 and 1933, indulged in a noisy rhetoric of the most unyielding militancy, so the Chinese, at the present time, spout words of revolutionary fire. In a previous chapter, I have asserted that in the Soviet case this rhetoric was a mask for both weakness and isolationism. It may also have been a public relations device with which to whip up popular alarm and enthusiasm and thus mobilize the masses for work. The fiery revolutionary talk of the early 1930's was not, however, supported by any meaningful action. Under the cloak of sharp but empty radicalism, the USSR continued to strive for mutually fruitful dealings with the capitalist world. Whether this strange contrast between words and deeds holds true also for China today is one of the most controversial of questions. The answer must, at least in part, be based on an assessment of the capabilities which China and the radical revolutionary movements throughout the world have today. Here one might argue that in comparison to the capitalist world contemporary China is even weaker than Soviet Russia was in 1930. At the same time, the global revolution of the late 1960's might be considered a more explosive force than the depression-ridden world of a generation ago, although historians might disagree with this statement. Prospects for revolutions today might be more propitious, among other things, because the heavy hand of the Comintern no longer lies on revolutionary movements to wreck their chances. On the other hand, the 1930's did not produce a global conservative power seeking to suppress revolutionary stirrings wherever they might occur, unless one considers the Third Reich a weak and abortive precursor of the United States in this respect.

One factor that does not fit into the comparison at all, and that has given novelty to the situation, is the hostility between China and the Soviet Union, a relationship in which their respective allies are, somehow, also caught. The two major communist powers are intensely nationalistic and are prone to identifying their own national interests with the assumed interest of world communism as a whole. They share a border thousands of miles long that is ill defined and was therefore bound to become the object of serious disputes. As for the Chinese communists, they doubtless have long and painful memories of insults, slights, and betrayals by their comrades in Moscow. Relations between the two parties have never been very happy; and in a number of crucial situations the leaders of the Soviet party have forced down their Chinese colleagues' throats policies which have had disastrous consequences. In times of momentous decisions, the Russian party has often dragged its feet. In short, feelings among the Chinese communists toward the party in the USSR must at best have been mixed. When Stalin died, it was natural for the Chinese to consider themselves the senior party in the communist world. But their assertions of independence and leadership were answered by sanctions, the most serious being the abrupt, and economically disastrous, withdrawal of Soviet economic aid.

On the Russian side, and among the communist leaders of Eastern Europe, some apprehensiveness seems to have developed, at the time of the Great Leap Forward, over the growth of a competitor of foreign race with an overwhelming reservoir of manpower, who operated by crude and harsh methods with which European and Russian communists no longer felt comfortable, to say the least. The result of these tensions has been open hostility between the two major communist powers.

Only a few years ago, most Western scholars still tended to maintain that, for the time being at least, the bonds of mutual interest tying the Russian and Chinese regimes together were stronger than the issues of controversy. Since then, the break has been revealed to be sharp; and today it seems irreconcilable. It came into the open at the Twenty-second Congress of the CPSU, meeting in Moscow in the fall of 1961, and has since taken the chronic form of a mutual campaign of vilification and denunciation. By now, the Chinese party defines the imperialist camp as consisting primarily of the United States and the Soviet Union. Nothing could symbolize the antagonism more dramatically.

The world of communist states thus is divided today into different types of regimes—European and Asian, industrial and pre-industrial, reasonably affluent and hungry; even perhaps conservative and radical. The picture becomes even more confusing when one adds Cuba to the group. Here, in a small Latin American country, where chronic economic problems were aggravated by American domination and a corrupt dictatorship, a typically Latin American revolutionary movement, supported primarily by the rural poor but opposed by the labor unions and by the Communist Party and led by an equally typical *caudillo,* battled its way to power in the name of radical democratic slogans. Once in power, it provoked the hostility of the United States by nationalizing business enterprises; and then Fidel Castro declared he was a communist and had been one for a long time, temporarily brought Communist Party members into his government, and announced his country's solidarity with the socialist bloc. But beyond Castro's obviously sincere antagonism toward the United States and the entire "imperialist" camp, and his commitment to socialism and national economic planning, his theoretical statements have not been much more Marxist or Leninist than they were before he changed (or revealed) his ideological allegiance. Also, beyond the nationalization of property and the attempt to reorganize farming on a cooperative or collectivist basis, the policies and programs of the Castro regime have not shown striking similarities to those of communist states in Europe or Asia.[2]

If Cuba is a communist country, then the meaning of "communism" has become exceedingly vague; it would include hardly more than anti-Americanism and the nationalization of the economy; and we might note in passing that the policy of nationalization, when instituted by the Castro regime, was opposed by the Cuban Communist Party. To this one must add that Castro has chosen to identify his regime with the communist camp, although he has turned out to be a fickle associate. Yet, in many salient respects he does not behave like other communist rulers. His authority is based more on "charisma" than on organization, more on his personal appeal than on an elaborate party, more on spontaneous emotions, including national pride and a defiant sense of collectivist independence, than on systematic indoctrination. Indeed, the one major preoccupation of all other communist regimes—the crash program of industrialization—is not shared by the present Cuban government, which has by now abandoned its brief but abortive industrialization program. The rapid differentiation within the communist world would then be attributable to the fact that in the Soviet Union the crash program has succeeded, so that the entire political system must now be restructured to respond to the needs of a mature and complex industrial society; Stalinist methods of management here have outlived their usefulness. In some countries of Eastern Europe, the Stalinist pattern was dysfunctional from the very beginning (except from the point of view of the Soviet leaders), because these countries already were highly developed and modern in many essential aspects. Hence communism, as a program of forced modernization, was entirely misapplied, and these countries now seem to be in a process of recovering from it. And in this process of recovery, each country is going, more than ever, its own way, at its own speed. In all communist countries, national interests and the national culture are asserting themselves and coming to the fore. The resulting trend toward greater differentiation is likely to intensify in times to come.

12

The Challenge of Communism

• Since the days of Lenin, the communist movement has
made impressive strides, even while its unity has disinte-
grated. Indeed, the increase in strength is one of the most
immediate causes for this disintegration. But the increase
has been rapid. The mere number of people under communist rule has grown enormously, and the achievements of
several communist states in building new political systems
and promoting economic growth should not be underesti-
mated, regardless of the price paid. Many leaders of the
communist world are more confident than ever that the tide
of history favors them. Many people in the so-called West
feel acutely threatened. How justified are they thus to feel
threatened?

There is no doubt that communist systems have managed
to coexist with capitalism, to stabilize themselves, and to
become world powers of significance. They have at times
evoked wide enthusiasm and are generally succeeding in
obtaining widening grass-roots support. To be sure, the relief with which vast masses in China welcomed the defeat of
the Kuomintang may by now have given way to regret; the
discipline of communes and construction armies may be attributable to terror rather than enthusiasm; economic austerity and thought control may be widely resented. In the

Soviet Union, little seems to remain of the enthusiasm which still moved many among Russia's younger generation at the time of the first five-year plan; and, despite careful indoctrination, vast masses of the Soviet population seem to be as indifferent to matters of ideology as are most Americans. Yet the Soviet population has nonetheless internalized significant portions of the socialist ethos; the recent successes of the Soviet regime in science, technology, and other areas seem to have given many people a strong incentive to be loyal, devoted, and cooperative. The mere passing of time makes the regime legitimate, and similar processes doubtless go on in Eastern Europe. Communist systems thus have stabilized themselves.

This growing stability, and the increased freedom of action which the regimes derive from it, may have divergent consequences. It may lead to a relaxation of tension and the growth of a spirit of accommodation; policy makers in communist foreign offices may convince themselves that time is in their favor, and that aggressive action may be too risky. The Soviet Union and its allies in Eastern Europe have publicly taken this line. The inferiority complex which forced communist leaders to be assertive, prestige-conscious, and stubborn in all dealings with the West may be on the wane; the strong can afford to be generous or flexible. On the other hand, the growing confidence of strength may make some communist leaders more cocky and demanding than ever before. It may be that they will continue to manifest both attitudes. Not even Stalin dared to make demands in such threatening language as Khrushchev did over Suez and Berlin. But neither would Stalin have dared yield to Western resistance with so little fuss as the same Khrushchev did in withdrawing his Cuban missiles and his Berlin ultimatum. And there remains the puzzle of the Chinese attitude; in words it is extremely militant, but Western politicians are kept guessing as to China's real intentions.

While some of the apprehensiveness shown by Western spokesmen focuses on the growing strength of communist states, others call attention to the link between these states and the major revolutions of our time—the emancipation of formerly dependent areas, the social upheavals in the so-called developing countries, and even the racial and class struggles and the unrest among the youth within the capitalist countries themselves. Although the popular imagination may still consider that a world-wide communist conspiracy is responsible for these troubles, it is obvious that they would occur with unabated virulence even if there were no communist movement at all. It may well be that many a leader in such rebellions has been inspired by the writings of Marx and Lenin or by the examples of the Russian or Chinese revolutions. At the same time it could be argued quite cogently that, had the Russian Revolution not taken place and had the Russians not interfered so much in the affairs of world communism, the global revolution would have gone on more rapidly and more successfully. Whether any similar statement can be made about Chinese interference in revolutionary stirrings abroad is not at all clear. However independent of communist initiative the global revolution may be, I would have conceded until a few years ago that the communist world is likely to derive greater benefit from it than the Western powers. But even this is today one of those commonplaces that ought to be reexamined. Certainly the great length to which some communist leaders, especially those of the USSR, have gone to discourage various revolutionary stirrings would suggest that, in their deeply engrained conservatism, they prefer a quiet world; they have a vested interest in the status quo; they do not wish to rock the boat; and even less do they wish to be embroiled by some minor revolutionary party in a conflict with the United States.

Americans apparently are beginning to realize that the revolution of our time cannot be fought effectively in the name of anticommunism. While communism may often emerge as the beneficiary of various revolutions (and even this is by no means the rule), it rarely functions as their prime mover. On the contrary, communists often become important only because the antirevolutionary forces insist on identifying all reform movements as tools of the communist conspiracy. Compulsive anticommunism also strengthens the very party it allegedly wishes to oppose by making more moderate solutions of acute social problems impossible. Yet even a communist victory (or, as many Americans would call it, a takeover) might in some countries come about whether the opposing forces make stupid mistakes or not. In today's world, it would seem reasonable to assume that the sphere of communist states will grow in numbers, despite Western efforts to "contain" this growth.

Among the scholars and public figures aware of this possible trend, a discussion is now beginning, however timidly, about whether such a development is cause for alarm. What is the threat posed by this possibility? What are the chief dangers that would result from its realization?

Without being a specialist in military affairs, I, for one, would be inclined to discount the strategic threat posed by possible further victories of communism, because of the remoteness of many areas from North America and Europe, because of the poverty of the areas most likely to be thus affected, and because of the nature of modern weapons systems, which depend less on remote land bases than armaments of the past. It seems likely also that an economy as wealthy as that of the United States could tolerate, without being shaken, the expropriation of some of its foreign holdings. We might have to pay more for tin, rubber, cinnamon bark, or coconuts; and the money would go into the treasuries of communist states rather than the cash registers of Western corporations, but that should not, really, be cause for national alarm. There remains the famous domino theory, which describes democracy somewhat like a besieged fortress, in which every government dependent on us is a vital section of the ramparts. Once one section has been breached, the entire wall will surely cave in. This theory, which usually is advanced without any supporting argument, seems to regard Western strength as ridiculously fragile and illusory. Against the domino theory one might argue that in fact North America and Europe contain immensely wealthy and stable communities which will be little affected by the nature of governments in other continents, even if Western actions could always determine the nature of these governments. The argument is strengthened by once again pointing

out that the communist world is no longer unified; hence the
Western powers can and must deal with its several members
more and more independently. One might even assume, with
a certain amount of assurance, that its disunity and heterogeneity will grow with the increase of its size; as more countries are added to the communist world, it will become less
manageable.

These speculations lead to a brief look at the entire world
situation at the time of this writing, in which one of the
outstanding facts is the changing nature of the cold war. For
about fifteen years, this antagonism between the two major
world powers and their clients seemed to be the principal
determinant of international politics, even though considerable numbers of people resisted (with varying success) being drawn into it. Notwithstanding the furor of the war in
Vietnam, however, the cold war in its old form seems to be
receding into the past. Its old form was related to the bipolarity of power in the world that had emerged from World
War II. This bipolarity is giving way to a pluralism of great
powers. Some new nations, or groups of new nations, are
beginning to make their weight felt. Meanwhile, the two
antagonistic blocs have lost their cohesiveness, and the disintegration of one has engendered parallel processes in the
other. Hence the stalemate of the cold war may be yielding
to the more flexible politics of maneuver which has already
begun to blur ideological lines. A French president can ini-
tiate serious negotiations with Soviet Russia, while a communist regime in Rumania engages in mutually fruitful dealings with the United States—the major powers seem to be
swapping mates. Groups of communist and noncommunist
powers may soon ally themselves against other groups of
similar composition, just as, in like fashion, a century after
the Reformation Protestant and Catholic princes began to
collaborate.

If the disaster of nuclear war can be averted, it is possible
that the analogy with the Reformation may become pertinent
in many other ways. In Chapter 1, I called communism the
puritanism of our century. We, of course, then are the Cath-
olics in that analogy. It is worth noting that puritans and

papists not only came to collaborate in politics; in time they came to live with each other. Even though the two groups maintain their doctrinal disputes, and even though they may vote differently in presidential elections, it would be difficult to establish meaningful differences between a Catholic and a Protestant way of life. In most important aspects they have become very much alike.

Communism and capitalism will retain differences in traditions and culture, major differences, perhaps, in the social structure and the functioning of the economic system as a whole, equally major differences also in the process of decision making, which is called politics and government. And yet, the common problems shared by all nations committed to twentieth-century industrialism and all it implies will grow in scope. If they are left to grow without major disturbances, perhaps communism and capitalism will gradually cease to present a challenge to each other. Perhaps one of the major tasks of our age is to seek a modern Peace of Westphalia without having to go through the nightmare of a modern Thirty Years' War.

Obstacles in the way of such a solution are formidable, and perhaps they should be seen as the most profound of all the challenges which communism presents to the West. On pages 8 and 74, I pointed out that communism was not prepared, psychologically or doctrinally, for prolonged coexistence with the capitalist world. From this I deduced a certain persistent inability for self-orientation, a mental block hindering understanding, a tendency even toward character traits which border paranoia. We should be aware that the West was no more prepared for coexistence with communism; hence, we too are threatened with the loss of our sanity. Communism has established itself as a successful alternative to our own way of life, to our own pattern of social organization. But our deeply engrained convictions make it almost impossible for us to acknowledge the possibility of a successful alternative. The moral challenge inherent in it is too great to be faced. The existence of a rival political order so shakes our belief in the virtues of our social system that many of us repress this knowledge. The resultant neurosis

takes the form of various delusions about the nature of contemporary world affairs. The principal function of these delusions is to reaffirm our shaken conviction that ours is the
best of all possible worlds. Since, moreover, on the communist side, the urge to flee from reality is equally strong, as
we have seen, the major powers in the contemporary world
seem to face each other in a stance that might best be described as reciprocal paranoia. Two nervous, shaken, trigger-
happy antagonists are facing each other with loaded weapons. Each *knows* the other will shoot first. Neither can do
anything at all without increasing the other's suspicions and
nervousness. Reciprocal paranoia may therefore make real
its worst fears.

Communism thus threatens our sanity, and the great challenge is for us to preserve it. It also challenges us not to
destroy our own way of life by the manner in which we
respond. This is an extremely complicated problem which
cannot be developed here. Suffice it to say that any attempt
to slow down the spread of communism must be guided by
imagination, empathy, generosity, and a deep commitment
to democratic values, if it is to be successful. Whether the
Western world can muster these qualities in its state of ideological shock remains to be seen. Moreover, to respond to
the challenge may require changes in the policy orientation
and management of the Western world which the nations of
the West are not prepared to undertake. This leaves two
alternatives: a conservative resolve to hold the line wherever
it can be held, or a militant determination to stamp out all
challenges by force. In a revolutionary world, the former is
self-defeating, and in the age of fusion devices the latter
may be suicidal. Both, moreover, are likely to help destroy
constitutional democracy in the West.

For the scholar and the student, the principal challenge
is not to view the phenomenon of communism through the
stereotypes and slogans engendered by the cold war, but,
instead, to develop views of a more independent sort. A
global, all-human point of view must be substituted for
opinions reflecting narrow national biases. The scholar, too,

must shed his provincialism. Instead of treating the communist world as if it were a unique phenomenon for which novel terms must be devised, he should apply the standard concepts of his discipline to the study of communist societies and thereby place such study within a genuinely comparative framework.

Notes and References

CHAPTER 1   Introduction

(1) Communist efforts to persuade distinguish different publics, for instance, when they differentiate between "propaganda" and "agitation." For a definition of these terms, see Alfred G. Meyer, *Leninism* (Cambridge, Mass., 1957), p. 150.

(2) See Myron Rush, *The Rise of Khrushchev* (Washington, D. C., 1958), which in its entirety deals with communist language as an esoteric code of this sort.

(3) "Ideology and Power Politics: A Symposium," *Problems of Communism*, VII, No. 2 (March–April 1958), pp. 10–35.

(4) See Harold J. Laski, *Reflections on the Revolution of Our Time* (New York, 1943), pp. 73–75; Eduard Bernstein, *Cromwell and Communism: Socialism and Democracy in the Great English Revolution* (London, 1930), pp. 26–30, and Leon Trotsky, *Whither England?* (New York, 1925), pp. 60–61 and *passim*.

CHAPTER 2   Marxist Theory

(1) Descriptions of the conditions of the working class in early capitalism abound not only in Marxist literature, beginning with Engels' *The Condition of the Working Class in England* (New York, 1958) and Marx's *Capital*, but are more familiar to us through the novels of Dickens, Victor Hugo, and others. For a more recent description of similar conditions in the United States, see Oscar Handlin, *The Uprooted* (Boston, 1951).

(2) *The Communist Manifesto* of Marx and Engels devotes a brief chapter to the utopian socialists.

(3) An interesting discussion of these elements in Marxism is provided in Vernon Venable, *Human Nature: The Marxist View* (New York, 1945). See also Alfred G. Meyer, *Marxism: The Unity of Theory and Practice* (Cambridge, Mass., 1954).

(4) The liberational elements in Marxism are brought out with greatest clarity, and with an emphasis that is controversial, in Raya Dunaevskaya, *Marxism and Freedom* (New York, 1958). See also Erich Fromm, *Marx's Concept of Man* (New York, 1961).

(5) See Meyer, *Marxism: The Unity of Theory and Practice.*

(6) For an introduction to Hegel's philosophy, see C. J. Friedrich's Introduction to *The Philosophy of Hegel* (New York, 1954); Herbert Marcuse, *Reason and Revolution: Hegel and The Rise of Social Theory* (New York, 1955); and Robert Tucker, *Philosophy and Myth in Karl Marx* (New York, 1961). For a convenient introduction to the Hegelian heritage in Marx, see Louis Dupre, *The Philosophical Foundations of Marxism* (New York, 1966).

(7) This brief account cannot possibly touch upon the very real philosophic problems created by Marx's attempt to fulfill philosophy by overcoming it. For works treating the problem, see Selected Readings on Marxist economic doctrines. Nor is this the place to treat the complicated relationship between Marxism and contemporary social science, a problem which I have treated briefly in "Marxism and Social Science," *Centennial Review,* Fall 1959, pp. 423–436.

CHAPTER 3   European Marxism, 1848–1914

(1) This idea is expressed clearly in *The Communist Manifesto*; in Marx's *The Poverty of Philosophy*; and in the essay by Engels on the *History of the Communist League*.

(2) George Lichtheim, "Marxist Doctrine in Perspective," *Problems of Communism,* VII, No. 6 (March–April 1958), p. 34.

(3) See especially Erich Matthias, "Kautsky und der Kautskyanismus," in *Marxismusstudien,* II, 151–197; also Karl Korsch, *Die materialistische Geschichtsauffassung* (Leipzig, 1930).

CHAPTER 4   Principles of Leninism

(1) Gerold T. Robinson, *Rural Russia Under the Old Regime: A History of the Landlord-Peasant Revolution of 1917* (New York, 1949).

(2) For a more detailed presentation of my views, and for sources, see Alfred G. Meyer, *Leninism* (Cambridge, Mass., 1957), of which the present chapter is a brief abstract. A discussion of the history of the bolshevik faction is reserved for the following chapter.

(3) See Erich Goldhagen's brilliant article on "Ideology and

the Transition to Communism," *Soviet Survey*, No. 28 (April–June 1959), pp. 56–63.

(4) V. I. Lenin, *Sochineniia* [Works] 2d ed., XXIII (Moscow, 1931), p. 220.

(5) See Adam Ulam, *The Unfinished Revolution* (New York, 1960).

(6) For books on communism which emphasize this Machiavellian morality of expediency, see Philip Selznick, *The Organizational Weapon* (New York, 1952), and Stefan T. Possony, *A Century of Conflict* (Chicago, 1953).

(7) Concerning the origins of the theory of imperialism in the writings of Hobson, Hilferding, Luxemburg, and Bukharin, see Meyer, *Leninism*, and Paul M. Sweezy, *The Theory of Capitalist Development*.

CHAPTER 5   History of the Russian Communist Party
up to the Death of Lenin

(1) In addition to the works by Radkey, Masaryk, Venturi, and Treadgold, cited in Selected Readings for Chapter 4, information about the *narodniks* is contained in Victor M. Chernov, *The Great Russian Revolution* (New Haven, 1936).

(2) Bertram D. Wolfe, *Three Who Made a Revolution* (Boston, 1955), has discussed these financial problems. They also receive attention in Leonard Schapiro's *The Communist Party of the Soviet Union* (New York, 1960).

(3) Merle Fainsod, *International Socialism and the World War* (Cambridge, Mass., 1935).

(4) See Isaac Deutscher, *The Prophet Armed: Trotsky 1921–1929* (Fair Lawn, N. J., 1954), for events leading up to 1921.

(5) For a summary of the issues over which opposition sentiment arose, see Alfred G. Meyer, *Leninism* (Cambridge, Mass., 1957), pp. 197–198, footnote. See also Deutscher, *The Prophet Unarmed: Trotsky, 1921–1929;* and Leonard Schapiro, *The Communist Party of the Soviet Union*. Full treatment of these issues is given in Robert V. Daniels, *The Conscience of The Revolution* (Cambridge, Mass., 1960).

CHAPTER 6   Phases of Soviet Rule

(1) Sidney Heitman, *An Annotated Bibliography of Nikolai I. Bukharin's Published Works* (Fort Collins, 1958), not only lists more than five hundred items of published work from Bukharin's pen, but also a number of unpublished dissertations and other secondary works dealing with him. Heitman's own views on Bukharin are summarized in his "Between Lenin and Stalin: Nikolai Bukharin," in Leopold Labedz (ed.), *Revisionism: Essays on the*

History of Marxist Ideas (New York, 1962). In addition, Julius Hecker, *Moscow Dialogues: Discussions on Red Philosophy* (London, 1933), and Raymond A. Bauer, *The New Man in Soviet Psychology* (Cambridge, Mass., 1959), present some Bukharinist ideas.

(2) *Capital* (Chicago, 1906), I, p. 784.

(3) *Ibid.*, I, p. 834.

(4) The term surplus alienation" is adapted from Herbert Marcuse, *Eros and Civilization* (Boston, 1956).

CHAPTER 7   The Stalinist Theory of the State

(1) "Cadres decide everything" was said by Stalin in May of 1935. See "Struktura otdela rukovodiashchikh partiinykh organov Ts. K. partii," *Partiinoe Stroitel'stvo*, No. 17 (1935), pp. 73–78.

(2) Khrushchev's pronouncements on the incipient transition to communism are analyzed in Erich Goldhagen, "Ideology and Transition to Communism," *Soviet Survey*, No. 28 (April–June 1959), pp. 56–63. The new platform ("Program") of the CPSU, adopted in the fall of 1961, which summarizes recent Soviet thinking about the impending transition to communism, can be found in numerous documentary collections, e.g., Arthur P. Mendel (ed.), *Essential Works of Marxism* (New York, 1961); or Dan N. Jacobs (ed.), *The New Communist Manifesto* (Evanston, Ill., 1962). For speculations by Western scholars on these developments, see W. Z. Laqueur and L. Labedz (eds.), *The Future of Communist Society* (New York, 1962).

(3) For a convincing attempt to decipher the esoteric code of communication used by the Soviet elite, see Myron Rush, *The Rise of Khrushchev* (Washington, D. C., 1958).

CHAPTER 8   Stalinist Society and Its Transformation

(1) For descriptions of the life of party members, see Raymond A. Bauer, Alex Inkeles, and Clyde K. M. Kluckhohn, *How The Soviet System Works* (Cambridge, Mass., 1956); Raymond A. Bauer, *Nine Soviet Portraits* (New York, 1955); and Raymond A. Bauer and Alex Inkeles, *The Soviet Citizen* (Cambridge, Mass., 1959).

(2) For works on the Soviet government see Selected Readings for Chapter 7.

(3) An interesting theory incorporating the selective enforcement of conflicting standards in Soviet administration is developed by Andrew Gunder Frank, "The Organization of Economic Activity in the Soviet Union," *Weltwirtschaftliches Archiv*, Vol. 78, No. 1 (1957), pp. 104–156.

(4) Merle Fainsod, *How Russia Is Ruled* (Cambridge, Mass.,

1953), sees the Soviet political system almost entirely as an instrument of control, neglecting the many other functions performed by its governmental institutions and processes. For a view of the Soviet system as the purest specimen of a new species of government, called totalitarianism, see Bertram D. Wolfe, *Communist Totalitarianism* (Boston, 1961).

(5) This idea is expressed most sharply in Isaac Deutscher, *Russia, What Next?* (Fair Lawn, N. J., 1953). It is evaluated critically in Barrington Moore, Jr., *Terror and Progress, USSR* (Cambridge, Mass., 1954). See also Bauer and Inkeles, *The Soviet Citizen;* Alfred G. Meyer, "Russia After Stalin," *Current History* (January 1956), pp. 1–7, and Marshall D. Shulman, "Changing Appreciation of the Soviet Problem," *World Politics* (July 1958).

(6) The relationship between the Soviet government and the peasantry is summarized in Herbert Dinerstein, *Communism and the Russian Peasant* (Chicago, 1955).

(7) For estimates of Soviet manpower losses during the war, see Alfred G. Meyer, *The Soviet Political System* (New York, 1966), p. 17, Note 4.

(8) Soviet wartime policies are summarized ably in Nicholas S. Timasheff, *The Great Retreat* (New York, 1946).

(9) A deluge of highly speculative and specious articles still continues to deal with the power struggles in the Kremlin following Stalin's death. One of the few convincing studies is Myron Rush, *The Rise of Khrushchev* (Washington, D. C., 1958). See also Leonard Schapiro, *The Communist Party of the Soviet Union* (New York, 1960) and Wolfgang Leonhard, *The Kremlin Since Stalin* (New York, 1962).

(10) See Selected Readings on resistance and revisionism.

(11) A convenient survey of policies pursued since 1953, and the various measures of relaxation included in them, is provided by Abraham Brumberg (ed.), *Russia Under Khrushchev* (New York, 1961).

CHAPTER 9   The Communist International, 1919–1943

(1) On the Treaty of Brest Litovsk, see J. W. Wheeler-Bennett, *The Forgotten Peace* (New York, 1939); also Deutscher, *The Prophet Armed: Trotsky* (Fair Lawn, N. J., 1954); Alfred G. Meyer, *Leninism* (Cambridge, Mass., 1957); and Louis Fischer, *The Soviets in World Affairs: A History of the Relations between the Soviet Union and the Rest of the World, 1917–1929* (2 vols.; London, 1930).

(2) On the German revolution of 1923, see Franz Borkenau, *The Communist International* (London, 1938), Chapter XIV; E. H. Carr, *A History of Soviet Russia*, Vol. IV, *The Interregnum* (New York, 1954), Chapters 7 and 9; Ruth Fischer, *Stalin and*

German Communism: A Study in the Origins of the State Party
(Cambridge, Mass., 1948), Chapters 13–16; and Jan Valtin, *Out
of The Night* (New York, 1941).

(3) The speeches made by Maxim Litvinov in the League of
Nations have been published in the English language. An authorized biography of Litvinov has been written by A. U. Pope,
Maxim Litvinov (New York, 1943). The official line regarding
communist policy in the period of the United Front is presented
in George Dimitrov, *The United Front* (New York, 1938). For
critical discussions, see Borkenau, *The Communist International*,
Chapter XXII; and, by the same author, *European Communism*
(New York, 1953), Chapter V.

(4) Communist activity during the Spanish Civil War has been
treated admirably in Hugh Thomas, *The Spanish Civil War* (New
York, 1961), which has a full bibliography. For French politics at
the time of the Popular Front policy, see Alexander Werth, *France
in Ferment* (New York, 1935); and J. Danos and M. Gibelin,
Juin 36: masses et militants (Paris, 1952). Also Franz Borkenau,
European Communism (New York, 1953), Chapters V–VIII;
Mario Einaudi *et al.*, *Communism in Western Europe* (Ithaca,
N. Y., 1951); and Hugh Seton-Watson, *From Lenin to Malenkov*
(New York, 1953).

(5) The effects of the Great Purge on foreign communist parties is described in Borkenau, *European Communism*, Chapters
VII–VIII, and in such eyewitness accounts as Margarete Buber-
Neumann, *Under Two Dictators* (London, 1949). See also Alfred
Burmeister, *Dissolution and Aftermath of the Comintern* (mimeographed; New York, 1955), and Ervin Sinko, *Roman eines Ro-
manes* (Köln, 1962).

(6) The technique of setting up so-called front organizations
is described in many books dealing with communism, especially
Stephen T. Possony, *A Century of Conflict* (Chicago, 1953), and
Philip Selznick, *The Organizational Weapon* (New York, 1952).
It is emphasized particularly in the confessional literature of for-
mer American communists, such as Louis Budenz, *The Tech-
niques of Communism* (Chicago, 1954); Whittaker Chambers,
Witness (New York, 1952); Benjamin Gitlow, *I Confess* (New
York, 1940); and Herbert A. Philbrick, *I Led Three Lives* (New
York, 1952). See also Max Kampelman, *The Communist Party
versus the CIO* (New York, 1957).

(7) A classic account of communist policies between August
1939 and July 1941 is A. Rossi, *Les Communistes français pen-
dant la drôle de guerre* (Paris, 1951) and *A Communist Party in
Action* (New Haven, 1949). For speculations and analyses of
Soviet motives in concluding the pact with Germany, see David
Dallin, *Soviet Russia's Foreign Policy, 1939–42* (New Haven,
1942); R. J. Sontag and J. S. Beddie, *Nazi-Soviet Relations* (New
York, 1948); Gustav Hilger and Alfred G. Meyer, *The Incompati-*

ble Allies (New York, 1953); G. Weinberg, *Germany and the Soviet Union* (New York, 1954); and A. Rossi, *The Russo-German Alliance* (London, 1950).

(8) No special treatment has yet been given to the activities of communist parties during the time the USSR was involved in World War II. Occasional remarks only can be found in much of the literature cited in the preceding notes, especially Borkenau, *European Communism*. It is regrettable that this important book is so unreliable because of its author's propensity for speculation and for citing anonymous references.

(9) On the dissolution of the Comintern, see the study by Burmeister cited in Note 5.

CHAPTER 10   World Communism since World War II

(1) The whole range of problems concerning the motives of Soviet and communist foreign policy during the last years of Stalin's life has been opened in challenging fashion by Marshall Shulman, *Stalin's Foreign Policy Reappraised* (Cambridge, Mass., 1963), a book which questions many of the stereotypes about Soviet policies and intentions to which the cold war gave rise in the West.

CHAPTER 11   Contemporary Communism:
                          Unity and Diversity

(1) See Franz Schurmann, *Ideology and Organization in Communist China* (Berkeley, Calif., 1966).

(2) See Theodore Draper, *Castroism: Theory and Practice* (New York, 1965).

Selected Readings

• The selected readings of the first editions are reproduced here with minor additions and changes. I have decided to retain this admittedly unsatisfactory bibliographic guide only with considerable misgivings. The reasons for my apprehension are many. The subject covered in this book is much too large to be studied adequately by one person. One person can never know enough to do it justice; he can never read even a fraction of the literature in the field, and that literature is growing rapidly. For many of the topics covered in this book by a single sentence, a mere phrase, or not at all, there are today entire bibliographies; and compiling bibliographies on some of these incidental subtopics is often a major undertaking in itself. Entire massive bibliographies exist, or could be assembled, for instance, on the following topics: the works of Marx and Engels; the history of Marxism; the life of Lenin; the Russian Revolution of 1917; the history of any communist country; the history of any of the major communist parties; the government, economy, and culture of any one communist system; the relationship of communist ideology and contemporary social science; and the relationship of communism and a host of contemporary social and political movements.

Obviously, one person will not be able to even keep track of the major publications currently appearing in the field. The study of communism has become a vast ocean of writings in which an individual may drown.

Because of this, any selection of books such as the one given here cannot be anything but capricious, personal, and inadequate. It must be described as containing those items which the author has had a chance to read and has found more interesting or more useful than others. Moreover, the selection is bound to be out-dated as soon as it appears in print. I make no apologies for the list and leave it in the book because an inadequate bibliography is perhaps better than none at all.

Marxist Theory

Source Material and Secondary Works

For handy bibliographies to the vast source material and secondary works on Marxism, see John Plamenatz, *German Marxism and Russian Communism* (New York, 1954); H. B. Mayo, *Democracy and Marxism* (Fair Lawn, N. J., 1955); Robert Tucker, *Philosophy and Myth in Karl Marx* (Cambridge University Press, 1961); George Lichtheim, *Marxism* (New York, 1961).

Iring Fetscher, *Von Marx zur Sowjetideologie* (Frankfurt, 1957); Iring Fetscher (ed.), *Der Marxismus: seine Geschichte in Dokumenten* (3 vols.; Munich, 1962) and *Karl Marx-Friedrich Engels* (Studienausgabe in 4 vols.; Frankfurt, 1966); Alfred G. Meyer, *Marxism: The Unity of Theory and Practice* (Cambridge, Mass., 1954); H. Arvon, *Le Marxisme* (Paris, 1955); Karl Korsch, *Karl Marx* (London, 1938); Arnold Kunzli, *Karl Marx: eine Psychographie* (Vienna, 1966); Jean-Yves Calvez, S.J., *La Pensée de Karl Marx* (Paris, 1957); M. Rubel, *Bibliographie des oeuvres de Karl Marx* (Paris, 1956); and Gerhard Lehmbruch, *Kleiner Wegweiser zum Studium der Sowjetideologie* (Bonn, 1958).

Marxist Economic Doctrines

The best summary of Marxist economic doctrines is to be found in Paul Sweezy, *The Theory of Capitalist Development* (New York, 1956). See also Henry Bartoli, *La Doctrine économique et sociale de Karl Marx* (Paris, 1950); Joan Robinson, *An Essay on Marxian Economics* (New York, 1952); Joseph Schumpeter, *Capitalism, Socialism and Democracy* (3d ed.; New York, 1950); and Maurice Dobb, *Political Economy and Capitalism* (New York, 1957).

Religious Criticism of Marxism

Marxism is discussed as a secular religion in Waldemar Gurian, *Bolshevism: Introduction to Soviet Communism* (Notre Dame, Ind., 1953). Similar ideas are expressed in Gustav Wetter, S.J., *Dialectical Materialism* (New York, 1959), and in J. Hommes, *Der technische Eros* (Freiburg, 1955). For further bibliography

of religious critics of Marxism, see Chapter XIV of G. Lehmbruch, *Kleiner Wegweiser zum Studium der Sowjetideologie.*

Philosophical Problems of Marxism

See Herbert Marcuse, *Reason and Revolution: Hegel and the
Rise of Social Theory* (New York, 1955); Gustav Wetter, *Dialectical Materialism* (New York, 1959); Sidney Hook, *From
Hegel to Marx* (New York, 1950); Louis Dupre, *The Philosophical Foundations of Marxism* (New York, 1966); A. James Gregor,
A Survey of Marxism (New York, 1965); Karl Korsch, *Marxismus
und Philosophie* (Leipzig, 1923); Georg Lukacs, *Geschichte und
Klassenbewusstsein* (Berlin, 1923); Max Raphael, *Zur Erkennt-
nistheorie der kontreten Dialektik* (Paris, 1934); and the extensive bibliography in Iring Fetscher, "Der Marxismus im Spiegel
der französischen Philosophie," *Marxismusstudien*, I, 173–213.

History of the Labor Movement, 1848–1890

On the history of the labor movement between 1848 and 1890,
see, among others, Paul Louis, *Histoire du socialisme en France*
(Paris, 1946); G. D. H. Cole, *British Working Class Politics,
1832–1914* (London, 1941); G. D. H. Cole, *A History of Socialist Thought*, Vols. II and III (New York, Vol. II 1954, Vol. III
1956); Max Beer, *A History of British Socialism* (London, 1940);
Alexander Gray, *The Socialist Tradition* (New York, 1946); Arthur Rosenberg, *Democracy and Socialism* (New York, 1939);
J. Lenz, *The Rise and Fall of the Second International* (New
York, 1932); James Joll, *The Second International: 1889–1914*
(New York, 1955); George Lichtheim, *Marxism* (New York,
1961).

History of Russia

For bibliographies on the history of Russia, see Paul L.
Horecky, *Russia and the Soviet Union* (Chicago, 1965), and *Basic
Russian Publications* (Chicago, 1962); Robert J. Kerner, *Slavic
Europe: A Selected Bibliography* (Cambridge, Mass., 1918);
Charles Morley, *Guide to Research in Russian History* (Syracuse,
N. Y., 1951); and Philip Grierson, *Books on Soviet Russia* (Lon-
don, 1943). General introductions to Russian history include V. O.
Klyuchevsky, *A History of Russia* (5 vols.; London, 1911–1931);
B. H. Sumner, *A Short History of Russia* (New York, 1949);
Valentin Gitermann, *Geschichte Russlands* (Zürich, 1944–49);
Karl Stählin, *Geschichte Russlands von den Anfängen bis zur*

Gegenwart (4 vols.; Berlin, 1923–39); Hans von Eckhardt, *Russia* (New York, 1932); Paul Milyukov, *Outlines of Russian Culture* (Philadelphia, 1942); P. I. Lyashchenko, *History of the National Economy of Russia to the 1917 Revolution* (New York, 1949); J. Mavor, *An Economic History of Russia* (2 vols.; London, 1914); Michael Karpovich, *Imperial Russia, 1801–1917* (New York, 1932); A. Kornilov, *Modern Russian History* (New York, 1916–1917); Sir John Maynard, *Russia in Flux* (New York, 1948); Bernard Pares, *The Fall of the Russian Monarchy: A History of Evidence* (London, 1939); Alfred Levin, *The Second Duma: A Study of the Social-Democratic Party and the Russian Constitutional Experiment* (New Haven, 1940). Two encyclopedias should be mentioned: *McGraw-Hill Encyclopedia on Russia and the Soviet Union* (New York, 1961); and *Everyman's Concise Encyclopedia of Russia* (London, 1961).

Russia's Revolutionary Movements

On Russia's revolutionary movements, see Richard Hare, *Pioneers of Russian Social Thought* (Fair Lawn, N. J., 1951); J. F. Hecker, *Russian Sociology* (New York, 1915); Oliver Radkey, *The Agrarian Foes of Bolshevism* (New York, 1958); Donald Treadgold, *Lenin and His Rivals* (New York, 1955); Thomas G. Masaryk, *The Spirit of Russia* (New York, 1955); Franco Venturi, *Roots of Revolution* (New York, 1960); Leopold Haimson, *Russian Marxists and the Origins of Bolshevism* (Cambridge, Mass., 1955); P. Scheibert, *Von Bakunin zu Lenin* (Leiden, 1956); Nikolai Berdyaev, *The Origin of Bolshevism* (Naperville, Ill., 1955); George Fischer, *Russian Liberalism before the Revolution: From Gentry to Intelligentsia* (Cambridge, Mass., 1958); Avrahm Yarmolinsky, *Road to Revolution* (London, 1957); Richard Pipes, *The Russian Intelligentsia* (New York, 1961).

History of the Russian Marxist Movement

Scholarly work on the history of the Russian Marxist movement is now coming out at an increasing rate both in the USSR and the Western world. The most recent is Leonard Schapiro, *The Communist Party of the Soviet Union* (New York, 1960). Previous works include Fedor Dan, *The Origins of Bolshevism* (New York, 1965); Arthur Rosenberg, *A History of Bolshevism from Marx to the First Five Years' Plan* (London, 1934); Isaac Deutscher, *Stalin: A Political Biography* (Fair Lawn, N. J., 1949), *The Prophet Armed: Trotsky, 1879–1921* (Fair Lawn, N. J., 1954), and *The Prophet Unarmed: Trotsky, 1921–1929* (New York, 1959); Adam Ulam, *The Bolsheviks* (New York, 1966); Bertram D. Wolfe, *Three Who Made a Revolution* (Boston,

1955); and Boris Souvarine, *Staline* (Paris, 1935). The most convenient guide to Soviet writings is probably provided by the journal *Voprosy Istorii KPSS*.

The Russian Revolution

Classic works on the Russian Revolution are Leon Trotsky, *The History of the Russian Revolution* (Ann Arbor, Mich., 1957); Victor M. Chernov, *The Great Russian Revolution* (New Haven, 1936); N. N. Sukhanov, *The Russian Revolution, 1917* (abridged from *Zapiski o revoliutsii*) (Fair Lawn, N. J., 1935); the first three volumes of E. H. Carr, *A History of Soviet Russia* (4 vols.; New York, 1950–1954); John Reed, *Ten Days That Shook the World* (New York, 1919). See also William Henry Chamberlin, *The Russian Revolution, 1917–1921* (2 vols., rev. ed.; New York, 1952); James Bunyan and H. H. Fisher (eds.), *The Bolshevik Revolution, 1917–1918; Documents and Materials* (Stanford, Calif., 1934); Leonard Schapiro, *The Origin of the Communist Autocracy: Political Opposition in the Soviet State: First Phase, 1917–1922* (Cambridge, Mass., 1955); and Oskar Anweiler, *Die Rätebewegung in Russland, 1905–1921* (Leiden, 1958).

The Civil War

On the civil war, see the works of Chamberlin, Schapiro, and Carr, cited above; also N. Kritsman, *Geroicheskii period velikoi Russkoi revoliutsii* (Moscow, 1924); Richard Pipes, *The Formation of the Soviet Union: Communism and Nationalism, 1917–1923* (Cambridge, Mass., 1954); John S. Reshetar, Jr., *The Ukrainian Revolution, 1917–1920* (Princeton, N. J., 1952); Firuz Kazemzadeh, *The Struggle for Transcaucasia, 1917–1921* (New York, 1951); James Bunyan (ed.), *Intervention, Civil War and Communism in Russia: April–December, 1918* (Baltimore, 1936). This list could be extended greatly. There is in addition an avalanche of documentary material, memoirs, and secondary accounts published in the USSR in recent years.

The Period of War Communism

For descriptions of the Soviet regime in the period of war communism, see the works on the civil war cited in Selected Readings for Chapter 5. On cultural trends, consult Rene Fülöp-Miller, *The Mind and Face of Bolshevism* (New York, 1928); D. S. Mirsky, *Contemporary Russian Literature* (Fair Lawn, N. J., 1925); Nicholas Hans and Sergius Hessen, *Educational Policy in Soviet Russia* (London, 1930); and especially N. S. Timasheff, *The Great Retreat* (New York, 1946).

The Trotsky Opposition

On the Trotsky opposition, see Deutscher, *The Prophet Un-armed* (New York, 1959); Souvarine, *Staline* (Paris, 1935); Ruth Fischer, *Stalin and German Communism: A Study in the Origins of the State Party* (Cambridge, Mass., 1948); R. V. Daniels, *The Conscience of The Revolution* (Cambridge, Mass., 1960); and Alexander Erlich, *The Soviet Industrialization Debate, 1924–1928* (Cambridge, Mass., 1960).

The Industrialization Period

For literature on the industrialization period, see W. H. Chamberlin, *Russia's Iron Age* (Boston, 1934); Maurice Hindus, *The Great Offensive* (London, 1933); John Scott, *Behind the Urals* (Boston, 1942), all of them useful eyewitness accounts.

The Collective Farm System

On the collective farm system, see Lazar Volin, *A Survey of Soviet Russian Agriculture* (Washington, D. C., 1951); David Mitrany, *Marx against the Peasant* (Chapel Hill, N. C., 1952); Fedor Belov, *A History of a Soviet Collective Farm* (New York, 1956); Naum Jasny, *The Socialized Agriculture of the USSR* (Stanford, Calif., 1949); Herbert Dinerstein, *Communism and the Russian Peasant* (Chicago, 1955); R. D. Laird and E. L. Crowley (eds.), *Soviet Agriculture* (New York, 1965); and R. D. Laird, *Collective Farming in Russia* (Lawrence, Kan., 1958).

The Great Purge, the Secret Police, and Labor Camps

On the Great Purge and the secret police, the literature is of tremendous bulk. An attempt to explain police terror as a functional aspect of the Soviet social system is made in Zbigniew K. Brzezinski, *The Permanent Purge: Politics in Soviet Totalitarianism* (Cambridge, Mass., 1956). A large number of conflicting explanations of the Great Purge are offered in F. Beck and W. Godin, *Russian Purge and the Extraction of Confession* (New York, 1951). See also Alex Weissberg, *The Accused* (New York, 1951); Nathan Leites and Elsa Bernaut, *Ritual of Liquidation* (Chicago, 1954); on the police system, Simon Wolin and Robert M. Slusser (eds.), *The Soviet Secret Police* (New York, 1957); on labor camps, David J. Dallin and Boris I. Nicolaevsky, *Forced Labor in Soviet Russia* (New Haven, 1947); also numerous eyewitness accounts such as Jerzy Gliksman, *Tell the West* (New York, 1948). There are a number of fictional treatments of the Great Purge; outstanding among them is Arthur Koestler, *Darkness at Noon* (New York, 1956).

The Cultural Counterrevolution

See Nicholas S. Timasheff, *The Great Retreat* (New York, 1946); Kurt London, *The Seven Soviet Arts* (London, 1937); Klaus Mehnert, *Stalin versus Marx* (London, 1952); Harold J. Berman, *Justice in Russia* (Cambridge, Mass., 1950); Raymond A. Bauer, *The New Man in Soviet Psychology* (Cambridge, Mass., 1959); Herbert Marcuse, *Soviet Marxism* (New York, 1958). A wealth of additional suggestions can be found in the chapters on philosophy, religion, social relations, science, literature, music, and other arts in the valuable bibliographic book, H. H. Fisher (ed.), *American Research on Russia* (Bloomington, Ind., 1959).

The Transformation of Marxism

On the transformation of Marxism, see the works by Marcuse, Mehnert, and Bauer cited above. See also Gustav Wetter, S.J., *Dialectical Materialism* (New York, 1959); I. Bocheński, *Der sowjetrussische dialektische Materialismus* (*Diamat*) (Bern, 1950); Max Gustav Lange, *Marxismus-Leninismus-Stalinismus* (Stuttgart, 1955); Henri Chambre, S.J., *Le Marxisme en Union Soviétique* (Paris, 1955); and the extensive bibliographies in the works by Wetter and Bocheński.

Dialectical Materialism and the Soviet Theory of State

The authoritative textbook on current Soviet ideology is O. Kuusinen (ed.), *Osnovy Marksizma-Leninizma* (Moscow, 1959), which is also available in English translation, *Fundamentals of Marxism-Leninism*. A companion volume of a more philosophical orientation is *Osnovy Marksistskoi Filosofii* (Moscow, 1963). Similar textbooks have been published in the field of political economy, public law and government, and a host of other areas directly related to the central themes of the ideology. Within the last ten years, an especially large volume of books has been devoted to the problems of leading the country from socialism to full communism.

English-language outlines of dialectical materialism by communist authors include V. Adoratsky, *Dialectical Materialism* (New York, 1934); Maurice Cornforth, *Science and Idealism* (New York, 1947); David A. Guest, *Textbook of Dialectical Materialism* (New York, 1939); and Howard Selsam, *Handbook of Philosophy* (New York, 1949); to which we might add the sympathetic treatment in John Somerville, *Soviet Philosophy* (New York, 1946). For critical treatment, see Gustav A. Wetter, *Dialectical Materialism* (New York, 1959); I. M. Bocheński, *Der sowjetrussische dialektische Materialismus (Diamat)* (Bern, 1950); and Max Gustav Lange, *Marxismus-Leninismus-Stalinismus* (Stuttgart, 1955). For ample bibliographical information about Soviet works on the subjects, see the work by Wetter cited above and Raymond A. Bauer, *The New Man in Soviet Psychology* (Cambridge, Mass., 1959). See also H. H. Fisher (ed.), *American Research on Russia* (Bloomington, Ind., 1959), pp. 68–70.

Stalinist Society and Its Transformation

History and Structure of the Communist Party

The history and structure of the Communist Party of the Soviet Union have been treated in considerable detail in Merle Fainsod, *How Russia is Ruled* (Cambridge, Mass., 1953), and Julian Towster, *Political Power in the USSR* (Fair Lawn, N. J., 1948), as well as in the work by Schapiro cited on p. 220. The party's function in a locally restricted area is vividly portrayed in Merle Fainsod, *Smolensk under Soviet Rule* (Cambridge, Mass., 1958). Exhaustive histories of the party have been planned for many years but have not been completed; for the time being, we have to study it through the use of biographies of Lenin, Trotsky, and Stalin, especially those by Deutscher, Souvarine, and Trotsky. John A. Armstrong, *The Soviet Bureaucratic Elite* (New York, 1959), deals with the party *aktiv* in the Ukraine; and the title of Sidney Harcave, *The Structure and Functioning of the Lower Party Organizations in the Soviet Union* (Maxwell Air Force Base, Ala., 1954), explains itself. An exhaustive bibliographic essay on Soviet sources has been published, though only in mimeographed form, by John A. Armstrong, *An Essay on Sources for the Study of the Communist Party of the Soviet Union, 1934–1960* (Madison, Wisc., 1961). See further Robert V. Daniels, "The Secretariat and the Local Organizations in the Russian Communist Party," *American Slavic and East European Review,* February 1957; also Louis B. Nemzer, "The Kremlin's Professional Staff: The 'Apparatus' of the Central Committee, Communist Party of the Soviet Union," *American Political Science Review,* XLIV, No. 1 (March 1950), 64–85.

Soviet Government

Soviet government is described in Merle Fainsod, *How Russia is Ruled* (Cambridge, Mass., 1953); Julian Towster, *Political Power in the USSR* (Fair Lawn, N. J., 1948); Derek Scott, *Rus-*

sian Political Institutions (New York, 1958); Barrington Moore, Jr., *Soviet Politics* (Cambridge, Mass., 1950), Chapters 11–12; and Alfred G. Meyer, *The Soviet Political System* (New York, 1965). Very brief introductions are provided by John N. Hazard, *The Soviet System of Government* (Chicago, 1957); John A. Armstrong, *Ideology, Politics, and Government in the Soviet Union* (New York, 1962); and Frederick L. Schuman, *Government in the Soviet Union* (New York, 1961). Bertram D. Wolfe, *Communist Totalitarianism* (Boston, 1962), provides an interpretation which might be balanced by reading Zbigniew K. Brzezinski, *Ideology and Power in Soviet Politics* (New York, 1962), as well as the discussion on the nature of the Soviet social system in *Slavic Review*, vol. XX, No. 3 (October 1961). For the development of soviets, see Oskar Anweiler, *Die Rätebewegung in Russland, 1905–1921* (Leiden, 1958); for local government organization, see Merle Fainsod, *Smolensk under Soviet Rule* (Cambridge, Mass., 1958); for electoral practices, George Barr Carson, *Electoral Practices in the U.S.S.R.* (New York, 1956).

The Soviet Economy

Harry Schwartz, *Russia's Soviet Economy* (Englewood Cliffs, N. J., 1954), although still useful as an introduction to the functioning of the Soviet economy, is outdated by now. But three excellent works are now available to serve this purpose: Alec Nove, *The Soviet Economy* (New York, 1961); Robert W. Campbell, *Soviet Economic Power* (Cambridge, Mass., 1960); and a symposium published by the Joint Economic Committee, Congress of the United States, *Comparisons of the United States and Soviet Economies*, parts I–III (Washington, 1960). See also Alexander Baykov, *The Development of the Soviet Economic System* (New York, 1946); Maurice Dobb, *Soviet Economic Development since 1917* (New York, 1948); and Naum Jasny, *The Soviet Economy during the Plan Era* (Stanford, Calif., 1951). Among works dealing with most recent developments, one might mention Harry Schwartz, *The Soviet Economy Since Stalin* (New York, 1965); and Jere L. Felker, *Soviet Economic Controversies* (Cambridge, Mass., 1966).

The headaches of a Soviet plant manager are described in David Granick, *The Red Executive* (New York, 1960); Joseph S. Berliner, *Factory and Manager in the USSR* (Cambridge, Mass., 1957); and David Granick, *Management of the Industrial Firm in the USSR* (New York, 1953). See also Alexander Vucinich, *Soviet Economic Institutions* (Stanford, Calif., 1952); and Gregory Bienstock, Solomon M. Schwarz, and Aron Yugow, *Management in Russian Industry and Agriculture* (London, 1944).

An interesting comment on the Soviet rat race is provided in Mark Field, *Doctor and Patient in Soviet Russia* (Cambridge, Mass., 1957). For a discussion of Stakhanovism and other devices for raising the productivity of labor, see Solomon M. Schwarz, *Labor in the Soviet Union* (New York, 1951).

Rewards

See Janet G. Chapman, "Real Wages in the Soviet Union, 1928–1952," *Review of Economics and Statistics*, XXXVI, No. 2 (May 1954), 134–156.

The rise in Soviet living standards in recent years is discussed by Alec Nove and a number of commentators in *Problems of Communism*, IX, No 1 (January–February 1960), pp. 1–22.

Regarding the growing literature on social mobility in the USSR, see Chapter 6 of H. H. Fisher (ed.), *American Research on Russia* (Bloomington, Ind., 1959), especially 86–96.

Sanctions

An interesting interpretation of Soviet criminal law is provided in Harold J. Berman, *Justice in Russia* (Cambridge, Mass., 1950). See also John Hazard, "Trends in the Soviet Treatment of Crime," *American Sociological Review*, V, No. 4 (August 1940), 566–576; and Mark Field, "Drink and Delinquency in the USSR," in *Problems of Communism*, IV, No. 3 (May–June 1955), pp. 29–37. The interpretation of terror as "prophylactic justice" is given in Jerzy Gliksman's contribution to Carl J. Friedrich (ed.), *Totalitarianism* (Cambridge, Mass., 1954). The functon of terror is analyzed in Barrington Moore, Jr., *Terror and Progress, USSR* (Cambridge, Mass., 1954); Zbigniew K. Brzezinski, *The Permanent Purge* (Cambridge, Mass., 1956); F. Beck and F. Godin, *Russian Purge and the Extraction of Confession* (New York, 1951); and, from a rather unusual angle, Nathan Leites and Elsa Bernaut, *The Ritual of Liquidation* (Chicago, 1954).

On Soviet labor camps there is a wealth of literature, such as Jerzy Gliksman, *Tell the West* (New York, 1948); Elinor Lipper, *Eleven Years in Soviet Prison Camps* (Chicago, 1951); and Albert K. Herling, *The Soviet Slave Empire* (New York, 1951). Joseph Scholmer, *Vorkuta* (New York, 1955) is recent enough to relate the disturbances that broke out in some of the camps after Stalin's death. A general treatise attempting to analyze all these accounts is David J. Dallin and Boris I. Nicolaevsky, *Forced Labor in Soviet Russia* (New Haven, 1947). Perhaps one should also mention a fictional account, Alexander Solzhenitsyn, *A Day in the Life of Ivan Denisovich* (New York, 1963).

For the structure of the police apparatus, see Otto Heilbrunn, *The Soviet Secret Services* (New York, 1956); and Robert Slusser and Simon Wolin, *The Soviet Secret Police* (New York, 1957). Of Soviet defectors who have described their activities under the Soviet police system, the most valuable book seems to be Peter Deriabin and Frank Gibney, *The Secret World* (New York, 1959).

Education

Literature concerning the Soviet educational system is cited in Note 13, p. 216, of H. H. Fisher (ed.), *American Research on Russia* (Bloomington, Ind., 1959). See also George Z. F. Bereday and Jaan Pennar (eds.), *The Politics of Soviet Education* (New York, 1960). Alex Inkeles, *Public Opinion in Soviet Russia: A Study in Mass Persuasion* (Cambridge, Mass., 1950), is a general treatise on the Soviet mass media of communication. See also Bruno Kalnins, *Der sowjetische Propagandastaat* (Stockholm, 1956); P. Babitsky and John Rimbarg, *The Soviet Film Industry* (New York, 1955); Merle Fainsod, "Censorship in the USSR," in *Problems of Communism*, V, No. 2 (March–April 1956), pp. 12–19; and Leo Gruliow, "How the Soviet Newspaper Operates," *ibid.*, pp. 3–11.

National Minorities

On national minorities, see A. G. Park, *Bolshevism in Turkestan* (New York, 1957); John A. Armstrong, *Ukrainian Nationalism, 1939–1945* (New York, 1955); Basil Dmytryshyn, *Moscow and the Ukraine* (New York, 1956); John S. Reshetar, Jr., *The Ukrainian Revolution* (Princeton, N. J., 1952); Nicholas P. Vakar, *Belorussia: The Making of a Nation* (Cambridge, Mass., 1956); Firuz Kazemzadeh, *The Struggle for Transcaucasia* (New York, 1951); Richard Pipes, *The Formation of the Soviet Union* (Cambridge, Mass., 1954); Frederick Barghoorn, *Soviet Russian Nationalism* (Fair Lawn, N. J., 1956); and the chapters dealing with national minorities in Waldemar Gurian (ed.), *Soviet Imperialism* (Notre Dame, Ind., 1953). A superficial survey reflecting the Soviet point of view is Corliss Lamont, *The Peoples of the Soviet Union* (New York, 1946).

World Communism

Soviet Foreign Relations

In previous editions of this book, I presented a brief selection of readings, as in the paragraphs below. Since then so much additional material has appeared that it might be wiser to eliminate this inadequate selection and instead list only bibliographies. I will let my selection stand, however, but will add two important bibliographies: Thomas T. Hammond (ed.), *Soviet Foreign Relations and World Communism*, a selected, annotated bibliography of seven thousand books in thirty languages (Princeton, 1965); and Walter Kolarz (ed.), *Books on Communism* (London, 1963).

An excellent introduction to the history of Soviet behavior in the world arena is provided by Alvin Z. Rubinstein, *The Foreign Policy of the Soviet Union* (New York, 1960).

On Soviet foreign policy in Europe before World War II, see Louis Fischer, *The Soviets in World Affairs: A History of the Relations between the Soviet Union and the Rest of the World, 1917–1929* (2 vols; London, 1930); Max Beloff, *The Foreign Policy of Soviet Russia* (Fair Lawn, N. J., 1947–1949); Mario Einaudi *et al.*, *Communism in Western Europe* (Ithaca, N. Y., 1951); G. Hilger and Alfred G. Meyer, *The Incompatible Allies* (New York, 1953).

On Soviet policy in Asia up to World War II, see the pertinent sections in the works cited above on the Communist International; also Allen Whiting *Soviet Policies in China, 1917–1924* (New York, 1954); Benjamin I. Schwartz, *Chinese Communism and the Rise of Mao* (Cambridge, Mass., 1951); Xenia Eudin and Robert C. North (eds.), *Soviet Russia and the East, 1920–1927* (Stanford, Calif., 1957); Conrad Brandt, *Stalin's Failure in China: 1924–1927* (Cambridge, Mass., 1958); M. A. Kennedy, *A Short History of Communism in Asia* (London, 1957); G. D. Overstreet and Marshall Windmiller, *Communism in India* (Berkeley, Calif., 1959); M. Masani, *The Communist Party of India* (New York, 1954); John Kautsky, *Moscow and the Communist Party of India* (New York, 1956); Rodger Swearingen and Paul Langer, *Red Flag in Japan* (Cambridge, Mass., 1952); Charles MacLane, *Soviet Policy and the Chinese Communists, 1931–46* (New York, 1958); Harold Isaacs, *The Tragedy of the Chinese Revolution* (Stanford, Calif., 1951); David Dallin, *Soviet Russia and the Far East* (New Haven, 1948); Walter Z. Laqueur, *Communism and*

Nationalism in the Middle East (New York, 1956); George Len-
czowski, *Russia and the West in Iran* (Ithaca, N. Y., 1953); Harry
Miller, *The Communist Menace in Malaya* (New York, 1954);
G. Hanrahan, *The Communist Struggle in Malaya* (New York,
1954); Malcolm D. Kennedy, *A History of Communism in East
Asia* (New York, 1957).

On the alliance with the Kuomintang and other features of
Soviet-Chinese relations, see the brilliant book by Allen Whiting,
Soviet Policies in China, 1917–1924 (New York, 1954); also Conrad Brandt, *Stalin's Failure in China* (Cambridge, Mass., 1958).
For documents, see Xenia Eudin and Robert C. North, *Soviet Russia and the East, 1920–1927* (Stanford, Calif., 1957); C. M. Wil-
bur, *Documents on Communism, Nationalism and Soviet Advisers
in China, 1918–1927* (New York, 1956); and Conrad Brandt,
John Fairbank, and Benjamin Schwartz, *A Documentary History
of Chinese Communism* (Cambridge, Mass., 1952).

The Communist International

The brief selection of readings presented in the paragraphs below could have been expanded at will. Instead of doing so, let
me refer the reader to the two major bibliographies listed under
Soviet Foreign Relations, above. It must be pointed out that even
these major bibliographies are inadequate. Neither includes articles, and the second one only lists works in English. Also, both
could not help being outdated, even at the moment of their publication. When journal material and pamphlets are added to the
bibliography, voluminous lists could be compiled on any one of
the major communist parties. See for instance Charles Corker
(ed.), *Bibliography on the Communist Problem in the United
States* (New York, 1955), a volume of almost five hundred pages.
One other bibliography should be listed, if only because it will be
easily accessible: Legislative Reference Service, Library of Congress, *World Communism: A Selected Annotated Bibliography*
(Washington, D. C., 1964).

Useful introductions to the history of the Communist Interna-
tional are provided by Hugh Seton-Watson, *From Lenin to Ma-
lenkov* (New York, 1953); Franz Borkenau, *The Communist
International* (London, 1938); G. D. H. Cole, *Communism and
Social-Democracy, 1914–1931* (London, 1959); Stefan T. Pos-
sony, *A Century of Conflict* (Chicago, 1953); Arthur Rosenberg,
A History of Bolshevism from Marx to the First Five Years' Plan
(London, 1934); and Ossip K. Flechtheim, "Die Internationale
des Kommunismus 1917–1957," *Zeitschrift für Politik,* VI (Neue
Folge, 1959), No. 3, 231–252. For documentary collections, see
Olga Gankin and H. H. Fisher (eds.), *The Bolsheviks and the*

World War (Stanford, Calif., 1940); Robert V. Daniels, *A Documentary History of Communism* (New York, 1960); and Jane Degras, *The Communist International* (Fair Lawn, N. J., 1956). See also E. H. Carr *A History of Soviet Russia*, Vol. I, *The Bolshevik Revolution* (New York, 1950); Robert V. Daniels, *A Documentary History of Communism* (New York, 1961); and Ruth Fischer, *Stalin and German Communism: A Study in the Origins of the State Party* (Cambridge, Mass., 1948); Ossip K. Flechtheim, *Die KPD in der Weimarer Republic* (Offenbach am Main, 1948); Leon Trotsky, *The First Five Years of the Communist International* (New York, 1945); Theodore Draper, *The Roots of American Communism* (New York, 1957); I. Howe and L. Coser, *The American Communist Party* (Boston, 1958); S. H. Sévène, *Les origines du communisme en France* (Paris, 1953); Gérard Walter, *Histoire du Parti Communiste Français* (Paris, 1948); and Michael T. Florinsky, *World Revolution and the USSR* (New York, 1933).

Communism in Eastern Europe

The wartime negotiations between Soviet Russia, England, and the United States are related in such memoirs as Winston S. Churchill, *The Second World War* (Boston, 1948–1953); Robert E. Sherwood, *Roosevelt and Hopkins* (rev. ed.; New York, 1950); James F. Byrnes, *Speaking Frankly* (New York, 1947); and Edward R. Stettinius Jr., *Roosevelt and the Russians* (New York, 1949). The case of Poland is discussed by Edward J. Rozek, *Allied Wartime Diplomacy* (New York, 1957). See the bibliography for Chapter V of Alvin Z. Rubinstein (ed.), *The Foreign Policy of the Soviet Union* (New York, 1960); and the works cited at the close of Chapter 24 of Donald W. Treadgold, *Twentieth Century Russia* (Chicago, 1959).

The most convenient introduction to the transformation of Eastern Europe into a group of communist governments remains Hugh Seton-Watson, *The East European Revolution* (London, 1950). See also R. R. Betts (ed.), *Central and South Eastern Europe* (Fair Lawn, N. J., 1950); A. Gyorgy, *Governments of Danubian Europe* (New York, 1949); J. Roucek (ed.), *Moscow's European Satellites* (Annals of the Amer. Acad. of Pol. Sci., Vol. 27, Sept. 1950); Doreen Warriner, *Revolution in Eastern Europe* (London, 1950); and Zbigniew K. Brzezinski, *The Soviet Bloc* (Cambridge, Mass., 1960). For treatments of individual countries, the list could be made very long. Convenient bibliographic information is given in H. Gordon Skilling, *The Governments of Communist East Europe* (New York, 1966); J. F. Brown, *The New Eastern Europe* (New York, 1966). See also "East Central Europe: Continuity and Change," *Journal of International Affairs*,

XX, No. 1 (1966), and Stephen Fischer-Galati (ed.), *Eastern Europe in the Sixties* (New York, 1963). Among the more important works we might name Otto Friedman, *The Breakup of Czech Democracy* (London, 1950); P. Barton, *Prague à l'heure de Moscou* (Paris, 1954); P. J. Nettl, *The Eastern Zone and Soviet Policy in Germany* (Fair Lawn, N. J., 1951); Henry L. Roberts, *Rumania* (New Haven, 1951); Samuel Sharp, *White Eagle on a Red Field* (Cambridge, Mass., 1953); I. Gadourek, *Political Control of Czechoslovakia* (Leiden, 1953). For bibliographical information, see also Jirina Sztachova, *Mid-Europe: A Selective Bibliography* (New York, 1953); and C. E. Black, "The People's Democracies of Eastern Europe," in Taylor Cole (ed.), *European Political Systems* (New York, 1953).

The early hopes for Europe's "own road" to socialism are treated incidentally in many of the works cited in the foregoing footnote. See also Adam Ulam, *Titoism and the Cominform* (Cambridge, Mass., 1952); C. P. McVicker, *Titoism: Pattern for International Communism* (New York, 1957); J. Montgomery, *Hungary, The Unwilling Satellite* (New York, 1947); D. A. Tomasic, *National Communism and Soviet Strategy* (Washington, D. C., 1957).

The break with Tito is traced on the basis of the correspondence between Belgrade and Moscow in Robert Bass and Elizabeth Marbury (eds.), *The Soviet-Yugoslav Dispute* (London, 1948).

The theory and practice of Titoism is described in the works cited above. See also Robert Bass and Elizabeth Marbury (eds.), *The Soviet-Yugoslav Controversy, 1948–58: A Documentary Record* (New York, 1959); H. F. Armstrong, *Tito and Goliath* (New York, 1951); V. Dedijer, *Tito* (New York, 1953); S. Clissold, *Whirlwind: An Account of Marshal Tito's Rise to Power* (London, 1949); F. W. Neal, *Titoism in Action: Reforms in Yugoslavia, 1948–1954* (Berkeley, Calif., 1958). An excellent bibliography is provided in George W. Hoffman and Fred W. Neal, *Yugoslavia and The New Communism* (New York, 1962).

For works on the Soviet domination and exploitation of Eastern Europe between 1945 and 1953, see the works cited above on the transformation of Eastern Europe; also A. Cretzianu (ed.), *Captive Rumania: A Decade of Soviet Rule, 1945–1955* (New York, 1956); C. Milosz, *The Captive Mind* (New York, 1953); Robert Slusser, *Soviet Economic Policy in Postwar Germany* (New York, 1953); D. A. Schmidt, *Anatomy of a Satellite* (Boston, 1952); W. J. Stankiewicz and J. M. Montias, *Institutional Changes in the Postwar Economy of Poland* (New York, 1955). The Cominform is treated in Franz Borkenau, *European Communism* (New York,

1953), Chapter 20, and in B. S. Morris, "The Cominform: A Five-Year Perspective," in *World Politics*, VI, 368–376.

The intellectual ferment and the revolts in Eastern Europe, 1953–1956, are the themes of the following works: Henry L. Roberts, "The Crisis in the Soviet Empire," *Foreign Affairs*, Vol. 35, pp. 191–200; Paul Zinner (ed.), *National Communism and Popular Revolt in Eastern Europe* (New York, 1956); Konrad Syrop, *Spring in October: The Polish Revolution of 1956* (London, 1957); Edmund Stillman (ed.), *Bitter Harvest* (New York, 1959); Imre Nagy, *On Communism; In Defense of the New Course* (New York, 1957); Tamas Aczel and Tibor Meray, *The Revolt of the Mind* (New York, 1959); Tibor Meray. *Thirteen Days That Shook the Kremlin* (New York, 1959).

Resistance and Revisionism

Apathy, malingering, delinquency, and other forms of escape, evasion, or rebellion are discussed in R. A. Bauer, Alex Inkeles, and Clyde K. M. Kluckhohn, *How the Soviet System Works* (Cambridge, Mass., 1956); Bauer and Inkeles, *The Soviet Citizen* (Cambridge, Mass., 1956); and Bauer, *Nine Soviet Portraits* (New York, 1955). See also Mark Field, *Doctor and Patient in the Soviet Union* (Cambridge, Mass., 1957); Joseph S. Berliner, *Factory and Manager in the USSR* (Cambridge, Mass., 1957); and the bibliographical information in Chapter 6 of H. H. Fisher (ed.), *American Research on Russia* (Bloomington, Ind., 1959).

Walter Z. Laqueur and George Lichtheim (eds.), *The Soviet Cultural Scene* (New York, 1958) concentrates its attention on evidence of intellectual ferment in the USSR since the death of Stalin. See also the quarterly publication *Soviet Survey*, and Leo Labedz (ed.), *Revisionism: Essays on the History of Marxist Ideas* (New York, 1962).

The current struggle against revisionism and the growing diversity of opinions on various matters can be followed by glancing through any recent issues of Soviet learned or political journals. Important articles are usually translated into English in the *Current Digest of the Soviet Press*. Some of the more interesting controversies and opinions are printed in the (apparently Soviet-sponsored) *Soviet Review*.

The Cold War

The cold war is treated in every book on Russia, communism, or world affairs that has appeared since about 1948. For a special treatment, see Kenneth Ingram, *History of the Cold War* (New

York, 1955); E. D. Carman, *Soviet Imperialism: Russia's Drive toward World Domination* (Washington, D. C., 1950); W. P. Davison, *The Berlin Blockade* (Princeton, N. J., 1958); Xenia J. Eudin, "Moscow's View of American Imperialism," *Russian Review*, Vol. 13, pp. 276–284; C. G. Haines (ed.), *The Threat of Soviet Imperialism* (Baltimore, 1954) and Hugh Seton-Watson, *Neither War Nor Peace* (New York, 1960). See also the extensive bibliography for Chapters 6 and 7 of Alvin Z. Rubinstein (ed.), *The Foreign Policy of the Soviet Union* (New York, 1960).

Regarding the breaking of the ice (the thaw) in the cold war, see the Columbia University publication, *The Anti-Stalinization Campaign and International Communism* (New York, 1957); Evron M. Kirkpatrick (ed.), *Target—The World* (New York, 1957); Bernard Morris, "Soviet Policy toward National Communism: The Limits of Diversity," *The American Political Science Review*, LIII, No. 1 (March 1959), 128–137; Harry Schwartz, *The Red Phoenix* (New York, 1961); and Wolfgang Leonhard, *The Kremlin Since Stalin* (New York, 1962); also E. L. Dulles and R. D. Crane (eds.), *Detente; Cold War Strategies in Transition* (New York, 1965); and Marshall D Shulman, *Stalin's Foreign Policy Reappraised* (New York, 1965).

The Soviet Image of the West

For systematic expositions of the Soviet image of the West, the reader will have to consult Soviet sources dealing with recent world history. American speculations about Soviet images, thoughts, and motives are presented in a convenient anthology in Alexander Dallin (ed.), *Soviet Conduct in World Affairs* (New York, 1960). Some selected pronouncements by Lenin, Stalin, and Khrushchev have been printed in Robert A. Goldwin and Marvin Zetterbaum (eds.), *Readings in Russian Foreign Policy* (2d ed., 3 vols.; Chicago, 1953). A more ample selection is provided in Alvin Z. Rubinstein (ed.), *The Foreign Policy of the Soviet Union* (New York, 1960).

Communist Parties of the Western World

On the communist parties of the Western world, see Gabriel Almond, *The Appeals of Communism* (Princeton, N. J., 1954); Philip Selznick, *The Organizational Weapon* (New York, 1952); Hadley Cantril, *The Politics of Despair* (New York, 1958); Wilson Record, *The Negro and the Communist Party* (Chapel Hill, N. C., 1951); John Gates, *The Story of an American Communist* (New York, 1958); Robert J. Alexander, *Communism in Latin America* (New Brunswick, N. J., 1957); Franz Borkenau, *Euro-*

pean Communism (New York, 1953); Mario Einaudi *et al., Communism in Western Europe* (Ithaca, N. Y., 1951); Morris L. Ernst and David Loth, *Report on the American Communist* (New York, 1952); Max M. Kampelman, *The Communist Party versus the CIO* (New York, 1957); William A. Nolan, *Communism versus the Negro* (Chicago, 1951); James Oneal and G. A. Werner, *American Communism* (New York, 1947); I. Howe and L. Coser, *The American Communist Party* (Boston, 1958); G. Walter, *Histoire du Parti Communiste Français* (Paris, 1948). Very ample bibliographical information on the communist parties of France and Italy is provided in the work by Einaudi and others cited here.

Communism and the Colonial Revolution

Works dealing with the relationship between communism and the colonial revolution are cited at the end of Chapters X and XI of Rubinstein (ed.), *The Foreign Policy of the Soviet Union* (New York, 1960). See also Robert A. Scalapino (ed.), *The Communist Revolution in Asia* (Englewood Cliffs, N. J., 1965); Doak Barnett, *Communist Strategies in Asia* (New York, 1963); and Cyril E. Black and Thomas P. Thornton (eds.), *Communism and Revolution* (Princeton, 1964).

Communism in China

The rise of Mao Tse-tung has been treated in Benjamin I. Schwartz, *Chinese Communism and the Rise of Mao* (Cambridge, Mass., 1951). See also Robert C. North, *Moscow and the Chinese Communists* (Stanford, Calif., 1953); Kuo-chun Chao, *The Communist Movement in China: A Chronology of Major Developments* (Cambridge, Mass., 1950); Edgar Snow, *Red Star Over China* (New York, 1939); and Charles MacLane, *Soviet Policy and the Chinese Communists* (New York, 1958); also Harold Isaacs, *The Tragedy of the Chinese Revolution* (Stanford, Calif., 1951).

On the causes and development of the Chinese Revolution, see, among others, Charles Patrick Fitzgerald, *Revolution in China* (New York, 1952); M. N. Roy, *Revolution and Counterrevolution in China* (Calcutta, 1946); and John K. Fairbank, *The United States and China* (Cambridge, Mass., 1958).

On the first few years of communist government in China, see Otto Van der Sprenkel, Michael Lindsay, and Robert Guillain, *New China: Three Views* (London, 1950); Peter S. H. Tang, *Communist China Today* (New York, 1958); Walt W. Rostow *et al., Prospects of Communist China* (New York, 1954); Frank Moraes, *Report on Mao's China* (New York, 1953); Derk Bodde, *Peking Diary* (New York, 1950); Richard Walker, *China Under Communism* (New Haven, 1955); H. A. Steiner, *Chinese Communists in Action* (Los Angeles, 1953); N. Y. Gluckstein, *Report on Mao's China* (Boston, 1957). The Chinese five-year plan is described in the more recent of these books, especially those by Tang and Gluckstein.

Excellent bibliographies on all topics related to current Chinese developments, including ideological, economic, political, and other matters, as well as the conflict between the Chinese and the Russian communist parties, are provided in the following: Allen B. Cole, *Forty Years of Chinese Communism: Selected Readings with Commentary* (Service Center for Teachers of History, Publication No. 47, Washington, 1962); George P. Jan (ed.), *Government of Communist China* (San Francisco, 1966); and Franz Schurmann, *Ideology and Organization in Communist China* (Berkeley, Calif., 1966).

Index